# TELEONOMY

# TELEONOMY

*Towards a Unification of Economy and Culture*

JOSEPH KEANE

# Contents

## PART THREE: TELEONOMY

First Printing, 2020

# I

# INTRODUCTION

As its title suggests, the following work attempts, above all else, to reconcile the doctrines of economy and culture, or of liberty and tradition. Attempting to unify two fields which rarely cross-pollinate, it is certain that many readers of what follows will be well-versed in works from one field, and less so in works from the other. In attempting to present an advanced work on both topics simultaneously, we have taken the risk of alienating or confusing the conservative reader in this work's first part, which is primarily economic, and of doing the same for the libertarian reader in our third part, which at times approaches an intellectual spiritualism. Any attempt to mitigate the risk carried by these complexities has presented the opposite issue: we fret to have written passages which, while helpful to the relative novice, might prove derivative to the erudite.

Where possible, we have chosen to lean on the side of brevity. It is not wished to present in six-hundred pages what may be concisely conveyed in half that number. Thus, what follows supposes a familiar-

ity with both the Austrian School of Economics and the general lexi-
con of philosophy, particularly that relating to epistemology. Despite
this, we have attempted to forego the unexplained use of the strictly
ideological jargon of any particular school, so as to avoid assisting in
the creation of a self-contained corner of self-referential intellectualism which might eventually become impenetrable to the unanointed
but otherwise studious individual. In attempting to satisfy these opposed conditions simultaneously, it is certain that we might in some
places treat improperly the attention of some number of readers.

This book is built upon a large mound of intellectual indebtedness. We here reserve special mention for two authors whose respective writings have inspired an appreciation of libertarian and
conservative thought to such a degree that without their respective influences this unification of the two would not have been attempted.
We owe an outstanding intellectual debt to Hans-Hermann Hoppe,
whose works first made it clear that the possibility of such a unification lay on the horizons of political thought. Secondly, a debt to the
late Sir Roger Scruton, who lays claim to influencing not so much an
intellectual framework as a sensibility which can scarcely be sensed
within the mechanics of orthodox libertarian thought. It is through
such a sensibility that the individual primarily convinced by the diverse modern theories of liberty might first come to understand his
field to be lacking in depth and direction. That is not to say that the
lens of liberty contains grave flaws in its essential structure. Instead,
the libertarian of high theory has often enough ignored everything exterior to a perfection of this lens' structure that he has actually forgotten how to properly look through it. Never considering his own
implicit perspective, he has often come to conflate that which *he* without fail sees through the lens with the nature of the lens itself. Thus,
his genuine analytical errors notwithstanding, the modern libertarian
has laced through his works countless implicit affirmations of moder-

nity which have, through time, come to bind liberty and modernity together as one.

Irrespective of the contents of this work, the libertarian and the conservative will agree with one another on one preliminary point. As matters stand, the prospects for securing that which we cherish seem dire. The direness of the situation appears only to grow with each passing year. Yet, despite standing united with respect to what they might detest, the two modes of thought seem incapable of coming together even to form a united resistance. If present societal directions are to continue, there can be little more wasteful than having each of these parties use their energies to nullify the works of the other. Thus it seems imperative that, insofar as such a thing is possible, the conservative and the libertarian should seek above all else the framework for a common ground.

Now, prior to embarking upon the task of the furthering of a science or the fulfilment of an investigation, it will always be proper to examine the true scope of one's subject matter. Should this groundwork labour be too often ignored, a whole science may run the risk of overshooting its own bounds. In doing so, it may become unable to recognise the fruit which it is properly capable of bearing, or may begin contorting itself in a wholly grotesque fashion in an attempt to extract from itself that which it in truth cannot yield.

The mainline orthodoxy of economics appears united on this one matter: the scope of the economic science is the understanding of either the laws or the historical tendencies discoverable with respect to the production of *physical consumer goods* - that the economic science spans from the purchase of the factors of production until the sale of the products thereof.

Disregarding exceptionally rare attention given to the barter economy, we may aptly encapsulate orthodox economics as the study of the monetary nexus and thus consider the orthodox conception of the economy to contain this very nexus and nothing further.

It is this conception that these writings aim to uproot - though not, as is now quite popular, so as to disparage the utility of the economic science itself, and to advocate for the position that we mix to the wine of our economic analyses a large part of the waters of this or that modern 'existential need'. Quite to the contrary, the arguments presented throughout this work serve rather to deal damage only to a profane economics which lacks both internal consistency and any rudimentary awareness of its proper scope.

Prevailing sentiment towards the economic science has seldom been so dismal as at the point at which these words were put to print. Those nineteenth-century spirits, liberal and hopeful, are now long forgotten. Freedom searches in vain for true political friends. Those few individuals presenting themselves as allies of freedom appear to writhe and cringe whenever their apparently liberalist slogans come into conflict with the genuine spirits of the age. This shows only that their pretence to liberty is farcical. This dwindling belief in the merits of freedom, caused by an increasing awareness of apparent incompatibilities between economics and a people's 'real needs', is far from harmless. The reader likely needs little reminding of the significance of the teachings of liberalism and the market in the context of the modern democracy – even a rudimentary understanding of the machinery of liberty serves to dispel the vast majority of governmental activities which have arisen in these most recent generations. Despite the pressing necessity of widespread economic understanding, the field appears entirely reluctant to come to its own defence. Most likely, it senses that the critiques levied at it cut right to its roots. Aware that it has little by means of defence, it instead pretends that the threat does not exist.

In order to have a place in the future of political discourse, economics must address the critiques of those who see it as little more than a series of state-directing abstractions, with no connection to the reality of human life.

Any reconciliation of liberty with the socialist perspective is naturally an impossibility. However, in this work's three parts, we shall attempt to convince the defender of libertarianism that his goals, properly understood, are in line with those of the cultural reactionary. Conversely, we wish to show those of traditionalist leanings that their ideals, far from requiring a utilisation of the modern state, can only be impeded thereby.

This task is to be completed through a critique of contemporary economics on its own grounds, leading to a synthesis of method such that the conservative position becomes entirely expressible by means of an expanded economic framework - through an understanding of the teleonomy.

# Part One: The Errors of Economics

**2**

# THE SCOPE OF THE ECONOMY

The prime confusion of orthodox economics lies in its conception of what precisely is meant by the word "economy". This foundational matter is one of vital importance. Arbitrarily limit the scope of the economy, as the economists do, and ever more holes will open up through which 'economic health' will be seen to be clearly incompatible with the ethical good. As a matter of example, to be later elaborated upon, a common critique of the market economy runs as follows: through nefarious and manipulative means, such as predatory advertisement, market entities lure individuals towards the consumption of goods which, in the long-run, render them worse off. Individual corporate entities can profit through this action, and, therefore, left to its own devices, the market economy will act such that it lures man into vice. Thus, state intervention is necessary to the end of ensuring that privately produced goods are conducive to the well-being of the consumer.

The orthodox economic and liberal responses to these claims are entirely lacking. We have heard too many times the claim that 'an individual's vice is a society's benefit' - alluding to the economic growth inspired by the consumer's addiction to vice. More bluntly, some have adopted the slogan that liberty entails "the right of each of us to go to hell in his own fashion". And so we must believe that society would be better off if all men were chained to insatiable vice - provided that they laboured endlessly to fund it.

Such inadequate defences necessarily arise from a dogmatic adherence to a position of liberty constructed upon unstable grounds. In particular, one could only make such muddleheaded claims under the implicit presupposition that the scope of the economy (and therefore the scope of economic analysis) extends nowhere further than to the point of the purchase of a consumer good. To illustrate this point, we shall apply the above written critique of liberty to an idea of economy even more arbitrarily limited than that of the economist. We posit an economy the scope of which ceases a number of stages of production earlier in the production process than the eventual sale of the consumer good. Thus, it encompasses no more than a region spanning from the first procurement of the factors of production, to the sale of some intermediate economic goods to a manufacturer who would later sell his constructed product to a retailer or directly to a consumer. Naturally, the retailer and consumer alike are excluded by this limited scope.

Take a clothes manufacturer. His position is such that he wishes to maximise his psychological profit; in this case, the tailor being Mammon himself, we can consider this to be synonymous with his monetary profit. Now, the suppliers of his factors of production, from the spinners of thread to his legal consultants, wish to maximise their profit at the expense of the tailor's pockets. They may mislead him, prey upon his lacking knowledge, lead him into binding agreements tilted ultimately to his own misfortune. We would be quite right in presuming that such practices occur quite frequently within the real world.

After the clothing manufacturer has made his purchases, the limit of this confined economic world has been met, and the economist's job is over. Any further developments escape our limited economic analysis, just as the post-retail elements of the orthodox economy escape the analysis of the orthodox economist. Fret not, a sociological critic steps in to fill this analytical void: "Manufacturers are being exploited all around! Merchants of parts and pieces routinely suppress the interests of the higher manufacturing classes through tactics of greed and a reliance on the ignorance of their patrons. Left to its own devices, the market economy seeks to maximise its own profits, to the eventual destruction of the collective well-being of the late-stage manufacturer".

Our limited economist retorts as follows, his arguments arising from the foregone conclusion of the goodness of his conceived economy: "While you have observed something quite real, you draw false conclusions from your lack of systemic analysis. In fact, we ought to see that one manufacturer's poor purchase is the general economy's gain! By purchasing such low-quality factors of production and lowering his own profit, the manufacturer is doing us the service of stimulating the economy through the injection of his labours and funds, which reduce unemployment and increase real wages". As all with sight can see, this economist can be easily shown to be peddler of the absurd through a simple universalisation of his position, that the economy must then benefit were all manufacturers to make a loss.

In order to properly defend against the critiques of the sociologist, the economist needs to expand his conception of the economy so as to draw closer to the point of ultimate exhaustion of all of the resources in play - an expansionary step precisely the same as the one required for a transfiguration of economy into teleonomy, the latter of which we may here define as the system of the totality of means interacted with by man.

Orthodox economics in its current state, which has properly integrated the stages of production up until the point of the consumer sale, may, through a consistent application of its concepts to its wider scope, confidently refute the absurd critique of the market economy given above.

When a factor of production is put to work at a loss, the economy suffers. The price of the input resource represents the present value of its alternative market uses[1]. To consume this resource and fail to generate a profit means that, *ceteris paribus*, the economy is damaged as a result of a manufacturer purchasing factors of production and therewith creating a capital product worth less than the sum of its factors. Being worth less than that which was consumed in its creation, we may be certain that the potential economic uses of the manufactured product are less than those consumed in its creation. From the perspective of the whole economy, we may by no means call these failures a 'stimulus to the economy'. On the contrary, it tranquilises the economy, reducing its productivity *when this latter is measured rightly in terms of its ends, these being consumer products, from which all economic activity derives its instrumental value.*

The economist, furnishing his point that economic losses are detrimental to the economy as a whole, does not then go on to call for government intervention for the purposes of 'outlawing' losses at the manufacturing level. His advice is, owing to his integration of wider parts of the economy into his analytical framework, quite to the contrary: firstly, we see from our expanded perspective that the economy functions such that whenever a loss is incurred by a particular manufacturer, that is, whenever a particular manufacturer is detrimental to the functioning of the whole economy, he directly and necessarily ends up with fewer resources with which to command economic activities in the future, and loses the interest of third-party investors and creditors owing to his inability to properly manage his finances.

Consequently, those manufacturers who source their produce from suppliers of inferior stock, or of factors otherwise inadequate for the manufacturer's purposes, gradually tend towards non-existence. Thus, the economy exhibits a permanent tendency towards ensuring that all entities intermediate in the production of any given good (that is, all entities active in stages prior to its purchase by the consumer) work to the ultimate, rather than merely immediate, benefit of their customers. For the economic power of any entity is dependent on how many resources their customers are able and willing to expend. Holding all else constant, then, we must admit that the predatory supplier, given that he generates losses for his customers, attacks the very source of his power in going about his activities. The most beneficial suppliers (again in terms of ultimate effect of the goods sold, rather than the customer's initial valuation), on the other hand, continually nourish their cause of existence.

Further, given that those entities which purchase the faulty goods are essentially less capable of making correct decisions than are their market competitors, we must expect a gradual production of correct decision-making in all aspects currently lacking, given that the production of this knowledge does not expend more resources than the possession of the knowledge itself creates. In other terms, the market economy will tend to immunise itself against any known predatory practices insofar as these practices are indeed of high detriment.

The economist claims not that no errors occur within the market, but rather that the market is the surest means towards the detection and proportionally apt treatment of the inefficient allocation of resources in the economy, *where efficiency is defined as the total production of consumer goods valued according to their price at the point of purchase.*

Orthodox economics claims now to derive its knowledge from a positivist-empiricist epistemological framework. It may be claimed that this is a new development, arriving along with increasing Popperian influences of the 1960s. Prior to that decade however, economics acted under very much the same presuppositions; while it had not yet explicitly identified itself with any particular epistemological system, and had yet to smooth away some its more antiquated edges, its method was certainly predominantly empirical. By way of example, the law of demand, that less of a good is demanded as its price rises (or, more strictly put, that no more of a good can be demanded due to an increase in its price), was seen as being justified in its validity according only to its representation in historical fact - thus only a law in the loosest sense. Orthodox economics has never conceived of its field as being the realm of the *a priori*.

Throughout its entire history the fundamental concepts of economics have been derived through empirical observation, abstracting numerous similarities from the phenomenological world without thinking it possible to grasp their internal essences (or thinking that such essences simply cannot exist). For example, the field's understanding of the phenomenon of interest is drawn wholly from the observance of phenomena deemed intuitively similar. As a result, its conception of interest contains little more than the nominal return on loans in the money market.

It is not possible to abstract from the produce of this methodology anything similar to a universal essence. Thus, given that these *a priori* essences (or essential economic categories) do indeed exist, the current approach renders itself liable to a failure to recognise the necessary scope of the applicability of its tools. From his approach, the orthodox economist is incapable of arriving at the position that the money-market loan interest rate receives its particular behaviour of interest from a manifold of isolatable categories, categories which are inherent in, and discoverable through, the qualities of purposeful action as such. Of particular magnitude, the loan market interest rate expresses, in a highly quantitative and visible manner, the time preference[2] of all involved actors - a factor necessarily present in purposive action qua purposive action. Without any faculty suited to the evaluation of its constituent parts, we would indeed be foolish to carry any faith that economics is fully aware of the scope of its whole.

Having measured the critique of our hypothetical limited economy against the arguments of orthodox economics, we may now, through this same method of an expansion of scope, venture to respond to those genuine critiques of the orthodox economy by means of a perspective more akin to that of the whole teleonomic system.

Thus, just as the economist denies that a manufacturer's loss is an economy's gain, we are not to claim that an interaction ultimately to the detriment of a consumer may be considered good from the standpoint of the teleonomy. Instead, applying concepts inherent in economic analysis, while expanding the proper range of their application to action as such, we will analyse the societal tendencies upon which liberty necessarily directs us.

Insofar as an individual acts in a fashion detached from the best possible action, he commits vice. Insofar as an individual, through his actions or otherwise, is recognised by others as being vicious, others will be less inclined to rely on him for the satisfaction of their own ends. In other words, should an individual be perceived to be incompetent, a perception presupposed by all attempts to solve this problem through infringements of liberty, this individual loses teleonomic value.

Those apparent exceptions to the above proposition arise from a misunderstanding of the terms here used. For example, a man may receive pity for his misdeeds. Yet insofar as this is the case - and we are here far from extolling any virtues of pity - the action which inspired pity must be seen as, in this limited sense, more successful. Man cannot gain from vice, and insofar as he receives any part of restitution for his action, this action loses a degree of its negative character. This holds even in cases where the absolute vices of another are perceived as being valuable to another, this occurring in cases ranging from blackmail to the sale of tobacco. In these cases, that part of the loss to the individual's reputation which is alleviated by his increased instrumental value to those malicious parties is inflicted instead upon the latter.

The implications of this loss are, *mutatis mutandis*, precisely those listed above with respect to the manufacturer. In his vice, the individual becomes diminished in his ability to exert an active influence over the teleonomy. The reader may need to be reminded that in making such a claim, we do so with respect to an inherent tendency, revealed through an examination of the principles at hand, rather than with respect to any particular snippet of the totality of effects of any given cause. Now, since an individual's teleonomic influence, or power, is the sum of the effects of his being on the totality of being (in the same way that an economic entity's power is equal to the sum of the immediate effects of his products on his customers), the tendencies active under a state of liberty must be such that those individuals who benefit from the viciousness of another are themselves subject to a reduction of power vis-a-vis the individual who coaxes others towards a more virtuous path. With relevance to the initial critique of economics, this means that those who promote vice through the sale of consumer goods must be drawing their power from entities tending towards social powerlessness. To think of this powerlessness solely in terms of the monetary is the habit of a mind afflicted by modernity's infatuation with orthodox economics, a habit from which the conservative anti-capitalist (or non-capitalist) is by no means free.

The above analysis must come into being through a consistent application of the true conceptual apparatus of the orthodox economy or monetary nexus. As such, any contingencies of their truths must be jointly shared. Either liberty, left to its own devices, ensures a tendency towards virtue on a cultural or teleonomic level, or the market is necessarily destructive not only to culture, but also to the economy itself. For now, a more complete justification and evaluation of the teleonomic view will be put aside until we have presented a systematic critique of both the flaws of orthodox economics as well as the insufficiency of all popular reactions thereto. What has up to now been said serves only as a first familiarisation with the thesis of this work.

Despite the intentional brevity of these initial points, and our intention to give these matters their due attention during later chapters, it would not be out of place to below provide a short defence against certain broader claims which have most likely already arisen in the minds of some, so as to more fully contextualise what it is we wish to critique, and what it is we seek to defend.

The first of these immediate claims comes from the more historically oriented, conservative critic. Whatever may be claimed with the above theorizing, is it not easily observed that there appears to be an inverse relation between the size of an economy and the strength of the culture which surrounds it? For, since the post-war period, economies have undergone a general liberalisation and expansion, while deep-rooted cultural standards have been subject to ceaseless and rapid decay. Moreover, those most representative of market freedom, the monolithic, international corporate entities, seem most responsible for the destruction of the distinctive character of locality, and are actively participatory in the creation and maintenance of progressive dominance of culture.

We disagree with nothing contained within this critique other than its presupposition that the twentieth century represents a period of increasing liberty. To the contrary, we wish to show it quite evident that the period in question exhibited only a tendency towards an increase in fraudulent liberty, a liberty for some at the expense of the gradual enslavement of others, a reality hidden by the facade of 'the democratic society'. The blame for this misconception of liberty, as we shall shortly see, can be in large part blamed on the economic profession itself. For now, let it be clear that the popular notion of a modern society characterised by liberty is wholly mythical. A near-majority of economic resources within those formerly liberal Western nations are now directly organised by state power, while nothing at all escapes the leviathan's more indirect influences. These countries define themselves by a governmental system which, in its supposedly 'ideal' form, ensures that any naturally forming elite subject to the continually envious, ignorant, and levelling whim of the demos. The public taste for liberty, and understanding of its rudimentary function, is non-existent in the European nations, and elsewhere swiftly receding. By sleight of hand, forces at work have given 'capitalism' a two-faced meaning: it represents both 'the current state of affairs' and 'political organisation according to liberty'. Thus, a predominant perception exists that the former is in fact the latter.

Speaking with respect to historical correlation alone, when properly aware of what is here meant by liberty, the observer would be closer to the truth in drawing a connection between the presence of coercion in routine society and the cultural degeneracy which follows. This point will be laboured at length in part two.

A second, more sentimental critique will accuse our initial claim of simply turning away from the reality of the suffering of the weak or misused. We do no such thing. We turn not away, but towards the future. An absolute similarity may here be drawn to the wish that the state interfere with industry by banning, taxing, subsidising or otherwise mandating the purchase of this or that factor of production so that incapable entrepreneurs may avoid the pain involved in a heavy loss. We may immediately feel pity for those entrepreneurs who continually lose money according to the latest changes and fashions; yet, far from turning a blind-eye to the plight of the entrepreneur, through our advocating for the system of liberty, we very much wish for the success of an entrepreneur *as a category of action or of individual*. New phenomena must continually arise; to step into the same stream twice is not possible. A manifestation of that which misleads will always appear, and that which misleads lies, in all cases other than mere fraud (which is another form of coercion against which we rally), within the misled individual. We seek not to implement a particularised, post-hoc societal shield, which serves only to blind society to its failure after having already paid the price of its inadequacy. Instead, we wish to act as the enemy of vice *as such*, so that men are in future times less subject to its evils. We wish to eliminate those traits in men which steep them in error. This can only be accomplished through the natural impediment of those in whom this trait manifests.

# 3

## THE VALUE OF THE ECONOMY

From the perspective of the proponents of its growth, the value of the economy lies in its ability to satisfy, through production, the diverse needs of man. The individual may only purchase that which he, at the point of the purchase, considers beneficial. This much is true. From this, it is supposed to follow that the enlargement of the economy's productive capacity, less any economic externalities hereby incurred[3], must result in a world more tolerable for humanity, a world in which all sorts of men can, according to their best judgement, more easily satisfy the requirements of their wishes. This is also true - subject to the qualification that this change be *ceteris paribus*. However, despite the fact that only this much more limited claim follows from the first proposition, the caveat is wholly ignored by the framework of the orthodox economist. This subtlety is fatal to the security of the economy's claim to value.

The economist would admit that certain actions are preferable to others from the perspective of the actor, and that any resource, given that it has value, may be used for the production of multiple ends. Money, being a resource, must have multiple uses, some better than others, such that, when making a decision to save or to spend, or to buy some fleeting entertainment instead of paying mounting debts, an individual may make faults. A resource's value is equal to the present estimate of the totality of its future function; a loss occurs to the degree that one misjudges this totality.

We above mentioned the fact that one may not consider the economy to have been bettered by the producer's mispurchases, say, the purchase of a dozen typewriters on the eve of the personal computer. We here consider purchases of equal price to be differing in quality, or total eventual value, due to the inevitable differences between expectation and reality which arise in the employment of any means. From the standpoint of economics, then, we must quantitatively discern between the utilisation of equal amounts of its base quantitative unit, money, based on the realised ability of each possible utilisation to satisfy a given end, which itself can only be valuable insofar as it is, in its totality, conducive to an even higher end. Therefore, the economy's value, under its own apparatus, cannot arise from the indifferent perspective of immediate purchase, but can only be infallibly valued from a position of hypothetical hindsight beyond the point of the exhaustion of the good's totality of effects.

Thus the chasm obscured from vision by the exclusion of the *ceteris paribus* caveat is that, by its own standards, the growth of the economy is valuable only if it does not come at the expense of man's ability to secure his highest good. If this capacity has been forfeited to a degree greater than the increase in the totality of the value of economic produce, then the economy has not grown in value. We must consider it to have shrunken.

While much of the above may seem quite obvious, we have intentionally repeated ourselves in our affirmation that the above is the necessary result of the presuppositions of all strains of the economic science. This has been stressed not in order to prove the contingency of economics to the conservative reader, but instead to the economist. The above being true, it must be the case that any work in the field which fails to take this matter into account is useless at best even by its own criteria - it is bad economics, in the same way that a work of physics which ignores the existence of movement can only be bad physics.

Given that the orthodox economy must derive any claim to value through its effects on the teleonomic whole, and since the conceptual apparatus of economics can only find its true consistency and universalisation through an expansion into teleonomics, we must wonder what the allure may be of those orthodox economic strains, and consider what benefit, if any, may be yielded from giving prime importance to a mere subcategory of the teleonomy.

Any science wishing to apply its theories to reality would be much benefitted by an ease of both measurement and application. Easily observed is that the monetary nexus conforms to a uniform commensurability, this being the very reason why it has been usefully established in all advanced societies prior to the domination of the eye of quantitative science. It offers apparently fantastic potential for assorted empirical testing. Contrary to this stands the absolute impenetrability of the teleonomy by number or any reduction to quantity. In the latter field, we may, at most, infer through our personal ethical understanding the personal effects of action on various and diverse subjects. Such knowledge must always remain uncertain, owing to the unbridgeable gulf between subjects that renders the essence of each phenomenologically invisible to the other. That the monetary nexus has grown is relatively easy to behold. Fathoming anything resembling the exhaustive effects of any influence on the totality of man, however, requires profound personal wisdom. Adding to this, we may be quite certain that the modern developments made in the field of multivariate econometric computation quite outstrip any gains in our intimate knowledge of the good life, so as to make the monetary nexus an increasingly more comprehensible subject for the popular mind than is living itself.

We must note, however, that the prospective ease of any statistical measurement of the economy is entirely dependent upon the validity of the application of an empiricist methodology to the field. From the perspective of an *a priori* methodology, this relation is quite inverse. For, this latter study having the purposive action as such as its entire scope of subject, no *particular* action can ever bring to light anything which truly qualifies as novel economic knowledge. Nothing essentially new is unearthed or distinguished by entering the monetary nexus. In other words, no fundamental category of action is ever present in monetary behaviour which cannot be present in behaviour which lies outside of all monetary considerations. As such, any application of *a priori* principles to the prediction of the monetary nexus *as such* requires caveats and abstractions which cannot be found among the categories of action itself. As an example, we cannot make any absolute application of our notions alone to predict whether a change in the rate of taxation has an effect on the monetary whole. In order to make statements of necessity in such a topic, we would have to deny the reality of anything exterior to the monetary. For, given the reality of existence outside of the merely monetary, an increase in taxation may cause an individual to work more, due to the fact that his reduced income has increased for him the marginal utility of additional wages, or, on the other hand, he may work less, as the aforementioned increase may be outweighed by the decreased productivity of his wage labour vis-a-vis leisure, this latter being non-monetary. This economic blindness of the thorough praxeological approach, however, has absolutely no bearing on its ability to prescribe *teleonomic* relations. In this latter field, we must admit that, regardless of the responsive actions of the taxed individual, the taxes inevitably cause a shrinkage of the teleonomy, the individual being forced to choose an alternative less productive of his highest ends. We may thus establish definite laws with respect to human action as such, but never with respect to any particular, objective subsection of human behaviour, whether this subcategory attempt to encapsulate man's monetary behaviour, his dietary habits or his sleeping patterns. *Economic* laws are an impossibility.

This notwithstanding, the distinction of our era's preference for empiricist scepticism above epistemological rationalism the present makes an increasing predominance of positivist methodology in economics an entirely unsurprising event.

Despite the joint conceptual and ethical supremacy of the teleonomic approach over the economic approach, it may nonetheless be possible for one to hold the latter to be the prime realm of interest of the science in question. It might well be the case that the losses incurred through an adoption of the economic approach, namely a sacrifice of conceptual consistency and a grander expanse of scope, may be fully outweighed by the resultant increase in the quantitative measurability of the remaining subject matter. Anyone taking this leap would have to hold on faith the absolute goodness of economic growth, or hold, at the very least, that we must always be in favour of a monetary advance of the economy. The adherent must do so, since, as an intrinsic part of his descent to the purely economic view, he would have to hold that we are wholly unqualified to make any definite judgement regarding both the merit of and the dynamic laws which expand to include that which lies beyond the economy. In this descent, the economist would be fully aware of the imperfection of his conceptual grounds, a destruction of truth in the name of pragmatism, as a means to the creation of state policy decisions which "follow the latest science".

This leap, the unequivocal and universal affirmation of societal subjection to the empirical aggregate statistics of the monetary nexus, the only possible means for the economist to refuse to eliminate the economic science and replace it with its superior teleonomic form, can know no half measures. Any deviation therefrom, no matter how slight, could only come about through an affirmation of that proposition which was denied in order to justify the leap in the first place; namely, the ability to accurately measure matters outside of the monetary nexus. In admitting that we *sometimes* ought to pursue a path other than that one which maximises the monetary, he is bound to fully endorse any methodology which may make measured reconciliation between competing claims of economic and cultural.

When giving attention to economics from the monetary empiricist perspective, we must possess a toolkit of interrelated variables measuring economic phenomena considered prime indicators, causes or consequences of economic health, which itself must be quantitatively ascertainable to a high degree and, as mentioned above, taken for a good-in-itself as matter of principle. Elevating this measurement towards intrinsic worth has necessary consequences - namely, the relegation of all else to the position of being mere means towards the enlargement of the chosen indicator of the monetary economy. The ends of man lie within themselves, in the satisfaction of the ultimate spiritual purpose, the essential fulfilment of which can never take the form of phenomena, and, as such, cannot be the postulated end of pragmatic, empiricist economics. The elevation of any empirical phenomenon to the level of end necessitates the liquidation of all which lies between this phenomenon and man's ultimate spiritual satisfaction. The further down this chain of means we fall in selecting our posited empirical end, the more we must tend to sacrifice. Enthroning in this most high of places the growth of the monetary nexus, we must expect the gradual liquidation of all which genuinely makes the monetary nexus valuable: man's ability to properly make use of this produce in such a manner that is conducive to his ultimate spiritual purpose.

This turn of events has indeed come to pass. For more than half a century, few powers have been able to compete with the gross domestic product for the title of prime end of statecraft. Those things which have come close to claiming this title are no less profane: inflation, interest rate, the unemployment rate, real gross domestic product or purchasing power parity, all aggregate measures of the purely monetary realm. Aside from being a sign of the times, this real elevation is bound to have degenerative consequences in proportion to the size of the state, or the willingness of a populace to have their state take upon itself the role of omnipotent solver of woes. On the other hand, the economic belief can have only limited effect on any society which gives its state little scope, for any attempt to sacrifice the cultural or spiritual to the monetary in a society of liberty, governed by conviction, trade and an organisation of one's own life, must be hit with the full weight of any residual spirituality within the civilisation at hand. In attempting to devote one's being to the enlargement of monetary productivity alone, one will inevitably be made fully aware of the sacrifices of family, private vocation and spiritual health which must be taken in order to walk the path of Mammon. The strength of these opposite and higher natural duties prevents this perversion of desire from taking deep root.

Before advancing, it would be wise to state that when discussing the effects of the mass adoption of any given belief, one must take into account the ability of the hosts of the belief to fully comprehend it in its full complexity and most perfect state. Many calamitous errors may be spawned from the contrary notion, which holds that should a land succumb to the tendencies of, say, nineteenth-century liberalism, then we must evaluate the prospects of this liberty as if each common man were to hereby become a Mill. To avoid such foolishness, we must make ourselves aware of those inevitable bastardizations and debasements of beliefs and ideologies which themselves, while perhaps false, contain in their purest forms a modicum of nobility and an admirable consistency.

Now, when a belief in the mighty good of the state is added to the presuppositions of the economic mindset, we must arrive at the conclusion that the end of statecraft is the enlargement of the economic aggregate. As a direct result, the aim of the politician becomes to act such that the voting public, or whoever else gifts him with stately authority, believe that he is acting so as to cause an improvement in terms of these aggregates. We stress that it is the appearance, rather than the reality, of causal growth of these statistics which is bound to drive the politician in the age of economics. For those reasons mentioned above, we cannot entertain the notion that the democratic masses will be capable of any form of erudite unanimity with respect to economic fact and fiction. To claim otherwise is an obvious absurdity given the inability of the faculty staff of any popular university to compile in any unanimity even a short list of supposed economically beneficial policy positions. Furthermore, it cannot be disputed that natural deviations from certain notions are far more harmful than equitable misunderstandings of other notions.

It is immeasurably less taxing, and far more common, to judge an action with respect to its immediate effects rather than with view of the totality of its effects. The politician whose rule brings swift riches will be adored, and he whose policies are accompanied by decline, loathed. Yet the latter's decline may be wholly the consequence of the former's prosperity. Conversely, the politician who refuses to usher in a prosperous present, so that he may instead ensure a stable future, is most often understood to be the harbinger of stagnation and enemy of the good of mankind, while he whose reign takes place within that more stable future will enjoy a full harvest of popularity and power.

As such, we must expect, as a consequence of the simultaneous beliefs of orthodox economics and the state as unrestrained public will, a *ceteris paribus* liquidation of the future in favour of the present. The goal being a maximisation of the monetary, this liquidation of the future will, as a matter of preference, not prey upon economic capital, since, while there is relevant gain involved in such consumption, the explicit destruction of any capital stock carries with it a degree of immediate loss with respect to the monetary nexus and its most popular forms of aggregate measurement. To ensure popularity, the state must increase the apparent value of its total capital stock, raise production, or both.

The present value of capital is determined by the interest-discounted value of the sum of its produce. Should the interest rate fall, the value of capital will rise, as interest is in essence determined by the value of future goods vis-a-vis present goods, or through the ever-present market for time. Should more savings appear, it is as a consequence of an increased willingness to trade present consumption for future gain, such that the present value of future productivity rises and the resources of society are directed towards the production of additional capital.

The state can only utilise this mechanism when it has the means to effect interest rate changes at its own volition. For the vast majority of human history, any such escapades, enacted to any large degree, were above the power of the sovereign. Fortunately for the state, and unfortunately for us, this function was gratuitously gifted to the modern national government at the beginning of the twentieth century in the form of central banking. The supposed independence of state and central bank is naturally a myth, as the latter may only exist as a consequence of the wholly revocable monopoly privileges bestowed upon it by the state. In any other sector, any claim of independence under such conditions would be rightly viewed as laughable naivety. It, of course, may only exist when understood to be furthering the long-term interests of coercive power. Further, figures of authority within central banks are naturally and demonstrably chosen from those allied with the state's objectives, central bank boards being dominated by a wide array of colourful figures of all backgrounds and creeds, such as direct state elects and the elects of the banks of the chosen few - banks which, to roughly the same degree as central banks, are entirely reliant on state favour for their positions of power. Should this much not provide the state with sufficient influence over central bank interest rates, it may regardless facilitate deficit spending, issuing bonds to banks which, when deposited at the central bank, act as reserves upon which banks may lend according to the current multiplicative of the fractional reserve rate - also set by the state - to the effect of manufacturing an apparent increase in the supply of future goods. This occurring, the economy undergoes a twofold effect. Its interest rates are artificially and temporarily lowered, creating the beginnings of an expansion of the capital sectors, and the consumer feels less inclination to store his money as savings, these yielding lower return, and instead acts in favour of immediate consumption. Since the state has no intent of either saving or investing in order to pay off its own debts, but achieves this instead by promising to bond-owners some sum of taxes extracted from the labours of future men, this bond creating action knowns only the limit of complete economic collapse.

This exploitation of its command over the supply of credit serves to cause cyclical periods of false boom and inevitable crash. To fully describe the subtleties of this process would distract this work from its supra-economic focus, since there can exist no teleonomic equivalent of the central bank. These intricacies having been better analysed in other works with which many readers are likely to be familiar, it will serve our current purposes to give here only a basic view.

The natural formation and maintenance of capital occurs when, due to a particular abundance of savings, the cost of using savings to produce some distant good becomes reduced to the point where the production of said good becomes more profitable than the production of some other more immediate good. This process requires that someone involved forego the consumption of some of society's material resources. That future product will be created either out of this unconsumed good and its dormant factor, or some other entity will begin to use these unused resources and free up whatever else he would otherwise have utilised. Either way, the person creating the future good requires the consumption of certain real resources to be foregone. When the state or a fraudulent bank provides artificial credit, however, no real resources are set aside. To the contrary, the lower interest rates resulting from this excess of credit must result in an increase in general consumption, meaning fewer real resources exist for the production of a larger number of real future projects. We would here experience an immediate halt if not for the secondary effect of monetary expansion - inflation. The first recipient of new money may use it before the general level of prices has adjusted to compensate for a higher amount of money per real resource. This being so, the necessary correction may be averted so long as monetary expansion continues. In this time, there exists an optimistic illusion of growth, due to the abundance of new capital ventures enabled by cheap credit. Once the interference ceases, which must occur should hyperinflation be avoided, those natural forces, unchanged by the events at hand will reassert themselves. It will be seen that there are insufficient savings to fund the new expanse of capital ventures, and the economy enters a corrective recession.

The cumulative effect of this will be, and has been, a concentration of power and resources in the possession of those few first beneficiaries of the fraudulent banking press, combined with a continuous wasting of society's scarce economic resources.

The state is not limited to a manipulation of the monetary market in its pursuance of the expansion of the monetary nexus (to the satisfaction of the voter). The primary method applicable, one which foregoes any necessity of economic recession in the near future, and one which would remain applicable even if all voters were to obtain a full comprehension of the entire corpus of economic truth, must necessarily be the liquidation of all that is 'non-economic', or of all that is truly valuable.

# 4

# CULTURAL LIQUIDATION

In order to completely grasp the implications of a liquidation of all supra-economic elements within our lives, we must attempt a proper elucidation of the exact relations between the economy and the teleonomy, insofar as such a commensurability is even possible. It must be noted at the outset that these two conceptions attempt to operate under entirely different ontological and epistemological suppositions. Economics attempts to find its prime matter in a phenomenological object-in-itself, while teleonomics looks to the universal nature of the subjective[4]. Difference between the two must be multiple of dimension. Further, as a modification of our previous metaphor which regarded the economy as being 'contained within' the teleonomy, it must be stated that it is impossible to express one strictly in terms of the other. An attempt to reconcile the two in these terms might be said to be similar to any attempt to examine the empirical particulars of the phenomenological world in order to make them strictly commensurable with analytical geometric ideas, such as the perfect circle. The orthodox economist would be akin to a man who asserts that the notion of the circle comes to its initial existence through particular 'circular' objects, and thus defines 'circular' in terms of those discovered objects. The 'perfect circle' would be, to him, an abstraction containing an inferior degree of being, or no being whatsoever. The teleonomic perspective, on the other hand, works akin to positing the nature of circularity, and of all other geometrical categories, as being inherent within the nature of phenomenological reality as such. It would assert that all phenomena must conform to those identities to which are presupposed by experience itself. With respect to the nature of shape, one would assert that since all shape must occur within space, and is unthinkable without it, all shape must confirm to the laws of space, whatever they may be. The laws of space – the laws of extension – come to be understood to be the laws of geometry, and thus the circle must be a form ontologically anterior to all that is seen to be circle-like. Thus, it is the object which conforms, and must conform, to the standards of ideal geometry. Any attempt to compare the 'economic' realm with the teleonomic realm, then, would through this metaphor be akin to an attempt to describe the exact differences between the empiricist circular object and the rationalist idea-circle. Naturally, no *a priori*, analytic list of differences may be drawn between the two, as such, in the same way that one might properly differentiate the ideal triangle from the ideal square.

Nonetheless, in an attempt to clarify the differences between the two as much as is possible, it will serve some utility to imagine the economy as being placed firmly 'within' the teleonomy, so as to search for anything resembling that sharp division of economy and non-economy which, while unreal in any categorical sense, must be said to carry some meaning with it insofar as each person carries within him an intuitive understanding of what 'economy' means. We are not transplanting the economy into the teleonomy so as to stealthily critique it from grounds upon which it would never stake its claims. To the contrary, it seems clear that, insofar as the economic science has permanent and unsolvable contradictions at its roots, these arise from its attempts to fix its views of object-in-itself into its conceptual apparatus arising intuitively from subjective and functional grounds. If anything at all, a transplant would give it a helping hand by allowing it some element of consistency. Economics being an unnatural science, it is impossible to perfectly transplant it into a natural system, and we can thus give no exclusive and exhaustive account of the differences between the two fields in question. At most, we can categorise those aspects of highest import with respect to the overarching subject of this work.

Insofar as a thing holds value without reference to its ability to produce consumer goods exchangeable for money, we may consider it supra-economic. A given object may be inseparably economic and supra-economic, or contingently one and then the other. A proper upbringing can be considered valuable from the economic perspective as it is expected to cause an increase in the total value of consumer goods generated by the child in the future. As a consequence of this upbringing, it may instead be possible for the child to care little about a striving for the material and the monetary, resulting in his living a more distant and contemplative life. From the perspective of all that exalts the monetary nexus, this latter effect must be seen as a misallocation of resources, as worthless, something which it is wholly desirable to liquidate. This needn't necessarily mean an erasure of all standards of child raising.

The degree to which any object works to grow the monetary nexus, or partakes in the supra-economic, is in a constant state of flux. As such, when examining historical examples of cultural liquidation, we must note that the manifestation of this need not appear to al-together destroy the structures, but often only transfigures them to-wards a spiritless profanity.

Hitherto, the general satisfaction of man came as a consequence of his dutiful actions towards his role, his community, his family and his one or many gods. Some of these vocations derive little of their value from their effect on the monetary, the rest derive nothing at all from it. As such, we must expect these aspects of human life to face a gradual liquidation in proportion to the will, and ability, of peo-ple and government, to elevate crude economic growth to the end of statesmanship. For the sake of conciseness, we take that as *culture* which these false economic times are destined to destroy. The famil-iarity of this concept, despite the elusiveness of formal definition, may allow it to be used to properly describe the totality of non-economic phenomena with little repudiation, and yet reiterate that, in employ-ing this term, we use it not to describe those norms which, while per-haps noble, are instrumentally effective as means to the monetary - such as, for example, that form of education which best breeds high computational intelligence.

The twentieth century may aptly be summarized as being the century of permanent revolution, the point at which long-rising pro-fane undercurrents of thought made themselves manifest and became truly for-themselves. The firm ground under which these currents did flow, and above which the whole, fragile edifice of tradition towered, held firm no more. The currents swelled and their erosion hastened, and, giving way, those immemorial pillars above, for long a source of quite some confusion, fell through to the abyss, eternally irretrievable, to the lament of only a short number of souls.

The implications of this, our age, are inexhaustible, and it is far beyond our current scope to give even a moderately sufficient ac-count of their perniciousness. Upon a brief survey of this landscape, there must become visible a contrast so stark, and hitherto quite un-fathomable, upon which we wish to comment: the emergence of the behemoth state, in both its quantitative scope and qualitative central structure. Initially the effect of cultural upheaval, and thereafter becoming themselves an active cause of additional degradation, the states of this revolutionary era possess a coercive density unsurpassed throughout man's entire civilised history. We wish to leave aside for now those totalitarian states which arose towards the first half of the twentieth century, for they represent something both statistically anomalous and, in a number of significant ways, express principles contrary to the nature of the present-day state. Instead, we shall focus on their tempered successor, the liberal-democratic-socialist amalgamation state which holds to itself the near-universal support of the modern political and ethical mind. Originally the bastard child of compromise born of those who held to the critiques, but not to the answers, raised by the purer strains of revolutionary socialism, this mode of societal organisation has only grown in scope and in overwhelming acceptance since its inception. Of remarkable note on this matter is the continuing exodus of the academic economist from the camps of thorough liberty, an exodus only partial on the 'merely economic' front, but one most complete with respect to 'social' aspects, to adopt the vocabulary of a certain strain of 'libertarian'.

A more universalised elaboration of the effects of coercion will be presented in the second part of the current work. For this moment, we cast our view towards the complicity of the economist in the liquidation of culture, a complicity made inevitable by his unjustifiable severance of culture and economy.

It was mentioned close to the outset of this work that orthodox economics has, since inception, failed to adhere to, or to articulate, the principles of its proper scope. It has, however, displayed a tendency towards a confinement of its efforts, and an increased but unspoken certainty regarding where it thinks its subject lies. Adam Smith felt it natural to focus on the monetary nexus in terms of tangible material resources and concrete example. Additionally, The Wealth of Nations is a work permeated with an underlying sentiment of the political, of international relations and of ethics, which served to embed the economic at least loosely within the fabric of actual life. Malthus articulated the relations between population and economy, which, despite a degeneration of methodology towards the wholly quantifiable, at least had in purview some sense of the oneness of the monetary nexus and culture. The narrowing of the economic mind is a particular manifestation of the decline of that ideal of intellectual breadth to which the renaissance had strived. At present, the economist is an extremely specialised statistician, for whom even talk of the whole monetary nexus is too grandiose. He prefers instead to scrupulously search for the historical trends of labour, or the laws entirely particular to farming root vegetables, or laws applicable to international trade. These sectorial laws, he admits, are not to be considered applicable to the national macro-economy itself.

Throughout the time surrounding the turn of the twentieth century, the internal intellectual conflicts of the economic science were reflective of the general dilemmas of the period. Those silent, implicit, rooted truths came before the judgement of a new wave of positive rationalism. In economics, this spirit manifested as the gradual solidification of the science into the forms of aggregate quantity. This advancement challenged the implicit presuppositions of the rustic economists, namely the nesting of the economy within, and in terms of, the life itself. While orthodoxy was busying itself with its own clarification, or reduction into nothingness, the discarded undertones of eighteenth-century economics became explicit in the subjectivist school. Attributable to Menger, the original distinctive feature of this school lay in its claim that the essence of economics lay in the

laws of the subjective and functional, rather than in any characteristic of the economic object as such. Despite a brief period of popularity through its refutations of the increasingly influential Marxist
schools, the subjectivist impact left little lasting mark on the orthodox
currents. The 1920s brought with them the rise of Mises and Hayek,
both, and especially the former, being rejected on methodological
grounds by mainstream academia for their apparent radicalism or absolutism. According to popular thought at the time, the economic science had successfully 'integrated' all that was useful in the subjectivist
stance of Menger with their models of materialist and objectivist em-
piricism. Since present economics, and perhaps the whole of modern
thought, contains as an essential component its continuous efforts to
flatten the qualitatively distinct into the quantitative and commensurable, this attempt to integrate snippets of subjectivist notions into
an objective framework is only characteristic. This pragmatic middle-
ground, with rapid movement, crowned itself sovereign just prior to
Keynes' General Theory, the immediate and absolute acceptance of
which proved that the science had irreversibly chosen the more profane of paths. From this point on, developments in orthodox economic
thought are simply not worth mentioning - they are merely appen-
dices to the General Theory, no more structurally revolutionary than
the dusting of a shelf. All consider the prime subject of economics
to be aggregates of homogenous physical units, the relationships between which are to be continuously refined through the latest correl-
ative analyses and then formed into some predictive graphical model,
new, in-vogue versions of which constantly appearing so as to meet
some political fashion.

It is perhaps unfortunate that the Keynesian methodology won
the adoration of the economic establishment, relegating the whole
Misesian alternative to abandon, recalling it only briefly to adorn the
footnotes of an introductory lecture on business cycle theory. Lament-

ing this, however, supposes the possibility of the alternative path, a thought quite obviously naive to those with an understanding of the depth of modernity's entrenchment in the popular spirit. To adhere to the Misesian would require at least some affinity with modes of traditional thought which, by the time of Mises, were nowhere to be found in the barren land of global intelligentsia. The domination of philosophy by modern science, of metaphysics by positivism, of absolute justice by pragmatism, a reality of order by one of chaos, and of object over subject. With these presuppositions, the choice of economic doctrine was as much as predetermined.

The Keynesians and their offshoots have played a large role in the severing of conservatism and liberalism. It made explicit the doctrine that the highest end of economics was aggregate statistics and the monetary, and required that the state have a leading role in this procurement, through active and drastic use of powers unthinkable for a state to possess a mere century earlier. It is true that states had often enough engaged in currency supply manipulation through means of the debasement of currency, but, as suggested by the fact that the term 'debasement' has now been replaced with 'expansion', the act of metal-clipping was seen as the mark of either a tyrant or a failure - by no means was debasement understood to be a country's medicine.

The rally behind the methodology, apparatus and conclusions of Keynes meant that the economic science was now wholly complicit in any defects hereby caused and could not but glide over these defects with the blind eye of ideology. This acceptance of a centralisation of economic decision-making power in the state was juxtaposed with a fast emerging contempt for the traditions, now superstitions and prejudices, of the masses, who, unable to run an economy for their own benefit without governmental supervision and balancing, may, perhaps, be in need of supervision and subtle contortion in other areas, too. In their treatment of women, perhaps, or in their dogmatic belief in the essentiality of national borders, or perhaps with respect to their inability to properly educate their own children. For why would it be so that while the natural interactions of man create periodic economic calamity, a fate only preventable by enlightened state intervention, he is in all of his other actions perfectly capable of self-governance?

The development of economic thought has as its driving force the gradual subordination of all thought to the prevailing fundamental presuppositions of the age. As epistemology has become positivist, economics has followed suit. Metaphysically, economics has, through its methodology, come to deny the reality of teleological causation in man, who may now be broken down into his constituent parts, modelled and predicted with, ideally and eventually, absolute certainty. Ontologically, economics identifies reality with the object and illusion with the subject; it is ethically nihilistic, it is reductive and quantitative. Sociologically and politically, it worships individualist rationalism. The quietude of the economist with respect to the erasure of the traditional is not a surprise.

The absolute incapacity of an alliance between this economics and conservatism is perhaps most obvious in the former's treatment of the family, specifically regarding all which relates to sexual essentialism or dimorphism and any of their societal implications. The belief in the absolute similarity of sexes will here be left aside, irrelevant as it is to the core of this discussion. This notion has, as of late, gained traction within economic academia, but remains an unessential part of economic dogma. The matter at hand is rather the different approaches taken to the utility of gender roles arising as a result of differences in analytical framework, rather than empirical happenstance. Even those economists who hold innate sexual differences to be quite real cannot defend against, and generally contribute to, the destruction of traditionally differentiated gender norms. It is telling that even Sowell, the best modern representative of any sort of conservative libertarianism on grounds of positivist economics, follows Mill in suggesting that an exorbitant and stagnation-inducing decay would follow from a separation of average woman from the forty hour monetary-nexus work week.

The historical state of the male sex, and thus the masculine principle, has been marked by its industriousness and proximity to the traditional economy. The economy and the reign of money are bound to appear with more fixity in areas of lower trust, intense calculation and distance of personal sentiment - the higher these factors, the more necessary the medium of money becomes for the facilitation of mutually beneficial interaction. It is for this reason that money rules much more in metropolitan than in rural areas. We say this not to slander money - it has its just place, being a highly useful means of rendering others useful without necessitating unworkable personal relations and risking that conflict hereby caused. An inability to work with those new, unknown, and transitory people by means of trust alone is quite unavoidable; it is possible to bridge this by means of money. The male sex has predominately situated itself further into this unknown, monetary-based society than has the female. A prime motive for his doing so has always been the provision for those with whom he interacts within relative safeness of the non-monetary sphere, this being his community, children, or wife. His participation in the *economy* served primarily the higher, supra-monetary end of the home (here understood to be those places in which man considers himself at home, rather than the house as such). The economy has its use for him insofar as it can be used to serve these and other non-monetary duties, objects of his adoration. Should these fields lose their splendour, the economy will cease to satisfy the depths of his spirit. Despite this, we see no reason as to why his activity within the economy would hereby decrease. A destruction of the home environment holds the same duality of consequence as does taxation - the deprived individual may work less, work being a less effective means of satisfying his highest ends, or work yet more industriously in hopes of hereby attaining that which he has lost - this loss being either monetary abundance, in the case of taxation, or spiritual contentment, with respect to the destruction of home. He must naturally occupy himself with something. Indeed, those characters which are formed by these possible responses, formally oddities, are now quite abundant. The man who works less, having nothing to work for, becomes the nihilistic eternal child to whom responsibility is anathematic, while he who works more, finding meaning nowhere else, becomes the labour addict for whom the notion of virtuous leisure becomes truly incomprehensible. Under this characterisation of the peculiar male nature, it becomes visible why the economist is bound to express a prejudice in favour of the more masculine patterns of behaviour. To make this clearer, we will make brief mention of the female role, which must be shunned to the degree that the masculine is preferred.

Being the maker of home, rather than the marker of consumer product, the traditionally feminine aspect will never contribute directly to the monetary nexus to any significant degree. Inasmuch as the monetary nexus is concerned, the value of the homemaker consists solely in her ability to inspire the monetary worker towards a higher productivity. As already mentioned, the role of the homemaker, enlarging the value of all which constitutes home, has an analytically ambiguous effect on man's monetary-productive behaviour. On the other hand, the existence of this role has a two-fold effect towards the *ceteris paribus* reduction of the monetary should the quantitative magnitude of the monetary be considered to be the ultimate end of the economy.

Whenever a service is performed outside of the monetary nexus, the nexus foregoes expansion to the degree that the specified service would have been monetised in the absence of any alternative of the more homely labours. If it were possible to reduce this aspect of the feminine role, the economy would happily grow in order to replace it. Additionally, the freeing of the woman from monetarily non-existent endeavours massively expands the amount of labour available to the service of economic activity, allowing for a great increase in cumulative economic product. As such, the economist qua *economist* must be expected to be a principled supporter of all measures which, through the state or otherwise, effect the elimination of the traditionally feminine principle. His perspective being only economic, we cannot expect him to stand to defend the elimination of the traditionally feminine role, which must be seen as a pure 'waste product'. Insofar as this role can be effectively eliminated by the state, it is bound to be seen by the monetary economist as another one of those inefficiencies, or irrationalities, of backwards 'laissez-faire' society, which, just like those real endeavours which underlie diagnostic aggregate statistics of the 'macro-economy', require continuous oversight such that economic growth be maximised to the ultimate benefit of us all.[5]

The manifest influences of cultural engineering in this area need little mention; whether one thinks them to be cause for better or for worse, they are visible daily to the naked eye for any and for all. The economy consisting of trade-offs, there is no reason to believe that the economist would demand an absolute levelling of the sexes. The traditionally feminine will be inhibited until it becomes too economically costly to invest in the inhibition of its more stubborn particularities. Latent femininity will reassert itself from within the monetary nexus, women gravitating towards a continuation of her traditional tasks, now performed within an impersonal, low-trust environment. With men this far unable to find the function of the feminine through any mutual dutiful relationship, he will seek it instead from within the economy itself. Man and wife, masculine and feminine, will tend to lose their unity of purpose; while originally serving towards the creation of a space more sacred, suited for the highest satisfactions of both kinds of spirits, these roles are instead to be allocated to the hired outsider, alienating the family from itself. For as long as the influence of the aggregate economic statistic holds sway in the minds of men, this development is entirely irreversible. Reassertion of those natural norms of the two spiritual roles would entail a grand and swift liquidation of the monetary nexus. Few are willing to entertain even the possibility of supporting such an 'economic catastrophe'. For now, we must continue to see the feminine outsourced and replaced, those would-be homemakers now labouring in the alien both for and as their own replacements.

The role most essential to the traditional feminine is that of the maternal. While mundane household duties may be yielded to the monetary with little pressure or loss, attempts to integrate the maternal into the economic must prove exceedingly costly, owing to the insuppressible reassertive strength of a property so fundamental. Nonetheless, firm movement in this direction has been made. There exists a chasm between parent and child on matters of education, and the maternal instinct has been increasingly satiated through more monetizable means, such as doting on infant animals.

When the mother plays the traditionally maternal role, the monetary nexus has diminished access to her labours and foregoes the monetisation of the task itself. Yet these are not the only monetary losses incurred by adoption of the roles of the mother and the father. More directly, and entirely unavoidably, the economy shrinks due to the very nature of childhood.

From the perspective of the monetary, the formative years of the child represent a pure liability. In accordance with our society's current organisation, the human being produces nothing at all for the first two dozen or so years of his life. During this time, it consumes a tremendous amount of resources which could have been more profitably invested elsewhere. While the presence of a child does appear to cause higher productivity in the father, this is more than offset in the economic withdrawal of the mother.

Now, population is undeniably necessary for production, and, after its period of incubation, the human brings to the economy resources far in excess of those consumed by it in its formative years. This alone, however, is not enough to guarantee that a healthy native birth rate, and the structures which support it, receive the approval of economic theory or the protection of the political classes tasked foremost to be guardians of the economy. To keep its primacy, this path towards the expansion of the labour force must also prove economically superior to any of its alternatives.

Luckily for the economist, it is entirely possible to increase the labour force without first incurring the major liabilities of childhood. Namely, a nation may instead have transplanted into it an adult population born from without. Naturally, the economist here expresses a preference for labour of the highest quality, for those in some way superior to the native labour force. Competition for the best of humanity running high, however, and the need for additional labour always somewhere abundant, the economist scruples not over the prospect of the importation of labour of the inferior quality. In many cases, an immigrant of lower average output per year than a native may nonetheless appear more economically efficient from the point at which the additional human unit first enters the national economy.

The market contains an extraordinarily useful mechanism for the economic valuation of future production, the interest function. Comparing one apple tree due to bear fruit in one month, and another expected to yield its first in thirteen, the interest mechanism acts, with good reason, to value the former more highly than the latter. An attempted elimination of all manifestations of the interest function would undeniably result in utter collapse, economic and cultural alike. Nonetheless, it must be made clear that grand problems are bound to arise should a society's diverse modes of valuation be transfigured and concentrated into the merely economic mode. Those sagely norms passed down as tradition, spawned either through the active influence of a virtuous elite, or otherwise the more accidental proliferation of a cultural trait the blind to the reason of its own success, often possess a great deal of farsightedness, a farsightedness which, while perhaps less valued by its modern recipients, regardless retains its original effectiveness. For example, the norms involved in the strength of the family unit may necessitate some general moral increase a number of centuries into the future. Should the norms governing the present well-being of family members be wholly integrated into the economy, it is highly unlikely that these aspects of foresight will be carried through into the conditions of the economic arrangement. The losses hereby occasioned must only become greater to the degree that the economic valuation of things is contingent upon the coercive actions of the state, a blind maximisation of the former necessitating an increase of the degenerative effects of the latter.

The economic mind will seek population growth through the metric of the would-be citizen's present, interest-discounted value. To demonstrate the effects of this, we will resort to some rudimentary numerical analysis: taking the first twenty years of an individual's life to average a net loss of 10,000 dollars per year, and an average of the following forty five years accruing a net profit of 20,000 dollars per year, we can, given a historically low discount rate of 2.5%, calculate the individual's economic value to be around 175,000 dollars. In absolute terms, he will, in the course of his whole life, generate 700,000 dollars worth of resources in excess to what he has consumed. A low-skilled migrant, on the other hand, may arrive in the host country at the age of twenty, and thereafter work for forty five years generating an average net profit of 12,000 dollars, yielding a lifetime profit to the economy of 540,000 dollars.

From a more long-drawn perspective, even one wholly economic, it is clear that, supposing any remote relation of the quality of a child to its parents, the former, native-born individual better secures a lasting prosperity. Yet, in interest-discounted terms, the latter individual brings an immediate wealth of around $330,000 dollars, making his importation worth ninety percent more the representative native birth. This figure understates the immediate economic benefit of the method of importation as such. The immigrant's value-additions become exhausted after forty-five years; the native's after sixty-five. After those forty-five years, we would, the individual's working life being exhausted, bring in a second immigrant unit, increasing the per-year expected return of the immigration policy by another half.

It must be added that this holds despite the fact that there exists no explicit market in capitalised labour, that is, no market wherein one may buy another's future labour decades in advance[6]. Instead, forecasted changes in future production are themselves capitalised in areas such as private bond markets, stock markets and other projections related to the rate of profit. It follows that, insofar as the maximisation of the aggregate statistic becomes an end of statecraft and of a civilisation's peoples, we must expect a continuous pressure towards the replacement of the native birth rate with immigration as prime means towards replenishment of the working age population.

These specific consequences of a drift towards monetary consciousness are not isolated - they act to exacerbate one another, hastening the advent of something akin to an irreversible decline. To the degree that man loses his highest spiritual ends, we can expect, and can easily observe, that he attempts to replace them with the monetary, and that array of things therewith purchasable. Should this occur, he will come to cherish, through his narrowing of consciousness, present pleasure and discounted values instead of those values which live beyond the span of his own individual life. In doing so, he must become complicit in, and actively facilitate, the destruction of the traditional family structure and the replacement of the native by the immigrant. Insofar as he lives in a state-led society, this transfiguration of the mind from spirit to matter must bring with it effects more dire.

Incapable of lamenting the severing of ties between one generation and that which comes next, current dogma serves quite well towards ensuring the severance of those connecting one generation and that which came prior. For one, care for the elderly within the homely environment falls to the same blows which eviscerate the role of the homemaker - children increasingly removed from the care of the mother and placed as one amongst three dozen in collective arrangement under the eyes of a salaried employee; the elderly removed from the care of their children, instead placed as one amongst eight dozen in collective arrangement under the eyes of some other salaried employee. Indeed, these developments are far more complete with respect to the elderly than to children. It is unthinkable to many that the future well-being of the parent may be, to any degree, the responsibility of the child. Far more destructive to the continuous family structure, however, is the source of those resources by which modern care for the elderly is supported.

The revolutionary century brought with it the emergence and expansion of the state pension as means of continuance for the elderly. The immediately apparent effect of nationalised elderly provision is that the welfare of the elderly becomes wholly independent from the financial support of the family unit. Rather than taking place through direct provision of his own family, the elderly individual now receives a minute amount of resources from every tax paying family. From the opposite perspective, the taxpayer is relieved of the duty of caring for his own parents, and instead becomes taxed so as to support all parents. The individual thus loses another reason to bring a child into the world, for one's own child will be of absolutely insignificant benefit to the longevity of one's elderly self in comparison to the sum of other peoples' children. Those children who continue to be born are less likely to be instilled with the same degree of filial duty as was previously the norm - to do so is simply less pressing.

These diminished bonds are further burnt, or ignited into downright animosity, through the suspension of the pension above the political arena. Similar to how the 'just price of goods', once much sought by primitive economists, is now understood to be wholly fantastical, it should be quite obvious that it is impossible to discover a definitively just rate of state pension payments. The young wish to not be burdened by higher rates of taxation for the sole benefit of the faceless 'ageing population', while the elderly wish to reap what they have many times been told constitutes their due. When money may sit with equal justice in the pocket of any man, each man sees an enemy in all those wishing to lay any claim thereto. Only when all recognise a law of belonging, of right, can the collective live in peace. The splitting of young and old is a remarkable political phenomenon, perhaps the most explicit (though far from the most latently intense) of present-day demographic divisions.

It is no longer rare to find political parties representing the interests of the elderly as a matter of core doctrine. The youth come to see the elderly not as those commanding respect and inspiring duty, but rather as a parasitic class. The burden upon youth becomes greater according to the development of this system, owing to its necessarily inhibitive effects upon the birth rate, as well as the fact that this mode of organisation only has reason to form when the bonds of family, and thus the incentives towards the creation of adequate future generations, are already considerably weakened. As a consequence of a qualitatively and quantitatively waning working population, each successive generation of elderly will tend to receive relatively less than the last, should the means of provision be held constant. In order to have their pension demands satisfied, the total amount of tax extracted from youth must increase. It is far from certain that higher tax rates can facilitate this to any great degree - increasing the rate of taxation often leads to little change on total revenue yield. Further, those paying most towards this enrichment of the elderly are precisely those closest to retirement, who, understanding their position, vote largely along the same lines as do those demanding the tax increases in the first place, making these party policy makers less likely to choose taxation as preferred means towards the satisfaction of the desires of the elderly. The tax demands of the aged may, on the other hand, be satisfied by expanding the number of taxpayers - not through births, this taking too long, but rather through the importation of labour. Thus, under the regime of state pensions, the elderly will find themselves complicit in the replacement of the native population. It is quite likely that this fact eludes them - the determinants of their pension funds' price increases are never as visible as the increase itself. All that is necessary is that they tend towards a support of those actions which bolster pension payments. Doing so, they indirectly support the most prudent means hereto.

The initiation of the public pensions scheme can be little blamed on the economic science itself, an initiative primarily backed by the early twentieth century progressives and the non-revolutionary socialists. The science did, however, fail to combat this emergence through argumentation from a teleological perspective, and so could form no alliance with the conservative faction. The attitude of the orthodox is more starkly in contrast to that laid out in this work when judging the public pension as it currently exists. At current, viewing the inverted pyramid of pension payment servitude, we are presented with a number of options: increasing taxes on the young, increasing immigration, increasing the age requirement for the claiming of pension returns, permanently increasing budget deficits or an elimination of the public pension as such.

The infeasibility of continuously increasing taxes on youth, as well as of endlessly increasing budget deficits, is something recognised by both the economic profession and our own stance. Looking solely to the monetary nexus, the options most appealing for the economist are those of immigration and an increase in the age requirement for pension eligibility, with a preference for the former. Explicit callings for hitherto unthinkable amounts of immigration have become standard course for the science. Its representative financial newspapers and international 'think-tanks', as well as the sway its 'expert opinion' holds over certain supra-governmental institutions (namely the European Union and the United Nations), give good testament to this. Not only would this approach rebalance the age demographics of the industrialised nations, but it would also provide the that economic growth spurt so much cherished by those holding present political power. It is presumably understood that this must be a continuous process, rather than a one-off transplant. Orthodox academia has come to believe that, once realising their industrial potential, populations cease to breed and then die out, their living standards collapsing under the weight of the aged. This proposed causation appears as necessary and inviolable as was once held to be the case of Newtonian physics. We must conclude, then, that the immigration approach will be repeated once the birth rate of the new nationals itself drops below replacement level.

It is here worthy of mention that economics takes up an absolutely anaemic defence against transfer payments in general, incapable of giving any real weight to the disruption thereby caused to the societal hierarchies created and maintained by a system of liberty, which produces as one of its most important qualities its allocations of teleological gravity, or societal decision-making power, just as how the economic market puts monetary resources at the disposal of those most proven capable of satisfying the material wants of man.

A monetary focused economics may or may not support the initial imposition of a public pension scheme, but still less will it support its removal once the inevitable crisis point is reached. This course of action provides very distant benefits to the monetary, negligible when capitalised, and to a degree foregoes an opportunity to adopt the more favoured solution of immigration.

# 5

MIGRATORY CULTURE

Before proceeding further with our analysis of the failures and resultant ill effects of orthodox economics, it would be wise to elucidate the concepts of culture and migration employed within this work, and to discuss the relations of these categories both to one another and, ultimately, to the teleonomy.

A culture is a distinct cluster of values behaviourally expressed by any multiple of related individuals. Being clustered, correct identification of an individual's participation in a culture presupposes the ability to predict, and to understand or empathise with, the actions of the individual so identified. In interacting with his environment, man experiences successes and failures. In recognition of his deviation from perfect action (or insofar as he considers his inferior outcome as contingent upon the past inferiority of his will), man experiences regret, and, herewith, changes his approach towards any subsequent event understood to be similar. This is the tendency of the spirit towards the good - man is of necessity a fallen automaton drawn, with success according to his merits, towards perfection.

Clusters of behavioural norms come into being through the systemic process of adaptation for success. Within the environment of human society, the success of any endeavour, and subsequent adaptation, is contingent upon the results of all previous adaptations of the society at hand. Oftentimes, then, a norm flourishes, and is successful, not because of its isolated, inherent superiority, but because it is understood by others. Without this, there could never arise language, manners, and etiquette. In lieu of that sum of previous human adaptations, mostly primitive, which resulted in the environment through which these mediums became capable of carrying any meaning, their attempted employment would be unthinkable nonsense. This is not to say that all norms of communication are equally good; rather that the utility of a mode of communication in a given circumstance, insofar as we consider only its communicative purpose, resides primarily in accepted custom. Those characteristic modifications which qualitatively distinguish the communicative forms rest on the foundation of the common acceptability of the substratum which they alter.

Other cultural norms are valuable not because they allow us to communicate something of import, but rather consist in this thing-of-import itself. To the degree that a norm consists in the object of communication, rather than the communication thereof, is the degree to which its specific form can reach equivalence with the intrinsically good. For example, in a world barren of translation, the learning of ancient Greek is quite as valuable as that trove of profound texts, Aristotelian to Pauline, to which one thereby gains access. Despite this apparent equality, the value of the language is contingent upon the value of the lessons learnable by no other means. The degree to which the *essence* of a norm holds value is the degree to which it must be distant from the merely communicative. The most universal formulation of ethics has but one form; the means of its communication are conceptually indefinite of form. As such, one must expect from all grand cultures a tendency towards a higher uniformity, in matters of intrinsic ethical or behavioural virtue, which is initially masked by the disparities of the culture's particular modes of communication, which can never be fully understood by one outside of the culture. The communicative culture works to direct the highest cultural ends unto those partaking in the culture, its particular communicative form continually adapting according to these people's general receptivity. These means, of course, barely consist in the form of explicit dialectic and syllogism. Rather, they are almost wholly symbolic or metaphorical.

Given the diversity of the human species in both body and soul, we would be foolish to presume that cultural norms of a specific people are properly understandable by those to whom it has never had the slightest particular adaptation. These outsiders may, as esoterics, be able to pierce through certain regions of a culture's communicative fog, and thereby catch for themselves a glance at its highest treasures. Even for the esoteric, however, the profundity of the communicative means themselves, latent in the symbol-culture, will never find full expression. They reveal themselves only to those for whom they were made. The degree to which one can be guided by the symbolistic is to the degree to which one understands it to be integrated, known and meaningful immediately upon its confrontation within one's soul, rather than coming to one as cryptic and alien, yet showing the faint promise of profundity. This confrontation's effects are largely determined prior to any explicit consciousness of the object, in accordance with the particular of the individual's supra-rational faculties.

Being present in an environment adapted to his particular sub- and supra-rational characteristics, man is shepherded by his culture into a fitting form of striving towards the apex of the cultural good. This cultural good is far more likely than any rationalised, post hoc alternative to be approximate to the highest good, and is certain to be so with a far more penetrating depth. Analogous to this is the nature of the fluctuating array of prices which makes up the market economy and administers its particular allocations. Here, too, we find an organic system which could never, as a whole, or by matter of principle, find itself inferior to a rationalised draft economy created without reference to the inevitable unknown, a system wherein every price point is chosen by the judgement of a centralised planning bureau. Cultures being particular to peoples, we ought to be utmost sceptical of any person's attempt to culturally reform the spring of that which is foreign to him. The peoples leading the reformation are not subject to the same contingent principles as are the reformed, and, as such, norms of interaction cannot be transplanted with any remote certainty, any more than a bridge of the Thames may be duplicated over the Nile and ensure a safe passage. Naturally, this applies to international as well as to intranational interference, the occupiers of a country's state system likely as different from many of the governed as a Dane is to an Arab.

Should all higher cultures, religions and spiritualities have a common ground, it is this: know thyself, serve the one above the many, sacrifice the many on the altar of the one, transfigure the unknown, become the One. This applies to the Abrahamics as well as to the Buddhists, the Stoic and the Nietzschean, the Greek and the Hindu. To pursue this matter more deeply would be to escape the scope of our present topic. As such, for now, this unanimity of opinion, the object of the highest various works of all cultures, will be taken as representing the ethical truths mentioned within this work's first two parts.

The human untempered by culture is closer to brute than to the man of our common experience. The behaviour of man, and his supremacy to the other animal species, lies essentially distinct from his biology. The configuration of the body is merely the requisite circumstance for his higher developments, which lie in the norms which he has arduously developed through his history. Should one supplant these norms, yet let man keep his native cunning, and he will fall far beyond the level of the brute, becoming diabolic. The great rationalist inversions of the revolutionary century testify to this. These grand inversions relentlessly stripped away all remnants of the old order and postulated a false God to sit in its place. Twenty-first century man claims to have learned from these events, believing now that these violent modes of revolutionary cultural idolatry are outdated. Instead, he endeavours to deconstruct his native culture's structures and unleash its human contents into some abominable formless shape. To this end, he feels that he is free when those frayed threads pulling him heavenwards finally yield to the forces of gravity, falling to the floor and, to his relief, out of his sight. In his directionless wandering, they tangle around his feet and snag on bush and thorn. He falls on his face and rejoices in his individuality.

For better or for worse, the nature of an established culture is the rejection of, and discrimination against, that which goes against its grain. The natural modification of a culture has always been a slow and attritional process, the most visible aspects of which are those swift collapses which follow the gradual erosion of a cultural structure's underpinnings. The more self-assured a culture is, the more indiscriminately it rejects difference. That which is doubted is easily toppled and cannot be held fast to in times of weakness, fear, or desire. That culture, which we may group as more-or-less 'Western', held assurance in itself until the middle of the nineteenth-century. Before this point, any doubt of its own sophistication, development and superiority is scarcely found. The native culture or way of being is undoubtedly supreme, its architecture the most sublime, its arts the most beautiful and its faith the most pure. This preference for self is not confined to these norms' geographical birthplaces. Should a group migrate to a foreign land in number enough to continue with its activities unimpeded by the restrictive exclusiveness of its norms, it will, given that it brings with it a cultural assurance, segregate itself from its host population and retain its defining characteristics for generations. This has been particularly notable in the Germans of Russia, the Irish in America, and the Chinese of the Malays. The effect is yet stronger with respect to the more highly normative. Religious enclaves are prone to segregated survival for many centuries. Not only when surrounded by the simply alien, but even when subject to persistent and violent persecution, has the self-assured religious spirit held firm and multiplied.

The tendency of self-assured belief systems to avoid disintegration, to retain identity and to congregate together very strongly suggests that the present cultural erosion has not been brought to pass by immigration. In demographic terms, immigrant populations of western nations hold identity with their ancestral cultures far more often than do the western natives - despite being fractional minorities in foreign lands. While mass migration may hasten the disintegration of a terminally ill host culture, it can only do so as do maggots to rotting flesh. Should one ever wish to stop the festering, something deeper must be redeemed. In order for us to have accepted the festering, something deeper must have been induced into giving way.

The story of the loss of western self-assurance is a topic worthy of a whole tomb. Its roots span many eras, and its development has mostly been authentic, decentralised, and unconscious. It is only in and after the revolutionary century that these tendencies have become manifest in a widely untaken and intentionally subversive effort. All reminiscent of the older order is to be torn down. All things vertical are to be remodelled horizontally. The guiding intelligentsia will form a monopoly upon vestigial verticality, and, once its goals are achieved, disintegrate itself into the uniform diversity of the flatlands.

The economist has, for the most part, remained outside of (or, more correctly, lagging behind) the core drivers of the valueless society. It is a testament to the inherently conservative and hierarchical position of the true economic science that all which even vaguely resembles it finds itself unable to conform to the postulates of the wider modern 'social sciences'. While much action has been spent to remove man from the science of his own action, only so much leeway has been gained. As of today, the economist has been unable to deny that indiscriminate resource allocation is untenable, and that discriminatory hierarchies are indispensable for the continuation of man; though to make such an explicit admittance would undoubtedly bring to blush many economic academics.

The economist has, however, consistently stood side-by-side with the new intelligentsia on matters of hierarchy and discriminatory judgement insofar as they do not affect the monetary nexus. His eccentric, capitalist beliefs by no means deter him from asserting that he is, on matters of ends, left-wing at heart. Unaware that his economic beliefs are strictly incompatible with egalitarian presuppositions, and that the rise latter will eventually result in the persecution of the former, he has supported the use of the state, and its many affiliated branches, for the erasure of those traditions which hold back man's monetary productive potential. Market economists have been far from inactive in the promotion of alternative family structures, alternative sexual interests, mass migration, forced diversity and a universal female participation in the monetary workforce.

In the previous chapter the realms of the familiar and foreign, homely and alien, trust-based and money-based, were briefly mentioned. All things home, and all things private, act as direct competition to the activities of the alien world of the monetary. Neither represents an inherent good; they are to be traversed such that they best complement one another. In a coercion-free teleonomic system, they tend towards that very state, just as how the fields of manufacturing and retailing exist symbiotically within the market system. Higher spiritual culture has always resided within the private and trust-based sphere. Were man's belief in his culture to topple, and its value for him to decrease, we would see in many a rise in participation in the monetary nexus, and in all a lower value attributed to the gift of life. The economist has admitted the use of the social engineering state by appointing the central bank as the economic man's protector. The same presuppositions permit the phenomenon of state-backed cultural liquidation.

Every major culture gravitates around its living ideal, a form of being or of action. These ideals are uncommunicable, as their exact form can never be repeated, lying in the perfect traversing of the unknown matter of life, a category which mutates when any part of it becomes known. This is the ideal man, who holds mythological prominence over the absolute, the highest good and the All. He is incomprehensible in our fallen state. The full profundity of this figure lies in the essence of his Act, rather than its material or sensual effects. It is because of this that all depictions of ideal man must ultimately be found, though to varying degrees, lacking. These culturally sacred figures, all aiming to particularise the meta-ethic, necessarily have shared traits. Foremost, they act such that every action secures the highest, time-independent good for the totality of being, and such that each heterogeneous desire is sacrificed to the homogenous path. This role of the cultural hero has never been to momentarily comfort, but rather to inspire others to act according to the Way. This Way, always shunning temporality and seeking the eternal, gives no value to pleasures of the moment, and asks others to do the same, asks them to break the dependence of their satisfaction on the immediate and worldly.

All positive and adopted systems of ethics hitherto embedded at the heart of a culture have thus found little greatness in the traditional economy. Instead, they have directed man away from it. From the perspective of economy-as-end, this is troublesome. In fact, the two are so opposed that the latter can only come gain prominence once the former has truly become uprooted. Insofar as a culture comes to view the economy as an inherent good, it will, knowingly or otherwise, hasten and permit the process of cultural disintegration and a retreat from its own particularisation of the meta-ethic.

It must be reiterated that the position held here is not that the economist has been actively rooting for the destruction of tradition in all of its forms; it is rather one of demand and the satisfaction thereof. No consumer knows the whole process of the production of any one good he consumes - yet this chain moves into place to meet his desire for consumption. Whenever man comes to elevate the value of the economic, the chain of its production will, unseen by man, begin to utilise the precious and sacred as a means of its production. The resource with the most potential in this matter is, and must be, man's aversion to error or to sin. For every barricade stripped away, man will attach more value to material goods, to the monetary, and to the means of their procurement, economic labour. Startling ignorance has often been shown in this field regarding the true worth of all beyond the monetary. The notion of the supremacy of the monetary, and even its universality, runs deep enough that advocates of inflationary policy will seriously argue that man needs his assets depreciated so that he feels desire to spend and to consume. This cannot be at the loss of nothing. Economists would do well to more often recall one of their supposed presuppositions: everything incurs trade-offs.

The intellectual classes may be characterised by an arrogant rootlessness, from which the economist cannot be excluded. Each sector of intellectuality decries as sentimental a particular segment of its wider opposition. In the case of economics, the sentimentalists are those whose beliefs in the sacred and private act to forestall the expansion of the economy. The 'inefficient', when referring to the private sphere, refers to action which does not put monetary earnings as its ultimate end. As such, the aesthetic, while to the teleonomy highly essential, is to the economist, especially when mingled with business, a mere waste of gross domestic product. Discrimination of peoples according to private reason or taste is also a sentimental and inefficient waste. In fact, anything which acts as a barrier to man's labouring for cash is deemed inefficient. This condemnation is often quite implicit, praising the streamlined, 'functional' and cultureless as models of efficiency to which we all ought to aspire.

In standing idly by as the culture around him topples, and by ushering in the monetisation of man as a means towards the securing of a growing economy, the economist makes himself the unwitting subject of his own much used quip, first levied at Keynes, mocking the absurdity the proposal that the economy may be bettered simply by digging up and filling in holes, or by throwing stones at windows. Instead of smashing windows, decultured man has been led to produce a future of dissatisfaction and regret, and, conscious of this regret, he returns to his labours in order to fund another dose of his consumption. All is valuable only as a means to the highest good. The consumption inspired as a consequence of the modern era is as beneficial to the true economy as those much-mocked holes are to the restricted economy.

Man's habitation of the private can be affected in two ways, the border between which is indiscernible but real. This is a division quite alike that involved in the questions of the sensitivity of feelings: is a person more volatile due to an enhanced ability to sense what exists, or due to a lower tolerance to that which is sensed equally by others. In the same way, the degree to which man occupies the private is dependent upon how he values that which he considers familiar, and a change in the familiar itself.

In a homogenous and self-assured society, the scope of the private is extensive. While not universal, its reach knows no bounds.

Where the foreign and monetary lie, the familiar remains always perceptible. A key aspect of this perception of social familiarity and belonging is the implicit understanding of a unification of purpose. The most sacred and personal of all private, social spaces become alien and desecrated whenever one feels that those with whom one shares the space are divided in purpose and hold animosity towards one another. The space ceases to be one's home.

In a united society, man understands that those around him, whoever they may be, are receptive to and approving of that which he holds dear. He can behave true to his identity, with little need to adopt an expansive persona. The populace shares the same fundamental ethical norms, the same symbology, the same religion and the same language. Utmost important for a unified society is the sentiment that our neighbour's property belongs to him alone. Should we see our neighbour and immediately reflect that what he possesses may instead further our own ends, then we feel resentment towards him, and wish upon him subjection.

In feeling a sense of solidarity with his fellows, the realm of the familiar and the private expands for man. As mentioned, the private realm has a diminished need for, and involvement in, the monetary nexus. The private realm is based on trust, and a mutual recognition of the malleability and ultimate beneficiality of the relationships which take place within it, which have no need for contract. Social interaction with the like-minded is highly conducive to a steadfast adherence to one's shared principles, and a natural remedy to doubt. The social activities representative of all healthy private spheres - communal meals, shared fasts, mass exaltation of the sacred - have always acted to calm man's desire for self-serving consumption, for vice, and held him fast to virtue.

The erasure of the intimate holds the honour of being one of the great tragedies of the revolutionary century. The murmurs of uncertainty felt throughout the nineteenth-century exploded into prominence with the emergence of two wholly novel dispositions: the intuitive supplanting of natural law ethics by the democratic will of the people, and, closer to our day, the acceptance of permanent and accelerating ethno-demographic changes and the notion of multiculturalism.

These phenomena could not strike at a healthy culture - but, nonetheless, their arrival does not necessarily signal that the host civilisation was bound regardless to endure a slow and sure death. There is a degree of causative principle at work. Cultural self-certainty ebbs and flows. The recreation of this certainty is the true meaning of the word 'integration'. The lands of Europe have not been lands of uninterrupted peace and unity. Grand and sweeping changes, religious or political, Lutheran or Napoleonic, by nature or by man, have stricken the continent since man first lodged his studs in its soil. Yet, after volatility, unity always worked towards its own reestablishment. Liberty ensures this tendency. It may not be the swiftest conceivable mode towards the reassertion of unification in the wake of a chasmic rupture, but it is certainly the surest. Excepting those grand and universal declines of the spirit, in the face of which neither liberty nor coercion can inspire a regeneration; excepting these, it is only when the mechanisms for the reassertion of unity face systematic repression that a civilisation cannot be expected to heal its own wounds. Such systematic forces are in the present era abundant and make the combination of democratic multiculturalism more certainly lethal. These forces do not manifest in shock events. Rather, they create continuous and barely discernible adjustments which show no signs of ceasing.

The fundamental deviation of the democratic spirit from the spirit of natural law which, more or less, preceded it, is this: that which 'belongs' to another under antiquated natural law is in fact the righteous property of oneself, or of one's demographic faction, should a large enough number of people desire it to be so. It may be held that the original proponents of democratic theory had no such universality in mind. This may be the case. Yet if we consider democracy to be that system under which the will of the quantitatively great decides what is to be done with the totality of resources at a civilisation's disposal, the ethical position of democracy's forefathers is merely incomplete. These partial democrats must admit the moral universal of their system and attempt to qualify it with their individual opinion, one of many, qualitatively indistinct within a democratic framework. According to them, certain resources are to be left with those who own them, an artificial nesting of the absolutes of natural law within the relativity of the democratic superstructure. They must admit, however, that the acceptability of this conception is subject to the approval of the masses; the democratic principle is anterior. The refusal to trespass within another's domain becomes immediately downgraded from a matter of sacrilege to a matter of calculated means.

The democratic spirit is a particular manifestation of that same spirit which makes duty itself contingent upon the judgements of an unlimited individualised rationality, independent of the actual scope of the genuine rationality of the judging individuals in question. This spirit served to remove one's fellows from the realm of ends, wherein the other was a subject with his own justifications, his own desires and his own goals, which, in certain circumstances, the totality of which constituting the study of absolute ethical justice, trumped one's own rational, individualised judgement *per se*. Instead, one's fellows were brought closer to becoming a means for the satisfaction of the ends of one's own personality. The scope of this change is naturally dependent upon the permeation of the democratic spirit within a people. It is interesting to note that, to this day, one views other with democratic or natural-law spirit in proportion to that person's proximity to one's own private realm - the abstract and unknown man being treated almost entirely under democratic suppositions, while the closest members of our families remain to us sacred ends with an inalienable domain of their own personal sovereignty. This domain necessarily exists for each subject, and one's relationship with an individual is drastically changed according to whether or not one recognises that person's sovereignty therein. If one recognises the validity of plunder according to popular opinion, then what barrier stands in the way of conscious manipulation and deceit? Should one wish to use either of these so as to secure the object of will of the masses, and thus one's own conception of the will of the masses, can a man of democratic spirit truly repudiate him on ethical grounds? Only an ethic with no sense of proportion would or could forbid lying to the enslaved.

The democratic principle is propagated by the spring of resistance to some perceived tyranny. Per hypothesis, this tyranny is defined consequentially, rather than as a violation of the sovereignty of the individual as such; for the proposed medicine against this tyranny is the permitting of the latter. Democracy, then, springs from the individualised rationality of dethroning the oppressor, identified by the masses, without reference to individual ownership rights. Must we be surprised when, following the universal adoption of this spirit, we experience endless dethroning of supposedly oppressive classes without any respect to these classes' property rights? As a result, we begin in nineteenth-century to distinguish the formation of interest groups segregated along various demographic lines, each led by their own particularised democratic ideology, all seeking to topple an identified oppressor for the apparent greater good.

A land of democratic spirit generates a permanent and lucrative position in society, the position of convincing others that the resources of their fellows would be better placed in their own hands, or, in the case of those who wish to avoid any sentiment of their own selfishness, into the hands of a deserving third party. This actor thrives on divisions cleaved between an otherwise unified people. If there are few such gaps pre-existing, it becomes lucrative to inspire their creation. The classic and most pervasive of these demographic animosities lies between the materially rich and the materially poor. Yet, despite its historical prominence, the chasm now preventing any sense of a unification of purpose between the rich from the poor is, in its magnitude, a particularly modern phenomenon. There have certainly in every age been have-nots who believed that they could obtain happiness only by possessing what lies in the hands of their perceived haves; yet this desire did not constitute the essence of the identity of the poor in question, as is now increasingly the case. The have-nots must first be convinced that the objects of the haves are potentially their own, and thereafter discover justification for this now possible transfer.

The first of these requirements was provided through democracy, the second through a vague 'class consciousness' later solidified by the Marxist framework. Through this latter, the proletariat-in-itself became for-itself, that is, learned of the exploitative nature of its relationship with its oppressor and thus demanded justice.

There exists a not uncommon conservative opinion that one may placate the poor in their consciousness of income inequity by maintaining programmes which diminish this gap. In this consists, perhaps, the most naive of all modern conservative notions. The supposed goal of this policy is the prevention of uprising and revolt. For this uprising to ferment, the belief must spread that the most resource endowed members of society own too much, and that justice would be served by giving resources back to those with fewer opportunities, or to those who perform the function of the labourer. The naivety of the conservative position lies in the belief that the intensity of this consciousness can be reduced by admitting its central premise, that a state of inequality has arisen as a consequence of injustice, while satisfying only a slither of those demands which therefrom follow.

It is instructive that, despite in recent decades reallocating a far larger amount of resources than at any other period in the history of man, the level of class animosity now exceeds that of any point hitherto. The simplest way to create an outrage is to spread a moral principle and then deny its satisfaction. It takes no historical revisionism to see that man with self-assured justification and power to plunder does in fact plunder and does not in fact cease until either his power of self-assurance begins to wane. Animosity between the haves and have-nots retreats only insofar as there exists a mutually recognised hierarchy between the two. Conservatives would do well to focus their efforts on a recapturing of that sense of duty and reverence which has evaporated, to their lament, between parent and child, old and young, noble and plain, above and below, rather than to direct policy which presumes the supposition that these relationships are unjust and exploitative.

As we ought to have learned through this last one hundred years, the plunder of the apparently unjust 'haves' does not stop at a mind revocation of their right to property or sovereignty. These 'haves', and their sympathisers, were, the central principle of their exploitative nature being admitted, repeatedly led to slaughter. These reminders are but fulfilments of the principles necessarily in play when one makes light of degrading the relationships of men from ones harmonious to ones of struggle. This principle has been starkly evident in widening all demographic cracks which have emerged in the democratic landscape.

The principles of the class dialectic were exported into the affairs of the sexes quite early into the history of modern demographic animosity. If proletariat and capitalist are bound by history to be locked in struggle, the benefits of one detrimental to the other, regardless of any particularising opinions or values of the individuals themselves, might something similar not be the case between man and woman, or between masculine and feminine? The 'woman question' became unavoidable by the end of the nineteenth-century. The feminine principle is economically unjust according to monetary standards, might it also be socially unjust according to cultural standards? This question settled, the opinion of the woman, as of that of the worker, became irrelevant. They must be made aware of their plight, and then - struggle! They must develop from women-in-themselves to women-for-themselves. Any woman who disagrees with these new-found notions must be seen as living proof of the rooted depth of the patriarchal presuppositions of her culture.

These ideas struck euphoria, providing meaning in a world increasingly lacking in it, and for a people increasingly incapable of bearing it. This strain of thought is remarkable for its secular religiosity. This is a result not of its rigid, structural and internally-referential dogmatism *per se,* the depth and initial impenetrability of which in present times appears to be tending towards that of Scholasticism, but rather of its genius moralisation of doubt itself. Where Christianity often took doubt to be the manifestation of an individual Luciferian sin, these modern schools take doubt to be a manifestation of the culturally prejudicial sin. For he who remotely accepts its ideological premises, doubt hereby becomes transfigured into its inversion, it becomes a mechanism for the reinforcement of belief. In doubt, one proves oneself right. It is in this psychological irrefutability, as well as in the obvious social importance and sense of purpose which they bestow unto the individual, that these doctrines have come to solidify into that chasm left vacant by the religious spirit. With respect to the 'woman question', democracy once again presented the primary means, and universal ethical justification, for this struggle's battle. We point out here that through the notion that a demographic must be coaxed from outside in order to cognise its for-itself, oppressed state, we are provided with a recipe for animosity of infinite variability.

It has been mentioned that the democratic society gives rise to a new class, the class of the political carrot-dangler. His job, his route to power, is to offer to the many of the goods of the few, and to convince the former that to themselves these well belong. This is no hard task. Any democratic state, no matter how restrictive, already employs this redistributive mechanism through both its inherent structural identity, which gives the power of the non-democratic few to the democratic many, as well as in its barebones particulars, in the democratic police, in courts, public roads and public works, or any other assorted 'necessities'. Considering this plunder just, will many be dissuaded from travelling further down the path of the democratic spirit, a spirit which has become, in its principle, an unquestionable idol? And so it seems that those highest in society, by whatever fashionable metric, become the political class' carrot. In reality, those peoples hereby plundered are seldom the most powerful. It is rather, this being especially the case in settled and long-established democracies, the most powerful who plunder those men one rung below themselves with the assent of the lowest. Thus the ironic tendency of these redistributive systems to consolidate an unchallengeable might in the hands of the highest echelons of the political class, usually constituted by the descendants of those few aristocratic families and orders of the pre-democratic world who had the foresight to seize the democratic blade pointed at them and to turn it towards the evisceration of their less fortunate class contemporaries. In the newly democratic world, attempts to reclaim what the demos have conquered are met with anger from those who believe that these things are now rightfully theirs. This animosity is by no means monodirectional. As the oppressed hate and plunder the oppressor, the oppressor begins to hate the oppressed.

In this ever-growing perpetual jostling, the sacred shrinks and the redistributable grows. This is merely synonymous with the universalisation of the democratic principle. Farmers plunder and curse the city dwellers, the city dwellers take up political weaponry against the rural, the rural plunder the rich, who recuperate their losses from the coffers of the middle classes.

Man's relation to a fractured society is wholly different than to one united. Coming into contact with a stranger, he can no longer believe in any concord of higher spirituality. The treasures of each of their respective souls likely lie in two entirely opposed hierarchies of value, in opposite schemas of the Good and the bad. These schemas collectively forming the political power of a democratic society, it is necessary that these men of contrasting ideals will come to treat one another less with mere indifference, and increasingly with a mixture of anger, distrust and condescension. Further, given the clan-base nature of a developed democracy, man will begin to view those on the other side of political fault lines as oppressor or as parasite - not because of the nature of his demographic or his action *per se*, but simply as a consequence of the threat posed by difference of opinion in the democratic society. This necessitates a higher failure rate for acts which employ more intimate, and more honest, modes of personality. Man must retreat into himself and thus develop his persona in his own stead. When this becomes general habit, spontaneous intimacy becomes a truly foreign phenomenon. With no hope for connection, and with expectation of mutually destructive inner convictions, trust fades, and the private sphere retreats. In concrete, this manifests itself in an inability to establish, and difficulty in continuing, any sort of community ritual. Community meals and fasts cease; when leaving one's house, it becomes unthinkable to leave one's door open or even unlocked; advanced security mechanisms become increasingly necessary. This latter is made more necessary by the spirit of which runs sits at the core of the democratic society. Accounts can less often be built on the credit of trust, and the striking up of honest conversation in public becomes more and more rare. This retreat of the intimate, the disintegration of man from his environment, must also affect man's works. He has trouble integrating his convictions into his working life, becomes ashamed, or fearful, of developing an environment or demeanour in his employed labours which bears any direct relationship to his most cherished beliefs. Thereby, he alienates himself from his produce.

The difficulty which any unity of higher expression faces in the fragmented world has grand effects on the ability of man to produce grand works, those through which he makes manifest and manifold the Idea of his culture. The crowning works of any culture are created by, and emanate, a deep-running and truly profound knowledge of the respective culture, its symbology, and its points of closest contact with the meta-Ethic. Those cultural creations which lack this third aspect are incapable of timelessness. This does not guarantee the timelessness of those works which lack it not. Should a culture lose its anchor to the meta-Ethic, it will naturally become incapable of preserving those works whose profundity lies in a fixed relation thereto. When civilisations undergo their great twists, turns and evolutions, the great monuments of the older era undergo the scrutiny of a regenerated eye. Given the tendency of cultures towards the one Good, and the general unison of diverse cultures at a higher level of abstraction, we can see the permanence of a cultural artifact's power as a testament to its function as a window into this highest Good, rather than as a portal to transient cultural fashions and misendeavours. These works act to rejuvenate the always fading past and take it by the hand into the unknown. Without this rejuvenation, the past is no more a spring of present life than a line is a shape.

As we have said, such a work cannot spring from the mind of a man without a profound understanding, and impenetrable conviction, of the central tenets of that belief which he wishes to enshrine. A person's soul can only obtain and hold onto such ideas within a single-minded and self-assured culture. If the environment of man continuously reflects back into him reminders of his ideals, he has much trouble ever losing them. In an environment barren of these points of reflection - an environment with an almost categorical overlap with the alien - man's single-minded idealism must tend to fade, finding refuge only in a self-built solitudinous privacy. Yet this privacy can never act as full substitute for the decentralised cultural interaction of the vital culture's public places. Left to only his current mind, and personally gathered reminders of his treasured ideas, the solitary man undergoes no process of continual refinement according to the impulses of the external vital culture. He rather, with his invisible idiosyncrasies, veers off into the unknown. The produce of such men has always been too esoteric, in both the actual and derogatory sense of the word, to be of any real worth for wider society or to inspire any widespread cultural rejuvenation.

While the ability of western man to create true cultural greatness was already much diminished by 1910, these later creations being less the image of the divine and more the image of an earlier image, we will not, for this moment, go much further back than this when making comparison between the present day and a now-lost era. To do so would widen our scope far beyond what is here called for.

The reflective cultural environment above spoken about is not exclusive to architecture and creative aesthetics. It also includes, perhaps as its greatest component, its people. While the former categories instil within the observer a reminder of his culture's higher ends and purities, a cultural people provide a similarly refining, but more strictly corrective, function, in forms both passive and active. The passive form consists in fear of judgement, based upon a person's expectations of, and reverence towards, the belief systems of those around him. Additionally, in having one of our fellows catch our attention, and in judging their actions, we indirectly judge ourselves more clearly. To witness a glutton while we ourselves are desirous of gorging allows us to see ourselves from another perspective, through which we can more easily dispel those subtle, internal lies constructed as shrouds for sin. This is passive, self-reflective social reformation. Passive reformation may also be other-reflective, mostly apparent in the behavioural changes man undergoes when he immerses himself within a group. With this, one takes the expected judgements of others and abides by them, at least outwardly, so as to leaven the social sphere and to avoid either conflict or judgement. One wishes, in almost all cases, not be neither a subject of mockery nor an obvious outcast.

The company of man also offers the active mechanism for the reinforcement of values - verbal communication. The prime difference between the active and passive is the much greater proclivity of the former to clearly provide entirely unknown information to the subject, while the passive strongly evokes and refines that which already lies within. The active mechanism is also much more explicit. In having foreign propositions brought for one's examination, and offering up one's notions for scrutiny, one's value structure undergoes a gradual sharpening, and, in most cases, a gravitation towards the cultural ethic or spirit of the times. The active method of interpersonal value reflection exists only insofar as all participants in a conversation lay aside persona and treat the other as if he were part of the private environment, or, which amounts to the same, insofar as one understands the other to share with oneself a higher ethical purpose. It is, as a matter of principle, always possible to recognise another as sharing one's highest ethical purpose, for the ethical imperatives of men command them all alike as rational beings, not disparately as individuals. Nevertheless, consciousness of this unity at this remotest level of abstraction is testing for an individual, and simply impracticable on the cultural level. The further away from this ultimate abstract we can move before locating the most concrete point of unity, the easier it is for one to instinctively throw off the persona in another's presence.

The fractured culture, then, necessarily entails a recession of the active form of interpersonal reflection and of the true personality. The notions of the previously unified culture cease in their development, and, in doing so, become less suited to self-defence against the ripostes of the emerging fracture-cultures. The shift of the shared space from the private to the unpersonal, combined with the knowledge of the divergence of one's higher values from those of one's contemporaries, leads also to a clear diminishing of the goodness of the passive, other-based form of cultural incubation. In his life's twilight, Marcus Aurelius lamented that within a word of imperfect people, the virtuous man must act in ways that he finds, in themselves, quite contemptible, in order for him to best carry that very torch of virtue. To be social in a sinful society, one must act the matter of the sin, though certainly not its intent, in order to not destroy one's affinity with, and ability to influence, one's people. Hereby the virtuous must subject themselves to temptation. They must lay their own hurdles, and many will inevitably fall to those vices from which they wish to protect others. So it is in the fractured democracy. From others emanates not the pressure towards the imperatives instilled in oneself by one's own culture, but rather, insofar as society has ruptured, the pressure to appear to hold behavioural standards at odds with one's own conscience. This urge towards conformity, often rational, inspires error insofar as it is a creation of the self-uncertainty necessitated by the times. When conforming due to this weakness, one later feels the regret of self-betrayal. Through these and such actions, man, creature of habit, undermines what remains of his own creed.

Changes must also take place within the passive, self-directed mode of reflection, for a person's placement of another within his frame of values is dramatically affected by the degree to which the former can properly empathise with the latter. We do not condemn rodents, for we do not understand them to be acting, teleologically, towards the highest good; our instinctive belief in this regard being determined by the concrete of one's internal value structures and modes of understanding. In short, one can only locate oneself through this form of reflection insofar as one sees oneself, one's potentiality, in the actions of others, whether judged good or bad. When we see ourselves in the glutton, we cannot help but feel both pity and a desire to hold fast to our own moral standards, such that we do not become alike the pitiful man. When we see ourselves in the hero, we feel the highest respect, and the very same determination to hold fast to our own moral standards, such that we do become like the hero. When we see a glutton, but do not see ourselves in him, we, if we admit him human, feel only confusion or an arrogant superiority. The same applies for the supposed hero who shares nothing of one's own potentiality - we deem him driven by vanity.

The retreat of intimacy, and thereby empathy, in the fractured world, then, leads to a nullification of the advantages of all modes of interhuman cultural incubation and personal refinement. Left in its place are isolated, arrogant individuals incapable of understanding, or properly communicating with, one another.

Interaction with humanity may be the most explicit form of cultural incubation and development, but it is not of sole import. Isolated from other forms, it is as sheet music to orchestra, or as commentary upon a poem. The other gem of culture lies in the environment bestowed to us by those of earlier times. The grand - cathedrals and masterwork sculptures - as well as the humble - commonplace housing, road paving and a balance of man and nature. Between the culturally reflective phenomena more easily categorized as either interpersonal or environmental lie instances which participate very much in both - dress code, table etiquette or intonation of voice.

Those works which mark the ages are called into being by a common spiritual movement. This consists of, as above mentioned, a profound and penetrating understanding of the to be enshrined moral system, untarnished by doubt. There is a second, lesser but quite necessary requirement: expectation of the social propriety of the work. A society incapable of encouraging the creative efforts of conviction will receive few great gifts, and the author who expects his works to be appreciated by no single soul will have trouble picking up his pen. The grand creator extracts the true form from the past and reinvigorates it with genius; yet in a fractured culture the past tends towards impenetrability, and the form of invigoration becomes more elusive. Simultaneously, man feels less assured, and is less practiced, in the expression of his intimate values while under this new public eye. As such, his works become less truly public, less cultured in a very strict sense. Even when the culture-spirit finds rare replica, the product carries little conviction or fittingness - its reconstructors may grasp the obvious and explicit, but cannot capture the spirit, which, owing to an inability to reintegrate with the past, will always and necessarily evade his grasp. This product must carry with it a unique form of lonely profanity; much is eerily corpse-like about this conspicuous replica.

Having little avenue in the public realm, the artist retreats to a private circle of acquaintances. His art will appeal to their idiosyncratic tastes and be marked in the eyes of the masses by an artistic disintegration of meaning, unity, and coherence. Though the public realm be left barren of aesthetic vitality, those objects of the functional world, which served as substratum for the aesthetic, will nevertheless still require production, destruction, and renovation, for the world continues to move. These more modern buildings will begin with an integration of the above-mentioned replicas, and become, with the passing of time, more and more the spawn of the growing mass persona, the orientation which, in everything it touches, sacrifices soul for utility. As this road becomes further travelled, the path of return becomes increasingly concealed, for these new creations will form the educative environment of coming generations, each more subject to the disintegrative sickness than the last, and each less and less capable of creating anything fit for public space on any level above the specifically functional. The new environment offers up no coherent theme, and its very essence rejects it being subject to the higher states of reflection. Anchor severed, with nothing in his environment which may recall to him his singular duties, the man of the fractured culture becomes subject to the most insignificant tides of fashion and impulse. No longer a sacred space, little resistance can be mustered against the addition to the public realm of the positively vicious or obscene, those 'attractions' which prey upon the vices of man and mark the completion of an absolute inversion. Instead of lifting man towards the gods, the public area becomes that which most assuredly submerges his spirit below his awakened animal instincts.

The arts of the private sphere continue in their involution. The prime string of coherence rests now in their conveyance of confusion and instability. While at first retaining some potential of profundity layered behind an ever-thickening wall of individuality, there comes a point when, no longer capable of understanding art to be measured by the absolute to which the old culture was, in its highest places, tangential, the ultimate principle of valuation becomes this individuality itself. Led by this notion, the arts comes to lose even the conviction of the artists, for his individuality must be measured in terms of an absolute 'emancipation', first from his culture, and then, this being exhausted, from his individual past. The active principle of absolute individuality tends towards an indiscriminate destruction of one's own creations. The steady footing of the father culture is now well and truly above him. While his forerunners were immersed in the waters of chaos, they could nonetheless touch their toes to bedrock and propel themselves with a lingering feeling of the impenetrable ground below. The later artists know no such thing. Persona begets persona, democratic spirit begets democratic spirit, and cultural decay begets instinctive decay. New modes of thought have come to entirely replace the old, these artists likely to have been raised by the progressive elite of the previous generation. The old methods appear wholly nonsensical, yet there exists nothing with which to replace them except a thin skin of muck, the immediate, the untested and the individually rationalised dozen-or-so conceptual relations which are created in attempt to fill the void left by the sunken past in which we see no bottom. These have no true symbolism, no environment, and no conviction; beliefs not enough to die for, but quite enough to kill for. For many of these, the only constancy of Being is its inconstancy, though some go so far as to deny even this. This belief in the sole truth of the absolute void becomes manifest increasingly in all forms of communication in what remains of the private sphere. The search for the serious, the real, that worth sacrificing; this search becomes seen as folly, and therefore suited only for fools. It is subject to a peculiar mockery, for, all mockery presupposing a solid ground from which to safely mock, this mocker must go on to mock himself. This inherently contradictory mentality can manifest itself in any form of action. Man intentionally 'fails', and, once recognising his intentionality, attempts to 'fail to fail', and so on. Thus there comes to prominence a culture of self-depreciation and of irony, which, like the attempt to look towards the peripheral of one's own vision, shifts its grounds whenever any such attempt is made, nestling one level of self-referentiality deeper. These expressions are not meaningless, but rather become quite lofty objects of contemplation when understood in the context of the author's singular intent. This is one of the true ironies of modernity, given that these expressions are idiosyncratic of those who laud the severing of the artist from his art.

The personality of the fractured society develops itself so, and so does the cultural environment shift from a subconscious reinforcer of value-unity and verticality towards a vacuous plane littered with ill-fitting, attention grabbing frivolities and assorted mockeries. For who would consider it their duty to respect and maintain that which has lost all sense of sacredness and importance? From a second angle, this rise of the persona is a simultaneous retreat of the private life's share of the teleonomy. In its wake lies the monetary realm, where interaction with others, rather than personal, intimate, and trust-based, becomes persona-rich, distant, and held together by coin. The world becomes truly metropolitan. The question ceases to be 'what can one find in social interaction' and becomes 'what can one extract from social interaction' The individual loses that which gave each new generation its spiritual footing, and finds his goals - all men needing goals - in the attainment of spurious short-term pleasures. He cannot forego them for he has nothing to which he can make them sacrificial. His spirit is driven by envy, ever fermenting in the democratic substrate which informs him that he may take what he wishes should he only raise enough ruckus in appeal to the now deeply embedded political demagogic caste. He can be expected to lust after a material shining of his now alien countrymen, with whom he will shortly after feign even the most common of pleasantries.

His subsequent labours far from being of higher worth, become more and more worthless, for all purchased therewith, that is, all which gives it economic value, can only build up a short-living Sodom. The morning after its consumption, its utility spent and its glamour forever gone, man is left split, half harking back to Sodom, his other half planning the route to Gomorrah.

The economy grows.

# Part Two: The Impotence of State Conservatism

# 6

## CONSERVATISM CONTRA LIBERTY

Having been led through the revolutionary century to our current position, where are we to turn? Those of a genuine conservative persuasion cannot but turn with disgust away from those proposals put forth by almost all vocal theorists of liberty and liberalisation, who have not, and can not, from within their theories, condemn the modern turn of events from any perspective satisfactory to this type of conservative.

There are also the many voices of a wilted democratic conservatism, or pragmatic conservatism, whose positions appear to be those fixed to the end of a fixed-length string tied around the ankle of an ever-marching progressivism. Many, aware of the futility of an active support of any current democratic party, patiently await the coming of a truly conservative political party, and ask that the likeminded, too, keep waiting, never perhaps suspecting that a utilisation of democratic means for long-term conservative ends may be as futile as eating broth with a fork. These voices of compromise and idleness appeal to very few of those more fixed conservatives seeking the genuine reversal, or hierarchical transmutation, of the damages done through the preceding ten dozen years. There exists much latent energy within the conservative wing which wishes to act, and it is drawn to that voice which matches the vigour, persistence, and radicalism of the progressive ideology. This voice calls for conservatism through force, an internal subversion or overthrowing of the democratic apparatus, duty through force and culture through force. This is the fascist position. While it exists to varying degrees, and while few explicitly consider themselves fascistic, it is nonetheless true that, as a principle, it is the near-sole source of present-day conservative or traditionalist vitality.

We reject the statist route wholly. While those who advocate for its implementation often have in mind a goal quite noble we wish to show that their suggested means are entirely ill-suited to the procurement of their desired "traditionalist" society, and pale in both reliability and potency when compared to the only possible alternative: the free teleonomy.

The fundamental differences between liberty and fascism are two. Firstly, in a system of liberty decision-making is predominantly decentralised and incremental. Fascist decision-making, on the other hand, is centralised and absolute. Secondly, in a system of liberty, one is always free to opt out of participation in any norm if he is willing to bear the cost of this. In fascism, one can be subject to norms despite one's active non-consent. One would expect, given these descriptions, that the fascist route is the clearly superior means to a securing of cultural unity and stability. This expectation would arise from a failure to consider that matter, so easily forgettable, which is essential to the suitability of any societal construction: the actual value judgements of those very real individuals who are to be ruled hereby. As we will see, these judgements continually assert themselves and attempt to form their own natural norms, whatever environment they may find themselves in. By ignoring these natural values and norms, the social engineer, like the sculptor who enraptured by the object of his ideal creation becomes blind to the properties of his marble, risks shattering that upon which he goes to work.

The decentralised society forms its norms procedurally at every level of interaction. The father exercises a degree of power over his son which cannot be exercised by his town's mayor or the father's workplace manager, despite the fact that, in their relevant areas, both the mayor and the manager hold significant power over the father. The overflowing of this latter power into the realm of the paternal relationship would be unrecognised by all involved, as all have an implicit understanding of the boundaries of a particular power. If one oversteps these bounds, be he a child, a father, a manager or a mayor, consequences will be felt. The child, overstepping his power over his siblings, is held in check by the father, who is aware that he, nonetheless, has no power to manually prescribe all individual rules of interaction between his children. Every individual has a limited sovereignty, in the society of free men, no man is slave, and, therefore, no man is god.

The formation of these norms is most visible when many individuals are simultaneously introduced to a shared unknown and begin the process of environmental discrimination. A fitting example would be the first morning of the school calendar year. Hundreds of youths come together into a wholly unknown environment oversaturated with information and interest. The new pupils evaluate their surroundings, teachers, and fellow children alike, and make an unknown number of unknown judgements, inspired by perceptions which they themselves could not begin to describe. Nonetheless, these judgements are synthesised, communicated, and refined. Hierarchies are established, and individuals feel friendliness or hostility to one another through differences as subtle as distanced observation of silent demeanour. Within a couple of days, most of the labour of construction have been completed, and a structure is quite rigidly set. A mutually recognised and intricately weaved hierarchy emerges. Groups form, and within each of these groups emerge leaders and followers. These minor groups are themselves sorted, as units, within the major structure. Almost all recognise, *and agree with*, the established order of dominance, yet none can explain it. Again, such an order is not absolute: recognising power necessarily entails a recognition of its limits. If breached, from these limits the unknown re-emerges: the chaos of conflict. The established conceptions are called into question, and the relationship at hand is examined anew. If this breach appears, to the mass of those involved, to be justified, then the power of the active, breaching individual rises, while that of the passive individual, whose power has been beached, falls. If unjustified, then the power of the initiator shrinks. In these transgressions, we need not suppose, and, naturally, do not condone, any violations of the genuine principle of freedom. Instead, here occurs a re-evaluation of that to which no individual has an inherent right, his authority over others. An increase herein may be a result of the display of some perceived nobility or courage, while a fall may arise from participation in some shameful behaviour, or a failed attempt at the assertion of one's authority. As such, the hierarchy is both highly fixed yet receptive to the integration to new information. It is also incremental - no one student can unconditionally command all other students. If the most popular attempted to, he would quickly lose that crown.

This mechanism, with few adjustments, is at play in all interaction. In fact, this hierarchy is implicit in all action as such, for it is by this that the particulars of ethics are constituted. By use of this example, we obviously do not mean that man is equal to the child, or that the structures created by the child are either infallible or worthy of emulation. It serves rather as a microcosm of the incremental, decentralised principle at work under the employment of liberty.

On the level of a whole society, this principle is immeasurably more complex, and far more robust against the tyrannic overstepping of bounds, which constitute those deviations from liberty to coercion. Within the level of analysis here employed, that of the school, we can view in action one more key function of the decentralised principle: self-segregation. This we saw in the separation into sub-groups earlier described. These naturally forming sub-groups are united by a clustered value structure, the essential seed of culture, and highlight an important example of the futility, and danger, of forcing unity between the voluntarily separate.

Each group has its own system of values, this including its own categories of virtue, mechanisms of hierarchy mobility and trials for the proving of an individual's worth. The values that apply quite aptly to one group may prove quite incomprehensible and truly unhelpful to another portion of society. One group may value intellect and educational attainment as a barometer of competence, a second may have a system of hierarchical mobility based almost exclusively on pure physical assertiveness. Both groups may be acting under correct moral structures. To admit as much is not to permit an instance of that much-decried "relativism" if we are to define this term in any way that does not allow it to cover the totality of human morality. The particular of human morality are contingent upon the nature of the human material thereby governed. A society incapable of rising to a higher intellectualism might to better to govern itself according to the rules of a well-defined hierarchy of intimidation than according to those of a botched and transplanted rationalism.

Two self-segregated groups naturally remain distant from one another, perhaps to the point of entire mutual seclusion. This is not the *creation* of difference and group identity, but rather a reflection thereof. Groups which adhere to wildly differing value hierarchies can seldom be successfully integrated, for, as this difference grows larger, the possibility of arriving at a mutually acceptable response to any given dilemma shrinks exponentially. If this self-segregation becomes repressed, and the peoples integrated against their distinct natures, their interactions must, being incapable of any compromise on joint grounds, be dictated instead by the iron fist, most often possessed by those who show no moral qualm regarding its brash and wanton utilisation. We see that forced integration results in the general subordination of the virtuous group to the vicious group.

This poses a grand danger to those who wish to interfere with the process of self-segregation. Such an interference is an essential part of the fascistic and progressive ideologies alike. The barriers of progressivism are manifold and omnipresent - they hope that by eliminating all expressions of in-group preference, they may improve relations of contrasting casts, an emulsification of peoples. What has rather happened, in those places of most singular and complete attempt, has been more akin to a blending of either bleach and ammonia or vinegar and milk, yet we see no signs of their ceasing. This is naturally a consequence of the progressive belief that all resistance is an affirmation of the need for further pressure. With respect to fascism, its resistance to self-segregation is inherent in its desire for national unification, most properly demonstrated by its insistence on a centralised and universal school curriculum and the absolute restriction of alternate methods of education, as well as in its general attempts to thwart outward expressions of contending value structures, attempts which range from overt state censorship to the behavioural rules enforced within public spaces. In funnelling the children of all creeds and castes into a mono-curriculum school system, the ability of families to segregate their children is vastly diminished. It is far from clear that this integration serves the intended purpose of an assimilation of the abnormal more than it causes the pollution of the purity of the orthodox children's educative process. The predominance of this latter effect is quite obvious with respect to those attempts to mingle castes or classes - the introduction of farmers' sons to elite schools does more to vulgarise the noble than it does to make kings from seed sowers. It would appear, too, that this is the case with the mixing of major and minor cultures.

This integration of education must also cause strife between the family unit and the state, which, the latter having the final say in all such matters, will result in a stripping of general educative power from parents and a bestowal of this power upon bureaucrats and central authorities. This seizure cannot be limited to the choice of schooling curriculum, but must, if admitted, extend to those forms of education which take place within the home. If parents are incapable of selecting for their children that school which best prepares them to serve society's interests, what reason have we to believe that they are remotely capable of properly preparing their children to attend, and seamlessly integrate into, the state's favoured schools?

Fascist methodology, insofar as it represses the expression of alternative systems of action of belief, works to mask and mingle those very opposites, which forbids nature from running its course, a course which will, even so far as the fascistic belief is concerned, select in favour of the supreme culture and against those values more vicious. As their plans stand, this mingling will result in a need for an increased level of centralised supervision: those individuals who formerly made themselves distinct their undesirability, expressing their inner natures within their self-segregated enclaves, must now, as far as is possible, in being blended in with the cultural mass, conform in appearance to its norms and leave the expression of their inner natures to within those circumstances unreachable by the watchful state eye. This calls for more invasive methods of searching, which reduce the dignity of the right-thinking individual and further concentrate the totality of societal power.

A society at liberty is further distinguished by granting all within it a freedom to fail. Yet again, this trait may at first glance appear to be solely negative, and, once more, such a conclusion arises as a symptom of the arrogance of the fascistic soul. For to view this as a negative requires, amongst other wholly untenable beliefs, the understanding that all useful knowledge, that is, all knowledge required for the governance of every action of every man henceforth, has already been discovered and is readily available within the wills of one's chosen state leaders. This is not so, and never shall it be. No culture is perfectly adapted to the present, and certainly not to the future, the future remaining, to a degree, inherently unknowable.

The rejection of the freedom to fail extinguishes the only mechanism by which the teleonomy may select for and disseminate traits in due accord with their successes and diminish their power in proportion to their failures. To go down this path is to deny the very process through which the fascist's much-admired traditions actually came to be. The existence of the family, for instance, was certainly not theorised *a priori* and then grafted onto a placid culture of uniform people-clay. The family rather came to prominence in a natural fashion, due to its fittingness to the circumstances of man - the refinement into a single entity of the masculine and feminine principles of being, and the ability for the new generation to reliably inherit the material and spiritual successes of their elders. Those who refused to adopt this arrangement exercised their freedom to fail, as did those who indeed acted first towards its adoption. The eventual consequence of this was that the teleological gravity of the former group shrunk, while that of the latter expanded. So has it been with all ebbs and flows of societal arrangement - the emergence of property rights, the refinement of language, the particularisation of religion and creation of ritual. Any advancement of the human species has come as a consequence of acting differently to what has to that moment been considered best, which leads us back to the law of knowledge which fascism, and central planning as such, must either kneel before or blithely ignore: that it is impossible to predict which of your currently held truths will be rejected or improved upon in the future, the knowledge of this being necessarily out of the reach of any given mind. It is the sin of pride; that which we now know is all that there is to know, such that all deviations must be forced to fit into our established schema.

The function of a freedom to fail exists within culture and economy alike, with roughly equal proportional importance. In terms of the latter, it is expressed through the entrepreneurial function. We may nonetheless excavate this function from its economic setting, and use it to refer to a particular disposition with respect to action as such, a disposition in which all men, from time to time, and degree to degree, must partake. Man has an idea which he believes may prove an upgrade to existing methods of action. The majority of these actions lead to failure, his supposed advancement in reality being retrogressive. The consequence of this failure is that the entrepreneurial man loses resources and is thereby less capable of further experimentation - a natural and necessary reduction of the influence of those with bad ideas, or, more essentially, a proportional reduction of the influence of negative entrepreneurialism as a class of action.

In the opposite fashion, it does sometimes happen that, through this mechanism, an individual lands a grand success, vastly improving upon existing methods of action. Through these successes, the particular entrepreneur, initially of little influence, becomes quite powerful indeed – that is, until he once again fails. This vertical mobility, the bankruptcy of Lords and enrichment of the nameless, reminds us of an ever-present truth: an era's giants, themselves granted power by the freedom to fail, will one day be dethroned by that power which crowned them, their own rise itself requiring the simultaneous toppling of that which was previously believed to be an eternally true, best possible mode of action. Any attempted elevation of the fascist position runs into the following paradox: the position must be argued for as it is currently unaccepted and shunned, that is, in order for it to become adopted, the marginalised and unaccepted opinion must be spread against the force of the current dominant cultural value structure. Though its merits are now unknown to society, and its proponents maligned, its adoption would nonetheless benefit mankind greatly. From the perspective of the modern fascist, then, a virtue of a free teleonomy would be that it would grant them the freedom to fail in the spreading of their ideals. Yet, admitting that society would benefit greatly from allowing a decentralised judgement of the popular and unknown to take its natural course, fascism then wishes to cull this very virtue as soon as the fascistic principle comes to represent temporal order rather than temporal chaos.

The virtue of any way of life was, at one point, entirely unknown to those who currently practice it. The only way for the unknown to become systematically drawn out of chaos and refined into a vital order is through the establishment or preservation of a system that permits deviation from the known good. The espouser of fascism admits this but adds the caveat that this hitherto ever-present epistemological reality has made an exception for him alone.

The defining claim of this order of belief, then, should not be seen in its concrete provisions, but in its supposedly categorical epistemological supremacy. For the defining position of the fascist is not that one thing is better than another, a mere judgement of value - for such a claim is required of all ideological stances, not only the fascistic; it is rather the difference separating the assertion of absolute, objective knowledge from the assertion of a subjective belief that one possesses knowledge. The former claim makes any freedom to fail an entirely negative trait. The claim announces an infallibility, while the latter synthesises current order with the reality of the ever developing unknown.

One would predict, however, that the conservative societal engineer would deny this epistemological position in all of its expressions other than in himself. In fact, he must deny its previous expressions, for only through their falseness could his own claim of the finality of knowledge ever have come to develop. He who holds any norm, and wishes to impose it coercively, denying by force deviations therefrom, must, in one of two ways, contradict himself from the start. For there was a time when this apparently perfect norm did not exist, a time when it was necessarily unthinkable, yet to be pulled into existence from the unknown by some cultural visionary or apparent deviant. The claim may have then arisen, prior the emergence of the fascist's chosen norm, that the then-present structure of values must be codified, centralised, and solidified, and that deviation therefrom be disallowed. The modern-day fascist must judge this claim's justness. If he denies its justness on the basis of the superiority of his own norms, then he contradicts himself epistemologically. Yet if he affirms the claim, then he advocates for a society in which that which he seeks to enshrine never came into existence, that is, he contradicts himself ethically.

Aside from its decentralisation, the free society harbours an essential variability of incrementality in its decision-making. Decisions are made on an incremental basis insofar as they synthesise all available information into a particular judgement rather than so as to fit an established universal principle. The most highly incrementally minded decision is also the perfect decision, the one which simply takes the entire of reality into account. Despite this, a higher weight given to the particular truths of a situation does not necessitate a more apt action, for the devil lies in half-truths, not in complete falsehoods.

Sins which result from the deviation from a subjective principle are the result of an increase of incrementality, an incrementality which integrates the immediate bodily pleasure of the erroneous behaviour which is ignored by the positive ethical principle. A greater level of preciseness is, in itself, neither good nor bad. It is a variable which, in unison with other such traits, constitutes a decision. Only in the context of a given whole can it be judged. An attempt to exercise a highly incremental ruling based on scant information is simply bad judgement. For example, each and every individual may be justified in making the decision of precisely when, and for how long, and at which rate, he will work overtime. One individual may work ten hours a week overtime during the summer months and none at all throughout winter, another may never work overtime, a third may work overtime whenever his evening schedule permits it. The information required to make these decisions is exceedingly rare: nobody could with good reason decide these matters other than the working individual himself and, if he is an employee, his employer. If this decision were to be decided on a much higher level of order, at the level of a central government, for example, the flexibility inherent in such an individualised decision would have to be foregone in order to secure any remotely orderly mode of decision-making. The information required for each of these decisions is concentrated primarily around those individuals who are thereby most affected.

To centralise such an apparently simple matter, one would need to either employ many thousands of individuals within a new state bureaucracy, the Department of Overtime, tasked with the analysis, processing and collection of all relevant information regarding any submitted request for a change in overtime hours, or, as is more likely, employ a short number of individuals who will draft fixed overtime hours applicable to every labourer under the state's legal authority, without exception. There are, on the other hand, situations where reasonable decisions may only be made at a significant distance from the individuals immediately affected thereby. These areas benefit greatly from a system of uniformity and predictability rather than selectivity and malleability. All successful military structures have contained a thoroughly robust and rigid hierarchy of command, in which the order of a superior is simply an unquestionable imperative. If an army had no central plan of action, but merely consisted of a congregation of isolated individuals advancing, retreating, and breaking line according to their particular individual judgements, the army would swiftly cease to be. In sacrificing much of its decentralised judgement, it gains the might of unified action and an internal predictability

There are some decisions that require such predictability that it is almost impossible for the individual to deviate from them at will. Certain 'actions' (or reactions) are so uncontrollable that it is not clear whether they ought to be considered behavioural norms or instead strictly biological functions. The yawn is a prime example. Another example, certainly more normative but no more effaceable, is man's tendency to sort himself and those around him into perceptual hierarchies of competence or dominance. If we may ascribe purpose to a quality so instinctive, we would say that the intent of such decision-making is the creation of a predictable schema through which subsequent decisions can be made which carry any degree of authority and weight, such that this phenomenon may be considered meta-decision-making. Without a stable superstructure, the problem of group decision-making becomes tremendously difficult. The methods employed for the judgement of dominance are remarkably consistent across all cultures and eras. This instantaneous recognition of status, which considers an unknowable number of variables, establishes with little delay a natural chain of command in almost all imaginable social gatherings. Where this instinct lacks unity disagreement must occur, and jostling, either physical or intellectual, must take place to the swift reestablishment of some form of order.

Considering the employed array of instinctive judgement criteria to be generally determined on a level above that of the particulars of the individual, we see this trait of the species as being essentially non-incremental on any explicit level. By this we mean that many aspects of the judgement of competence cast from one individual onto another are independent of his particular rationalisations. To allow the particulars of these judgements to proceed immediately from the rational justifications of each particular individual would be so detrimental to the functionality of complex social interaction that these particulars have, for the proper generation of our species, remained much aloof from the domain of reason. A man who had to continuously and consciously will the coordination of his vital organs or the proper function of his nervous system would be similarly useless and would not survive. If the unity of judgement implicit in the discrimination of competence were shattered, then the process of arriving at generally agreeable dominance relation would become immeasurably difficult. Even if a momentary success were achieved, the volatility of judgement, and residual minority disagreement, would ensure continuous eruptions of higher conflict, escalating swiftly from stubbornness and arrogance. The strict necessity of such a mechanism is more easily demonstrated by viewing its implementation from a distance, rather than, as we are wont to do, from immediacy of our own society, an established structure built thereupon, wherein, as a result of its ubiquity, isolation of the principle becomes difficult. For our distant ancestors, the absence of this primitive and seemingly barbaric instinct would have led not only to mere inefficiency, but to calamity. Our differences may, in some cases, when only a small number are divided, be settled verbally. Without developed language, the prospects for a race incapable of instinctive establishment of dominance are more dire. To create the preliminary structures necessary for societal organisation, such a species must resort ubiquitously to bloody force against its own ranks instead of implicit and peaceful signalling. The exceptional disadvantage incurred by any species lacking in such universally accepted cues of dominance explains why very few such species of a complex order can be named. From the historicobiological perspective, it is unlikely that man could have ever come to be without this universal "centralisation" and inflexibility.

For any given category of decision, there exists an optimal distance away from the immediate judgements of each individual thereby affected. This degree is not knowable in any abstract fashion but is rather slowly discovered while traversing the endless road towards the development of being. Nor is this degree remotely static. With any change in the totality of present human knowledge, this optimum degree undergoes some shift. Technology which increases the ease of distanced observation allows decisions to be more efficiently centralised, whereas an increased complexity or urgency of any area of human life naturally favours a more incremental mode of decision-making.

The grand flaw of central planning lies in its essence, its irrevocable transferring of decision-making from smaller units - individual, family, business, or community - to the absolute largest, most distant unit, the central state. Decisions which were previously determined at the point of action or in anticipation thereof, liable to immediate adaptation to the intricacies and idiosyncrasies of any smaller unit's circumstances, are made unresponsive to that very information which allows the decision to be made to the benefit of the unit.

A fine example of this is the decision-making involved in the education of a child. The uniformity of educational standards sought by all forms of central planning ideology comes at the expense of the power of the family. Acting under the dubious presumption that state planners are as likely to be acting in a child's best interests as are the child's own parents, and also allowing the planner to possess a far stronger faculty of judgement than the parents in question, we are nonetheless unable to conclude that the planner's choice of action for the planner will be better than that of the parents. There exists such a tremendous gulf of information separating the parents' and the state's knowledge of the particulars of the child. The parent has direct experience of the manner in which the child interacts with the world, its aptitudes and weaknesses, like and dislikes, and, a factor so highly important and yet wholly forgotten by the modern busybody ideologue, the opportunities forgone by the child and those around him should the child focus solely on a formal education.

There was a time not too long ago when a universal and mandatory minimum educational age of sixteen would have entirely demolished the ability of many families to continue their own existence. It is a fact that less well-off families had (and, in the absence of enforced uniformity, still could have) their greatest salvation in their children's labour. These families, farmers or workshop labourers, indeed often birthed children with this exact labour in mind. It became the final cause of the child's existence. Without the assistance of the child, or the expectation thereof, the child would not come to exist, and the parents would be unable to support either those children or themselves.

This is but one of an unknown number of matters of potential import which are taken into incremental consideration when the educational decision is made at the level of the family. More importantly, this relevant information only exists on this level.

Were a representative of the central education board tasked with choosing the best course of action regarding the education of a single child, it would necessarily be at an informational deficit unless the decisive bureaucrat could somehow obtain at his disposal all experience exclusive to the parents. This level of information would require the bureaucrat to expend his entire labour on the educational direction of a number of children countable on a single hand. At this point, however, the established system can no longer be considered remotely centralised, for there is no central ruling principle determining the education of the nation - unless a higher level decision maker becomes designated and strips the powers of the bureaucrat here discussed, who at this point has become a pseudo-member of the family. Should this step be made, we would revert back to our original position of the ignorance of the judging unit, with the addition of the exorbitant cost of paying a significant portion of the population to act as some cumbersome division of bureaucrats permanently stationed within every child-bearing family.

It is certainly the case that the vast majority of decision-making would be most efficiently carried out at neither extreme of the spectrum of incrementality. No decision which takes into account all variables can ever be made; no decision which takes into account only one variable has any use. This poses a question similar to one with which the economist is decidedly familiar: how much land, and how much labour, ought to be utilised in the production of a given good? He would answer as follows: through the existence of a system of signals which indicate, as far as mankind is aware, the relative values of marginal units of inputs and outputs, or of means and ends. Within the monetary nexus, this is the matter of the price system. Its function is broken down insofar as there exist forces which can acquire and utilise resources without incurring the trade-offs inherent in those resources' utilisation, and insofar as there is no reward allotted to those who discover and exploit price differentials between inputs and outputs.

The universalisation of this claim, as best demonstrated by Mises, offers one of the unbreachable systematic rebuttals of the socialist economy, or, more precisely, of statist economic centralisation in general. This argument can be summarised thusly: the core goal of socialism is to remove all 'surplus value' extracted by the capitalist and to have the otherwise-exploited labourer capture the entirety of the value of his work. This is to be achieved by making capital own-erless, or, what amounts to the same, owned by all. This 'all' is to be represented in the state by a centralised allocator of capital and land, who, despite having ultimate discretion regarding the allocation of the nation's capital, does not receive for himself any of the revenues generated by the actions of the labourers upon the capital. The Mis-esian epistemological critique of this proposal is that the socialist sys-tem, given that factors of production cannot be purchased, rented, or owned, necessarily lacks markets for capital and land. Lacking mar-kets, and therefore lacking a genuine price system, complex economic calculation becomes impossible. Whether wood or iron should be used to create a number of houses poses an unsolvable dilemma when the relative values of all three of these objects cannot be known; it is as if society simply loses a faculty.

To believe that the prices of these items could be discovered through back-tracing multivariate algebra on a grand scale, given the input data of consumer prices, is to severely misunderstand both the role of the economic entrepreneur and the nature of the price sys-tem itself. Even should this impossibly complex multivariate algebra be computed to perfection, showing the profit margins of all possi-ble combinations of inputs, of which there are an indefinite number, and even if the allocator were capable of assigning "purchasing power" (or allocative weight) to each labourer in accordance to the exact pro-ductivity of his labours, the system would still be lacking any consid-eration of the fundamental entrepreneurial function. This function is the purchase or allocation of resources in anticipation of a method of economic production *which exceeds in efficiency all those methods which currently furnish the particular ratios of the economic price system.* It is a purchase now based on the subjective anticipation of the confirmation of data which, at the moment of the purchase, *does not yet exist.* The entrepreneur acts according to his own suppositions of future price data which is, definitionally, not traceable through any form of mathematical computation of current consumer price indexes. Further, the socialist system contains absolutely no means of calculating the rates at which capital ought to be exploited and replenished, for it contains no interest markets and no prices for savings, thus no market of time as such. It is not coincidental that this central planning ideology has no conception of the inherent future uncertainty of being - this is a necessary flow of thinking, a requirement of belief therein.

This Misesian critique of economic central planning contains an additional, implicit insight which, however, is incapable of full expression when presuming the domain of the critique to extend no further than the bounds of the monetary nexus, or to the limits of strictly "economic" decision-making. This insight, and the entire Misesian critique, refers to the universal reality of active being, such that it undermines not only the premises of the socialist system, but those of the cultural authoritarian too.

The entrepreneurial function is, rather than a description of a certain historically established financial position or occupation, a category of action as such. It contains all behaviour which works upon newly created action-schemas, rather than pre-established connections and valuations. All actions combine with both categories of values, novel and established, to some varying amount. Insofar as an action occurs by means of values detached from those established by the individual or his society, or, in more instructive terms, insofar as an individual acts chaotically rather than orderly vis-a-vis historical valuations, the action is entrepreneurial. As such, the entrepreneurial action bears a substantial overlap with the category of genius, the latter bearing an additional qualitative distinction.

Action essentially combining dried-up, solidified remains of old action with a degree of chaotic inspiration, it should be clear that all genuine economic entrepreneurialism is only such insofar as it partakes in this latter aspect of action as such, containing no significantly distinct essence of its own. When such an entrepreneur purchases inputs for the sake of the production of some output, and, successful in his endeavours, benefits *ceteris paribus* from a higher profit margin than could be found elsewhere in the economy, he receives this benefit from his positive use of the chaotic action category, as a trailblazer in a hitherto unknown mode of industry. In beating this path, he cannot avoid alerting the less sagely or courageous investors to the prudence of his ways. Those who wish to survive must follow his lead and funnel their resources into those newly carved channels to the point of their maximum potential. In this way, the meritorious entrepreneurial action disseminates its immediate benefits to the capable and sways the economy towards the more efficient servicing of any given want.

The same function exists on the cultural level. In fact, the bulk of entrepreneurial activity occurs without respect to the monetary. Every acting individual employs the entrepreneurial function, to differing degrees, and to varying success. The most pure examples, though, are found in those acts which may possibly create acclaimed, landmark works of intellect and culture, for the very essence of such tasks, independent of the quality of their product, lies in their employment of existing means for wholly unforeseen ends; pulling eternally possible conceptual apparatus and value frameworks out from the temporally unknown.

Socialism works to entirely remove the entrepreneurial function from the productive economy, for this action can only be undertaken by one who owns some economic means of production and expects some benefit from their utilisation. The ultimate principle through which Socialism destroys economic entrepreneurial activity is that it coerces man in his monetary-focused endeavours, be they productive or consumptive, or, in other words, that it deprives man of capital ownership. The state of maximum possible utilisation of the entrepreneurial function is the one wherein coercion is absolutely absent, or where property is absolutely private.

To this point the entrepreneurial function has been here spoken of irrespective of its qualitative function. It would be prudent here to introduce this qualitative distinction before fully analysing the interrelations of entrepreneurialism and state conservatism. Naturally, not all deviation from a previous norm can be positive. It seems likely that the vast majority of abnormal decisions have additionally been bad decisions, for the active individual himself and for society wholly. Ultimately, an action will be embarked upon if it is deemed by the actor to be in his interests, irrespective of the degree of moral sentiment contained within these interests. If society is to gain from the entrepreneurial, it must ensure that the negative effects thereof are returned to the original actor rather than to those around him. Insofar as this is not the case, the individual will act in such a manner that is detrimental to the health of the cultural system but beneficial to himself. A society which cannot prevent its own citizens from plundering cannot wish for long survival, and every self-serving action at the expense of the whole is, to this degree, a form of plunder.

A healthy society must further secure that the betterment of the position of the whole is in the interests of the individual. This may be achieved through a unification of moral purpose, bringing man into greater sympathy with his fellows, and by instilling a system of incentives and punishments such that man acts for the good, and against the harm, of others. If the general interests of the individual and the whole are aligned, the entrepreneurial benefits created by the individual, for the individual, will prove to also be the boon of those he thereby effects.

On the 'economic' level, the entrepreneur is responsible for all innovation which has taken place since the start of man's interaction - the first fire, the first sword, the first book; the first murder, first fraud and first ideological possession. The first category of innovative endeavours can be taken to represent the produce of entrepreneurial man when his interests are aligned with those of society, the latter representing what is produced in a state of antagonistic interests.

A key requisite to the fruition of positive entrepreneurialism is to create a distinction between what one is justly allowed to utilise to one's own ends, and that which one may not use. These boundaries must, too, be physically defendable. As a result, man must, in order to benefit from such a society, use that available to him to create something which his fellows think should be of benefit to them. When those boundaries of property become non-existent in the eyes of men, these men become to one another a resource like any other, to be forcibly plundered, from which some desired resource is to be extracted and processed. This situation is in stark contrast to that of the socialists, wherein man may not have capital resources at his own disposal, and wherein the activities and labours of man are not carried out on the basis of agreement, but of command. The positive entrepreneurialism of truly socialist states must be trifling.

A more hidden benefit of the entrepreneurial action is its continuous reallocation of economic resource directive power according to historical entrepreneurial success. This is the active mechanism for the determination of the decision-making structure within a society of liberty, or the society of fixed, inviolable private domains. Every entrepreneurial success, judged by the standards of individuals in proportion to their own prior successes through this system of judgement, increases the entrepreneur's ability to direct material resources, his subsequent wealth, and as such his proportion of societal economic decision-making. Inversely, the man who allocates resources inefficiently loses his power in proportion to his waste. This decision-making is also highly specific and incremental - he who has a grand history of success in one industry will be met with due scepticism, and this fewer resources at his disposal, should he wish to enter another specialised sector of decision-making.

# 7

## BUREAUCRACY

The working of centralised economic decision-making stands in exact opposition to the mechanism above described. There exists, insofar as economic decision-making is carried out by the state, no decentralised and incremental feedback mechanism whereby the state's failures subtract from its influence and its successes add to its power. Its method of resource accumulation entirely bypasses all market tests, for it takes rather than convinces. As a result, resources are not placed in the hands of those deemed, by the incremental mechanism, to be best suited towards their disposal. Further, as a consequence of the destruction of the profit motive, the state official ceases to gain nor lose in proportion to the judgements of the historically successful. As such, the state apparatus is absolutely shut off from the forces which direct the entrepreneurial function in such a way that it be aligned with society's revealed preferences. Additionally, coercive orientation must prove to be inherently revolutionary, that is, rationalistically anti-traditional.

Every structure of allocation has an accepted standard whereby positions of influence are established. The economically centralised state is no different. The structure of state decision-making is the strictly hierarchical bureaucracy. The internal rules of bureaucracy act to compensate for the information shortage necessitated by a lack of price data, as well as in adaptation to the centralisation and uniformity which is inherent in, and often the goal of, state planning. The actions of a bureaucratic worker can never be evaluated for their economic productivity, and, as such, a vertical movement in the bureaucracy must, at every level, occur according to a set of criteria free from the censure of those who strikes at the inefficiencies of marketable corporations with marketable products - the investor and the consumer.

The articulated aim of every rung in the bureaucratic structure is its adherence to the purpose of its establishment, execution of the passed-down will of the chief-planner, the highest authority. The ultimate goal is assigned, with little regard for its trade-offs, by highest command and passed to high command. High command can begin to understand the desired goal and apply it via more concrete instructions to the rung directly below, and so forth.

The instructions of the lowest bureaucratic units must be the most specialised, and these individuals must be largest in number. In order for their work to be appraised, they must condense its particulars and return them up the chain of command. Again, those bureaucrats second closest to the ground must do their own condensation, and properly pass the information upwards. This is to be repeated until whatever is left of the multitude of particulars finds its way, in easily communicable form, to the eyes or ears of highest command. Each bureaucrat, possessing far more knowledge of his particulars than do his superiors, sits in a personally exploitable position vis-a-vis his private sector counterpart. Since his superior is, by nature, incapable of verifying and receiving the whole of the subordinate's findings, the individual can synthesise the information at his disposal into the form most compliant with his superior's wishes. These exists an unbridgeable gap between each level of the bureaucratic pyramid, which is subject to no systematic mechanism acting towards its minimisation. This concentration-induced gap occurring at every level, the highest command is certain to receive, in all of his reports, inflated opinion of the successes of the state's operations. The bureaucrat will use all freedom available to him to refine from his excesses a performance which, where possible, leaves out all that reflects badly on his status.

In order to alleviate this informational gap, stricter and more definite standards and rules must be put in place than would ever be workable within a comparable structure rooted in the soil of liberty. Should the market arrive at an organisational model which contained a retention rate of total information of, say, some fifty percent, we may, for demonstration purposes, suggest that a similarly oriented bureaucratic structure, would mandate that eighty percent of all total information must be provided to one's supervisor. This is the only way through which a bureaucracy may properly reduce the abuses which occur at each of its stations. It requires a massive elongation and bloating of the bureaucracy's mid-sections. In order to present to highest command a one thousandth part of that sum of information available to the lowest bureaucrats, given a one-half-per-layer rate of compression, a bureaucratic structure requires ten rungs. Narrowing this loss to one fifth, the structure comes to require thirty-two layers for the same ultimate output. Should we calculate from this the total amount of labour required for the functioning of a given operation, a society governed bureaucratically would require the employment of its entire population for a sum of tasks which could be otherwise accomplished through the employment of only forty percent of the population through the structures of liberty.

Naturally, these crude figures are not here mentioned so as to insinuate any measure of the absolute quantitative difference between these two modes of order. Rather, these figures assist in demonstrating quite how large a difference may result from the seemingly insignificant truth of the informational mismanagement necessitated by the incentives inherent in the bureaucratic structure, and the manpower required to cover up these cracks.

A grand advantage of the price system is its efficiency in compressing information. A bureaucratic structure may, through the eyes and under the judgement criteria of the highest bureaucrat, seem quite efficient indeed - yet it is highly possible that if the same bureaucracy were monetised and subject to price calculation, it would find itself to have been operating wholly prodigally. This underlying reality would remain ever unknown by the bureaucratic mechanism. This way, the price system continually works to trim the fat between production and ultimate command, freeing up for better societal utilisation those individuals sitting comfily in bureaucratic middle-management. The key difference is this: subject to the price system, high management can make sweeping decisions regarding company direction, production cutbacks and expansions, and employee utilisation, with a large, synthesised abundance of extremely low-cost information. This information is also judged and independently verified by all forms of investment markets, such that any hidden important information undergoes a process of systematic uncovering. The bureaucratic leader, on the other hand, simply cannot judge the productivity of his own base, for the structure's criteria of judgement, decided partially by each level between the highest and lowest bureaucrats, does not allow for any real commensurability into that sort of information which the highest bureaucrat is capable of judging. At most, the bureaucratic leader may receive some significant information regarding the suitability of the whole structure beneath him to its own purported ends.

Only the leader of a structure of liberty may receive along with this information any notion of the value of these ends themselves. Without this knowledge of the value of one's ends, any idea of the value of one's means contains only the pretence of societal usefulness.

Through its rigidity and inability to calculate, the bureaucracy acts as one of central planning's most fervent assaults on positive entrepreneurialism. The only room for entrepreneurialism in a bureaucratic system is a genius in deception and smoke screens. The state's neutering of the entrepreneurial good, of the inspiration whereby all that is valued finds its temporal conception, is not limited to its activities within the formal economy. While the explicit nature of the price system makes its own absence highly visible, the kernel of the state's disruption of the entrepreneurial good actually lies elsewhere: in its use of coercion, the enforced destruction of the incremental, decentralised and weighted method of societal governance which makes up the, most stable, most productive and most ignored system for the organisation of man - the system of liberty.

As earlier mentioned, the concepts useful in application to the economy are fundamentally grounded in action qua action, and, as such, the proper methods of economic analysis are applicable also to culture. The processes described above, regarding the entrepreneurial action and the epistemological nature of hierarchical structures under centralised economic rule, are of direct relevance to a study of cultural centralisation.

The system of cultural centralisation exists primarily in the form of an attempt to eliminate the existence of certain behavioural traits. More rarely, it exists as an attempt to directly encourage alternative norms. The command of state conservatism must be, as previously mentioned, distant from the peculiarities of each concrete action, and thereby universal in nature. These dictates are highly distant from the universal ethical command, unutterable but perfect, the commandment for perfect action variable for each and every endeavour. Instead, they will form rules for action, necessitating or forbidding some interaction with an object, untailored to the detailed circumstances and moral subjectivities of those ruled and judged. Therefore, they are liable to inhibit entrepreneurially positive actions in addition to those targeted negative deviations. The degree to which a rule prohibits negative deviations while restraining as few as possible positive deviations is the degree of goodness of the rule.

Any rule may be executed from a stance either more particular or more universal. A particularisation of a rule will attempt to free those positive actions which a more universal rule would condemn, while continuing to punish, as much as is possible, those actions at which the rule takes direct aim. Conceptually, all rules permit indefinite particularisation. Unfortunately, particularisation comes at a price which men are quite often justly unwilling to pay. For example, prohibiting copious alcohol consumption acts to prohibit a higher ratio of bad actions to good actions than does a rule which bans alcohol consumption as such. The latter rule, however, is likely to prevent a higher absolute quantity of those actions which both rules ultimately wish to prevent.

Man being imperfect, he needs a degree of pre-established guidance in his action; he needs order, so that he may avoid his own naive destruction. The questions which any given culture must ask itself are three: given the necessity of such orderly norms, by which mechanisms are these to be constructed, amended, and enforced?

The statist position is for an entity chosen by some electorate, be this the demos or the party, to take the role of the ultimate creator of certain cultural standards. We proceed primarily with reference to the democratic means, given this former's general predominance. The proposed manner of this cultural creation is exceedingly simple: the governing entity will attempt to enshrine, in universal code, the cultural ideas of those whose support gave them power. The entity may, additionally, conjure up its own norms, unthought of by the body of its advocacy, and bring them into enforcement, for the protection of those who cannot themselves act better. The acceptance of this principle at once brings to power a strangely revolutionary and egalitarian universal masquerading as conservative: that the 'willpower' behind norm creation become entirely detached from historically established allocations of societal power and influence under the preceding system of relative liberty.

Insofar as those who desire change are to create their ideal government according to a standard that does not, at every change of power, cause a civil war, we are to see the criteria of governance become power through quantitative support. Should this system be implemented in its ideal form, the support of the bottom half of individuals, in terms of prior teleological gravity, would be strong enough to overthrow the notions and norms of the superior half. Almost assuredly, the quantitative mass of historical failures would be able to subordinate the qualitative elite. These few could not, by themselves, and in their agreements, ever be expected to voluntarily submerge themselves into the political movements of the masses below. In doing so, they would cease to be elite. Rather, the masses will use their democratic power to force the aristocracy into submission. To where, indeed, did the landed elites and natural aristocracy flee during the revolutionary century? When not simply hung, they themselves chose to bear the mask of the demos, their children raised with the soul of 'the people'. At our present point, there exists no discernible 'natural elite' outside of those few individuals who embody the ideals of the masses. There being essentially two types of modern man, the hedonist and the asset hoarder, there are accordingly two castes of modern elites, both wholly democratised. We find the former type of modern individual to worship the eternally subversive celebrity, whose power comes from their imagined indulgence in vicious pleasures and a freedom to act at every moment with an arrogant vulgarity, this latter quality taken to be a sign of their emancipation from the restraints of the 'authoritarianism' of the culture which the nihilist loathes and blames for his failings. The asset hoarder, on the other hand, celebrates the corporate savant, who has sold his being entirely to the pursuit of the proliferation of some new gadget and accordingly develops a large market capitalisation for the company in which he holds a large sum of shares.

This aside, we must ask ourselves who has most to gain through the existence of some power to enforce universal cultural standards from the ballot box or the parliament houses? We would be horrendously naive to believe this power immune to hijacking by those who, ultimately, have most to benefit from its immediate control, those who seek to auction its massive leverage to those who can most profit, in money or in status, as a result of its enforced, sweeping changes. For the benefit accrued to each politically influential individual though the state conservative's universal laws is relatively small when compared to the gain which one may accrue to oneself by using one's political power for the furthering of one's own private ends. The regular citizen's vote or involvement in the enactment of some politically conservative state, qua hypothesis, benefits all other citizens' positions as much as it does his own, such that, of all good therefrom resulting, his own share is miniscule. On the other hand, there exist, for every potential universal law, specific parties for whom the direct impact is tremendous, those who gain or lose a grand amount of societal power as a consequence of the systematic changes of man's behavioural preferences brought in through the new edicts of the state. Each action requires an object of preference, and a grand shift in the utility of object classes, the existence of other people here inclusive, requires an equally grand shift in the status of those who can procure or provide those objects. These interests have been present, active, and perniciously influential in all coercive apparatuses hitherto constructed. The have frequently succeeded, and, as we will see, must necessarily tend to succeed, in diverting the course of state power towards the opposite of its established purpose, a subversion which inverts a circumstance of the impediment of the one for the benefit of the whole, into a circumstance of impediment of the whole for the benefit of the one. For which person of one million could recognise, let alone strongly mobilize against, a subtle change in the source of the papers from which he reads his morning news? On the other hand, which industrialist would not have his life significantly altered if the state were to contract his paper mill for the provision of the whole nation's newspapers? Additionally, it is quite obvious which party is in a position to benefit the individual statesman more highly. It is quite obvious, too, then, that should rules regarding the production of newspapers be set by the state, these rules will be drafted by the papers' makers and their respective capital interests, rather than by those for whom the newspaper is actually produced.

But let us here exclude from authoritarian conservative statecraft all remote possibility of outside, non-governmental influence. This excluded, man is involved politically on a fairly standard position of some measure of cruder self-interest mingled with a part of genuine morality. In accordance with this political involvement, he expects the state to protect society. The highest actors, representatives of the people, mobilize the resources of the state as best they can into a form where in the people's best interests are put into effect. To this end, numerous bureaucratic departments are established, funded by the state treasury. Each department is tasked with enforcing provisions to ensure proper conduct in its respective area of society - familial relations, the usage of mind-altering substances, sexual activities, gambling, and so on. What can be expected to become of these structures after their initial establishment?

Societal structures are, of course, formed and manned by people. This is simple tautology, but, nonetheless, many seem to frequently forget the fact. It is one of vast importance. Where the actions of a structure are governed wholly by the underlying behaviours of those who staff it, it is of utmost importance to understand the value hierarchies sponsored by the characteristics of the structure. We engage in this analysis ubiquitously, and often to the point of simplistic reductionism, when we deal with organisations of liberty. All understand that, with respect to the market, an entity's survival is inextricably linked with its prospective monetary profit. Hereby one can explain, and predict, the actions of the economic entity, or those individuals who lead it. This insight greatly assists us in understanding the entity's labour hiring patterns, its marketing techniques, the structures of its affiliated legal entities, and so on. Despite its situational ubiquity, this analytic approach is rarely used when discussing non-market entities. It appears that, according to common understanding, while all business behaviour is governed by the self-interested profit motive, thought to be ultimately contrary to the public good, the actions of governmental agencies adhere as best they can to the 'will' of the country's populace, or, rather, to what that will would demand if stripped of all vice and ill judgement. Should the state or its branches ever not act such, the *individuals immediately responsible for the fault*, wherever they may be found, and in entire contradistinction to the structures themselves, are presumed to be the root cause of the opposition of interest between the entity and the public good as such. Should these individuals be extracted, the structure will once again set to work, towed by its bindings to the perennial leash of justice.

This is entirely false. It so happens that the prime bureaucratic motive is in fact far inferior to the profit motive of private enterprise, both for the securing of the organisation's final cause - its reason for establishment - and for the general well-being of society. We must ask ourselves: in which ways does the bureaucratic system encourage man to behave? In our analysis of these large peculiarities, we begin with the incentive structure of the standard, non-directive bureaucrat of middle-management. Further, let us presume - quite aside from the actual probability of the matter - that, in its initial, new-born state, the bureaucracy is almost exclusively manned by duty-driven, virtuous individuals. Of course, it is unthinkable for this to be the case in a society which is so destitute of common moral standards that it requires such revolutionarily enforced moral direction from above.

In a bureaucratic system, certain traits bring with them a propensity to a rise in the hierarchy, while others do not. The most inherent difference between the success of the bureaucrat and of the private employee lies in the respective systems' approach to the entrepreneurial action. The bureaucrat's success is officially measurable in no manner other than his satisfaction of predefined, rigid lists of criteria and goals. These goals are set by higher command yet contain insufficient information regarding the complexities and opportunities of the subordinate's full circumstances. Since the bureaucrat aims to maximise these criteria, and since these criteria, in unison, require a departure from the level of information and variability visible through the prospect of profit, the causal factors hereof being indefinitely large and indefinitely sensitive, we must conclude that the fundamental incentive structure of the bureaucracy causes hierarchical selectivity against innovation and the entrepreneurial spirit alike. All entrepreneurial behaviour entails trade-offs. If the innovative produce of such behaviour goes unrecognised by the system's established rules, despite its eventual utility and superiority - a likely fact given that such produce is, necessarily, a leap ahead of those very rules - then positive entrepreneurialism will be prohibited. This trait of bureaucracies tends to reinforce itself over time, as promotions are granted to, and therefore rules later written under, the unimaginative, uncreative, and quite mediocre.

This tendency towards a mediocrity-enforced solidification is not the only inherent effect of the bureaucratic upon the entrepreneurial. Aside from a prohibition of the positive form of entrepreneurialism, the bureaucratic also works to inspire an abundance of entrepreneurialism's strictly negative aspects. This negative aspect tends to manifest itself when success for a given person or within a given system can be best obtained through ingenuity at the expense of the ultimate good. A pertinent example is the process of cultural liquidation itself. When the goal of statecraft becomes aggregate statistic, genius in the liquidation of culture becomes the manner of highest success for the statesman. In other words, the virtue of the position itself tends to become at odds with true virtue.

The bureaucratic structure systematically and inherently provides a reward structure far departed from that of the society of liberty, which, as we shall later endeavour to show in proper detail, tends towards an optimal utilisation of all human knowledge, primarily distinguished by its free allocations of teleological gravity. With its rigid and epistemologically incomplete rules of conduct, the bureaucracy bestows reward upon those who can sacrifice that-which-is-not-measured for that which is, the former category always including, above the formal specifications of any given task, the appeasement of one's superiors. The point made here is not that private or natural hierarchies and structures are exempt from exhibiting any particular, isolated characteristics here discussed. It is rather that the inherent nature of state bureaucracy excludes much relevant information which would have been contained within an equivalent structure of liberty, and, thus, ceteris paribus, rewards vice. As with the reduction of positive entrepreneurialism we can expect this increase in negative entrepreneurialism to exacerbate itself and irreversibly solidify its results within the structural rules of the particular bureaucratic body. Thereafter, those few dutiful state servants attempting to adhere to the original 'spirit' of the entity, acting above and beyond official stipulation and seeking societal good as such, rather than ascension in the bureaucratic structure, increasingly sacrifice their ability to meet the criteria for bureaucratic promotion and influence. To the degree that the system has lost its freshness, the impediment accrued to the moral must increase, for any bureaucrat's subordinates will give to him increasingly restricted, to-the-mould information, manipulated according to the inherent blind spots of their superiors, while, simultaneously, the former bureaucrat's own superiors will have increasingly little enthusiasm for any potential bureaucratic philanthropy, this superior wishing rather to see by-the-book results. The philanthropic 'revolutionaries' will be rooted out by the natural bureaucrats, for they have been placed in an environment which selects against them. Irrespective of the magnitude of their own virtues, these non-conformists can fare only as well as can a lion deep at sea.

The bureaucratic structure contains within its framework a further difference of import - its lack of reaction to the inefficiencies inherent in a gargantuan size, which act to encumber, and often entirely topple, the lumbering behemoths of the private sphere. While public structures become more swiftly and surely burdened by the immobilities of centralised decision-making than do private structures, entities within the latter sphere are not immune to this dulling of their sensitivities. A stark difference, however, lies in the treatment of these nonadaptive giants by the relative environments in which they spread their roots - the market of state desires versus the market of private desires. These differences stem from two distinct areas: the obtaining of investment capital, and the funding acquired through the provision of relevant services. Should an entity lose its means of sustenance, it will quickly cease to be.

The bloated private firm, with a large qualitative distance separating the knowledge of the board of directors and that knowledge necessary for efficient organization and production, incurs many of the disadvantages inherent in the bureaucratic framework - the reliance on overly strict adherence to established rules, inflexibility of direction, internal mobility according to an appeasement of the particular tastes of one's own superiors rather than the tastes of one's consumers. A larger firm's directorship naturally faces more difficulty in its quest to route these inefficiencies and secure optimum profits. Yet centralisation offers its own natural benefits The large entity is capable of offering economic reliability to both customer, through recognition of identity, and to supplier, who incurs a lower cost when routinely supplying large amounts to specific customers in an orderly and predictable fashion. It has also, having navigated and succeeded within its own market, synthesised the efficiencies of present-day industry standards into its structures and mechanism, so stands to be a beacon of established knowledge. Given that centralisation is not an inherent evil, but rather presents a nuanced matter of particular costs and benefits, the situation calls not for a universal condemnation, but rather for nuanced evaluation of its utilities on a case-by-case basis - a proportional loss of disposable resources for those giants who exceed their optimum points of magnitude and centralisation, through a contraction of the veins of investment or a consumer distaste for the declining quality of the entity's final product.

The market mechanism for the judging of an entity's produce is contained within the purchasing trends of those who are ultimately to be served by the product, the consumers. These individuals judge according to their own preferences whether or not a product is well-suited to their person. Inefficient entities produce inferior products and lose their streams of consumer income. The ultimate means whereby investment capital flows into a new or established venture are predictions of an entity's ability to create products judged worthwhile by their ultimate consuming beneficiaries. Ventures judged to be undervalued receive increased funding and can thereby expand their operations. This undervaluation consists in the perception of an investor that the total amount of assets at a business' disposal is currently disproportionately low relative to the judgments of the general consumer regarding the utility of the products produced by these assets. The investment, then, serves to enlarge the productive potential of the company such that the economy can expand its production in those areas where such an expansion causes the highest perceived gain to the consumer. Through this mechanism, voluntary consumer purchases act as vital information for the diversion of society's capital reserves into those areas which most require expansion, from those areas which most require contraction. These judgments can fail. Yet this is not, in the market, a cloud with no silver lining. Human existence will always be a venture in failure, in imperfection. What renders it worth bearing is that there exists, inherent in the failure, the fruit of salvation - information pertaining to what has been done wrong, and, therefore, what could have been, and should soon be, better done. All systems create errors; worthwhile ones tend toward self-correction. So it is with the voluntary capital market.

Investors who have made historic malinvestments receive inferior or negative returns on their asset allocations, while those who have demonstrated a keen eye for appeasement of the consumer receive an accordingly increased share of return. This way, the market not only selects for the fitness of investments, but also for the fitness of investors; such that there exists a tendency for the mechanisms of capital investment, and the funding of society's ventures, to be placed in the hands of those of demonstrated aptitude.

The bureaucratic world knows no such corrective mechanism. Firstly, the monetary customer of the bureaucracy is not the claimed ultimate beneficiary or consumer of its end products: state schools are not funded by pleased parents, regulatory bureaucracies are not funded by the customers of the product thereby regulated, and so forth. As such, the bureaucracy is stripped of one of the two organic corrective mechanisms working upon it towards the refinement of its established purpose, an organ ever active with respect to all truly private enterprise. Having only this vein remaining, all funding of bureaucratic entities must take the route of top-down investment - to some degree similar to capitalist investment, yet here the 'investor' is categorically blind to that information which, in the market, is provided to him by the consumer. As already mentioned, it is impossible to measure a bureaucratic investment's success, as there is no return thereto commensurable with the cost thus incurred, and so there can be no way to properly compare the results of the investment, insofar as these may even be measured, with the alternative possible uses of the invested assets.

A second vital difference with respect to the second sustaining vein lies in the medium of top-down investment particular to the bureaucracy - it must be funded through taxation. This fact severs all remaining participation of such an entity in those revitalising currents in the entities of liberty are bathed.

Taxation entirely voids the mechanism for the gradual refinement of the investor and decision-maker. Rather than a gradual and permanent shift of funds towards the historically successful, the taxation function, which primarily draws its funds through a punishment of the most competent investors, suffers no loss for malinvestment and receives no gain for successes. Its treasury is not stocked by a history of sound decisions, but rather by a continuous stream of plunder from those who *have* made sound decisions. Lacking any mechanism for gradual refinement in this department, one can expect, from yet another angle, the bureaucratic system to tend, vis-a-vis liberty, towards the selection of unfit individuals at the head of its hierarchies, in this instance with respect to those who prepare and dispense treasury funds.

Given that the large state cannot invest its funds according to price data, it must make its investment choices through another mechanism. Not only within a single bureaucracy must it make this choice, but also between multiple bureaucratic structures, all of which will be vying for increased funding in order to expand their activities, which are potentially unlimited. The challenge posted to the treasury is this: given that we cannot aim for a monetary return, how are our accumulated taxes to be allocated? The only measure to fall back on is an indeterminate one, unbound to any commensurable criteria: which sector appears to be most lacking?

The chief representatives of each bureaucratic structure secure their funding by convincing the treasury of the direness of their particular situations. Those who do their best to appear 'underfunded' receive the highest proportion of taxes. As such, in order to have command over as many resources as possible, the bureaucrat must make his current supplies appear rather bare - he has a systematic incentive to inefficiently utilise that which is available to him. This strategy can only be a successful one in a realm where inputs and final products cannot be commensurably compared. The treasury stands in absolutely no position to judge whether or not three schools are more necessary than twelve bridges. This information, to the small degree that it actually exists within a priceless system, is contained within the various experiences of a great number of low-ranking bureaucrats. With this in mind, how is a treasurer to act when he hears from a senior educational bureaucrat that, despite previous calculations which had projected that prior funding would be sufficient, one school remains half-built and another understaffed? The source of the problem is entirely obfuscated from the treasury's position, yet he is led to understand that a two percent funding increase will serve to get the job done. On the other hand, the bureaucracy for the construction and maintenance of bridges has completed its duties well within its budget. As such, it has no ability to leverage the treasury for increased funding, and, in fact, may even have its remaining resources siphoned off into the apparently lacking educational sector. Further to this effect lies public opinion: the public sees not bureaucratic inefficiency, but rather the reckless parsimony of the treasury withholding necessary resources from vital services and institutions. Even the hardiest state is ultimately led by the strength of public opinion, as is the most frugal of state treasuries. Along with this bias in favour of the inefficient, the public is bound to carry with it a bias against the novel and the new - the entrepreneurial idea being initially palatable only to a select few, and appearing to the rest to be pure wastefulness.

Contrasting this state of affairs to the investment market reveals a stark difference: the company spending above and delivering below its predictions will systematically lose investment capital, rather than accruing thereby. Of equal import, those investors gullible enough to believe fabricated justifications for routine underperformance must find their own financial positions wilting. Contrarily, firms which produce more for less receive, rather than the hacksaw of the state, immediate flows of investment capital with which to expand their operations.

During the revolutionary century, the gradual bloating of the state hierarchy became, as was necessary, all too apparent. The world-shaping liberal nations of the nineteenth-century have now all become remarkable by the sluggishness of their vital organs. They consume more than was hitherto thought possible, yet, quite masterfully, out of this abundance create arrangements through which they are less potent in their societal works than at any point prior. The funding of policing has increased manifold, yet the ability of the police force to prevent crime has dwindled, and the just restitution of the victim thereof has simply ceased completely to be a function of state security. Educational funding has increased exponentially, while pupils reach the adult age less skilled and less wise, while pure educational attainment, and standards thereof, routinely fall. Bureaucratic agencies appear to have become more productive only in the exploitation of their own positions: doing less while receiving more. Such is the iron law of bureaucracy

Up to this point, we have refused to allow our hypothetical state actors any particular selfishness, a factor which has particularly influenced our leniency with respect to the ultimate dispensers of the state's funds. However inefficient their actions may be, we have mostly analysed individuals with a strong sense of duty, albeit in circumstances which hinder their ability to act as well as they otherwise might have been able to. If taken truly, this is a naive presumption. The potential of the seats of state for covert abuse must be addressed in abridged form before moving on.

The primary lure of power in the modern sovereign state, servant of the people's best interests, is that the resources thereby obtained and utilised are not one's own. To the contrary, state actors' lifeblood is tithed directly from the populace through wounds which do not clot. In addition, even though their usage the state actor does not become the owner of these resources, he acts only as their temporary caretaker. Sense of justice aside, then, the state actor has little to gain from utilising these resources in a manner ultimately productive for those whom he claims to represent. He cannot gain from public prudence, especially if he is not the public-facing embodiment of the state, but nonetheless possesses the power to dictate society's resources to the benefit or detriment of others. This puts him in a remarkably profitable position, for he may dispense of that which is otherwise quite meaningless and valueless to him, and in return be bestowed with the graces of the elite. He has acquired his position for he is judged the man most capable of making decisions which others could not make. This, combined with the necessarily opaque nature of the effects of his decisions with respect to the bureaucratic structure, gives him large liberty to act as an unscrutinised and invisible dispenser of public funds. This being his nature, it is only natural that he become crowded by parties vying, with some great success, to carry an influence over his power. Even with a pittance return on each pound of lavish spending and contractual liabilities, the representative can elevate himself from the position of a mere caretaker, who owns nothing at all, to a member of the elite with which he consorts. A historical account of such hereby elevated fortunes would demand its own separate work. The corruption of positions of political power is no consequence of the abominable morals of select individuals. Rather, the processes by which such positions come to be filled ensure that morally minded candidates incur increasing concessions when pursuing the position from which they may enforce their dutiful moral notions. Even in a state entirely departed from the democratic system, the candidate must shape his appeal to those not so interested in his particular notions of morality - he must shackle himself with practicality.

The individual of most repugnant moral character[7], which includes an adeptness in deceit, will have the fewest scruples in trading the employment of his political power, the expenditure of unowned resources, for renown and influence. For the moral candidate, political power holds a value independent of the value of that for which it may be exchanged. For the immoral candidate, the value of political power is subject to no such restraint. Immoral candidates will be more willing to auction off their potential future political potency in return for a higher chance of political success, through campaign funding, the appeasement of departmental bureaucratic leaders, or concessions to rival, powerful ideological circles. Yet once this step has been taken, the relatively moral candidate finds himself with quite a dilemma: he, now at a disadvantage, either concedes to the immoral those stations of power, or makes concessions of his own. But for every concession made by the moral candidate in the name of the greater good, the position for morality in government as such becomes still more dire. The playing field once more level, the original position is once against returned to, and the immoral candidate will once more deviate with little hesitation, any crumb of political power being worth more to him than the sum of moral causes which by that power may be served. An identical scenario will cause identical decisions. The eventual result of this is an electoral system wherein the normal course of events in the acquisition of political power, irrespective of the morality of the candidate himself, is the auctioning off of that power to various private interests. Candidates, even those of good intention, serve primarily as the choice vehicle of special interest groups, and serve only secondarily to the attainment of their own political preferences. This effect is quite symmetrical: those third parties vying for the public purse will obtain an advantage over those who do not. As such, they proliferate, and those parties unwilling to meld with the state begin to fall away. The 'private' sphere, something which can never truly exist within a state-led society, becomes, at its corporate heights, entirely intermingled with the political process. Those companies which secure a position as favoured contractor of the state, or who manage to persuade a state representative to pursue this over that, will inevitably come out ahead of those who categorically refuse to make use of such means.

Such mode of routine affairs can only be worse than the alternative of liberty much maligned by the statist conservative, for if private interests are unfit to "rule by consent", that is, grow through the voluntary purchases and investments of the marketplace, then what are we to expect of that mode of organisation which ensures that the most morally apathetic leaders of these despised corporations may rule even without consent?

Having spoken about the inevitable development of particular positions of state power, we next seek to understand the extent to which state conservatism, in its purest forms, can be expected to lay claim to the resources of the ruled peoples, and, subsequently, how this claim will tend to affect the dynamics of the society as a whole.

The prime necessities of the conservative state are its director-ship over the enforcement of security, courts of judgement and the creation of legislation. Exterior to this are a plethora of accessories aimed at particular social engineering, some of which shall be visited later.

Without the ability to enforce its laws, the state could not exist. As such, it must have a tax-funded division of public security. Tellingly, this function is in modern times only known under the name of 'law enforcement'. As a result of its tax funded nature, the cus-tomer of state security must ultimately be the state. It will only serve the public contingently, that is, insofar as the public affects the state in the latter's function as a customer of state police.

The effects of this tax funding are manifold and far reaching. Of course, this necessitates a participation in all of the defects of the bu-reaucratic system and of the political game laid out above; increasing expense for decreasing output[8], an absence of entrepreneurial direc-tion and an unpunished participation in power politics.

The particular details of state-funded law enforcement, how-ever, deserve deeper scrutiny, for it is often held that state ownership of law enforcement is a point of uncontested necessity, something which allows society as such to exist in a state of peace and which cannot be left to the whims of voluntary man. Such a claim is rather contrary to the general disposition of the roughly liberty-minded conservative thinker, for many such theorists hold this position despite admitting the otherwise almost-universal inability of the state to 'solve' societal problems.

The truth is, however, exactly opposite to what the 'small state' conservatives do suggest. Due to the very fact that law enforcement makes up much of any society's essential framework, it is imperative for any free society that the procurement of such security never be monopolised by the caste of coercion.

# 8

⟨❧⟩

# THE PREMISES OF
# STATISM

Throughout this continued critique of the state as a means to conservative ends, one must be sure to keep in mind the preconditions of state direction which so often escape the consideration of those who seek 'solutions' therein.

Man, for whichever reason, appears to possess much more intellectual thoroughness in his analytical critiques of some category of free behaviour than in his advocacy for some sort of coercive fix. He often treats the real dynamics of the latter as if they were some direct manifestation of his very own political desires, with a potency dependent only on his sheer force of will. When confronted with what appears to be a societal problem, perhaps quite deftly identified, he frequently resorts to what appears to be a very simple solution: he calls for it to be outlawed, as if the complexities of human behaviour should become so simple were one only to invoke the state. Similar approaches to other dilemmas seem to us quite absurd; should they be heard spoken, one might even presume the speaker to be talking in sheer jest. Can we imagine a citizen of Stalinist Russia taking the grave risk of confiding in his friend his desire to be free from the regime's tyranny, only to hear back "we need to ban the regime"? After passing laughter at his response, we come to realise that he was actually quite serious. The confidant genuinely believed that he had solved the dilemma. Could one respond with anything other than a confused 'how'?

Perhaps it is time to ask this question more consistently. Without an answer to this question, we must treat such 'solutions' as no more than disguised preferences, a Trojan horse of ends inside which a whole host of spurious means have been smuggled.

How much contrast we can see between our acceptance of the simplistic 'outlaw it', and our endless, scathing, and often quite justified, critiques of the itself simplistic 'liberalise it'? This error of thought is nowhere as ingrained as in the discussion of civic morality, the norms or laws of public behaviour. There exists the following, almost universally presumed equivalence: if something is bad, the state must ban it. Drug usage is bad, ban drugs; pornography is bad, ban pornography, immigration is bad, ban immigration. Even now, as a result of the implication that such things ought not to be banned by the state, the reader may be preparing to read, and perhaps preparing to loathe, some crafty defence of these listed activities and objects by virtue of the reader's distrust of the author's chosen means. There will be no such defence. It is simply our opinion that the will-to-ban can be nothing more than a superfluous non-solution, which has no apparent effect other than to distract the believer from the complexities and underlying processes of the matter at hand, and to divert his will away from more potent alternatives.

To return to the question of 'how': how does one propose that a ban of a societal plague be introduced? The obvious answer is through instating some form of government which also wills such a ban. Quite right, but once more: how? And the answer to this second 'how' makes visible a slight-of-hand method whereby the Bolshevik position enters the debate on terms wholly different from those of the proponent of liberty. The Bolshevik argument takes for granted a society capable of installing his preferred ruling party, which the man of liberty is left to make do with the current defective society as the clay to which his ideas must give form. It is as if the losing player in a game of chess were to switch out all his pawns for queens, with the justification that his prime goal is 'win'.

It is rather obvious that current society provides insufficient material for the enactment of any of the grand proposals of the conservative. This is nowhere better evidenced by the public-facing behaviours or personas of the state representatives in whom the public continuously place their faith and for whom they cast their votes, and in those political promises which best attract the bestowals of political power. Two questions, then, must be directed towards the state conservative: firstly, if a grand change is to be effected in the political (and thereby also moral) persuasions of a people, which means are suitable to the task? Secondly, does this method not partially rely on an affirmation of the processes which the state conservative tends to decry as unfit for the task of inspiring socially conservative tendencies?

The options left open to the conservative for obtaining the statist seat of power are also two: an uprising against the state and its progressive supporters, or the voluntary persuasion of those who, at present, disagree with the conservative ethos.

The opportunities for the former means are so laughably dire that the path merits little attention. Conservative behaviour has very little popular support and bolsters very little by way of might. Further, given the present-day interrelations of global military might, one would expect any such 'uprising' to be held not between a people on one side and its established classes and state on the other, but rather between an insignificant, single-digit percentage of the peoples of a single nation versus, should the situation call for it, a military coalition of the global order. Once more, any chance at overthrowing any modern-day state apparatus would require a societal material far more aligned with the interests of the state conservative than is actually the case. As such, the state conservative must inspire, through entirely voluntary means, a grand stirring in the hearts of his countrymen in favour of those behaviours which he finds dear enough to advocate that they ought to be the object of universal, coercive enforcement.

This point is, of course, no particular critique of the conservative standpoint itself. It is rather a critique of the uneven ground upon which the liberty-coercion debate is far too often waged. Rather than the question be framed with the state conservative already equipped with a society entirely moulded to the requisites of the enactment of his desires laws, and with the conservative advocate of liberty left to explain how present, decadent society may become conservative through solely voluntary means, the question must be posted as follows: given that we agree that voluntary persuasion must be used to inspire a grand change in the morals of our society, what justification is there for a departure from these means, once they have been proven successful, and a placing of the further and ultimate realisation of conservative morality in the hands of the state?

We must, then, when involved in the trial of liberty against coercion for the securing of moral strength, begin our analysis from the point of a society capable of calling into being a series of conservative-directed state legislations, one where the majority of individuals stand in favour of such transformations. This majority will not be ashamed of its views, and, as is highly likely, will not have arrived at them through wholly intellectual means. At no point in human history has a national majority been swayed solely by axiom and deduction. As such, this hypothetical conservatively dispositioned society, the only valid grounds for any comparison of conservative statism and liberty, must possess not merely intellectual, but also cultural dominance.

It is not new knowledge that revolutions are ushered in by laying a new, countercultural, unshakeable bedrock in the hearts of a society's children. This method has during the last hundred-or-so years remained quite unutilised by the conservative, likely because the ever-presence of conservative education prior to the twentieth century left him somewhat blind to its necessity, and incapable of its active imposition. The norms which such conservative 'background radiation' had instilled within the peoples of a culture became so intertwined with the peoples of the nation that they became mistaken as intrinsic aspects of the civilised human spirit. Established orders tend to become blind to their core foundations, and accordingly fail to come adequately to their defence. This is their eternal point of weakness, the point at which the true revolutionary must strike - those axioms of instinct and feeling, felt by even the adult dissident, upon which the intellect then builds. Unfortunately for modern dissidents, the instinctual axioms of the modern world, its notions of difference and disparity, and also the ethics thereof, are perhaps better protected than the foundational axioms of any historical society. The state holds an increasingly absolute monopoly over the fabrication of such immovable axioms in the minds of the youth, using means, such as the public school, which, lest we forget, were originally established with the aim of security universal conservative values.

The point of analysis must then be a society which has already embarked upon a refashioning of the foundations which replaced those which fell into the chasmic abyss since the middle of the nineteenth-century. The task of reaching this starting point, a task quite frequently neglected by the state conservative due to its necessarily supra-state processes, will here be postponed, meriting more detailed attention in the current work's final section. For now, we analyse what the state is likely to effect in a society which has become capable of injecting into it a conservative impetus.

The fascistic method of norm propagation may be summarised as the universal enforcement by a tax-funded policing service of the norms desired by a central legislative power. The grand differences between such an organisation and a market organisation are twofold: the customer of the entity is the state, rather than the public, and that the particular manifestation of the organisation's behaviour is governed by a universal, rather than incremental, order. This latter is what is meant by national sovereignty. When a sovereign force demands that the public not become intoxicated, the mandate is applicable without discrimination. The further a 'court of judgement' becomes incremental, the more often the cultural norm shifts from a condemnation of the *object* to a condemnation of an active violation of the golden mean – in each action, neither too much nor too little.

The tax funded nature of the fascist proposal is of grand consequence to the plausibility of its beneficiality, for the police force becomes a particular manifestation of the bureaucratic structure, and thereby partakes in all of its faults - its rigidity, inability to innovate, tendency to consume more and to produce less, as well as a gradual concentration of power at the disposal of those best at working to the benefit of the eternal bureaucratic principle, rather than that of those whom it purports to protect.

These matters carry such importance to the sector of policing not only due to the instrumental nature of the service itself, but also because of how quite innovative such a service must be to remain remotely effective. We talk here not necessarily of grand innovations, but rather of continuous minute adjustments. The police force must continually adapt itself to decide which usages of which objects are ultimately bad for society. The wider the state conservative net of social engineering is cast, the more it relies on incremental and continuous adaptation for its effectiveness. If its scope is simply to prevent murder, its rulings may be wholly universal - killing an innocent is punishable. In banning weaponry? Perhaps this rule is best kept partial. To ban alcohol. Ought this rule be universal? Exclusively for children? Should alcohol only be allowed at special occasions? Or exclusively as part of the holy sacrament? To ban laughter: never? At a funeral? During an important, radio-communicated speech of a war-time leader to his troops, which may result in national calamity if misunderstood or poorly followed? To ban words?

The somewhat older 'small-state' notion of policing has tended to stay close to the areas of norm enforcement which demand relatively little nuance - and for good reason. Not only is the creation of nationally universal law with respect to nuanced cultural norms an exceedingly difficult task, but it also happens to be the case that nuanced norms are most subject to variance, a variance which, in itself, is neither good nor bad. The north of a country sees a funeral as a joyous celebration of the gift of life; to the south, it is rather a time to grieve the disappearance of a soul from temporality. Which norms ought a police service to enforce in these ceremonies, should this be deemed a place proper for state intervention? This example may be extreme, yet the principle applies to all matters wherein this decision is to be made. Not only do norms vary spatially, they also vary temporally. Is the set of norms which governs acceptable behaviour of an infant still a good set when applied universally to adults? Is this set of norms 'worse' than another set which applies to adults? If so, why not apply adult norms to infants? The same considerations must be made when comparing cultures.

Given the contextual and highly complicated nature of norms of action, through which mechanisms is the state police force capable of making decisions beneficial to society? The most efficient form of law enforcement would be one whereby the correct decisions of the agency, from a perspective of ultimate teleological benefit, become instrumental to that organisation's growth. Any decisions which are ultimately detrimental to society would bring direct harm to the enforcement agency in proportion to the damage done. Further, the ideal agency would have at its disposal all information necessary for the making of those decisions which it is tasked to make. We mention this ideal not with any remote claim to its plausibility or to advocate for its immediate establishment, but rather as an immovable standard by which all such agencies ought to be judged.

State law enforcement is almost wholly untethered to the first half of our ideal. As will be elaborated, this is intrinsic in the fact that it grows through appeasing the treasury, not those whom it is functionally purported to serve. This can be best viewed through an isolation of the primary function of norm enforcement from the agency's secondary function of the amendment of the list of norms to be enforced.

If we presume that absolutely all consumption of alcohol is bad, and that all consumption of alcohol is for that reason to become a punishable offence, this matter will become clear. Firstly: how much are the police to be allocated by way of resources in order to punish those who consume alcohol? If this turns out to be too much, or too little, how are we to know? If we are gracious enough to admit that the police force may have the faculty of detecting their quantitative potency, let us say that ten thousand pounds has been added to the police's budget, through which they can prevent five cases of alcohol consumption per year. Is this a good allocation of resources? Who is to judge, and how? The first question we can only answer insofar as we are capable of comparing this allocation's benefit to that of all other possible allocations - say, building two houses, employing six labourers to grow, harvest and transport food, so on and so forth. We have, however, gotten ahead of ourselves, and have once again mistaken 'a good allocation' for 'a moral allocation' - the latter statement does away with the pertinent question: 'for whom'?

A good allocation of resources in the police by the treasurer is the allocation which best meets the latter's ends. We must remember that the higher we look in the bureaucratic hierarchy, and the more fully solidified bureaucracy at which we look, the more we ought to expect to find those whose core behavioural trends lie entirely detached from the public weal. Bureaucratic systems display a continuous exhibition of Gresham's law, only with respect to labour rather than to coin. As such, we may expect the public-serving bureaucracy to become increasingly diluted into a heavy alloy of vice and complacency, as truly good labours sink beneath the experience of the merely adequate at best, or the underhanded at worst.

The head of the police force, having convinced the treasurer's hand that ten policemen are worth more than a tenth of a bridge refurbishment or the installation of ten dozen street lamps, is keen to employ such resources to his own benefit - as are all men. Yet according to the peculiarities of his position, his benefit is rather discordant with our own best interests.

When compared to, say, a majority owner of an exchange listed corporation, it is clear that the head bureaucrat's selfish urges are not, like those of the businessman, cut back by the double-edged sword of judgement. Every penny spent for the sake of private passion instead of public product comes to effect the businessman's profit forecast, directly reducing his future incomes of cash through investment, as investors prefer those businessmen capable of distributing the means for the satisfaction of private passions to the sum total of shareholders. Further, the businessman is held back simply by the fact that he owns some part of that which he is consuming, therefore he suffers a loss inherent in every expense. The bureaucrat is subject to no such restraint.

Let it be posited that the bureaucrat is good of heart and wishes to elevate his position such that he may become a more brilliant beacon of virtue. How is he to usurp those who use the public fund for personal power through bribery and fraud? As we have said: unless he is a true visionary and uses means which the statist decries as incapable of inspiring real societal change, he must himself offer up part of the public fund for auction in order to arrive at a competitive range of power. The only land in which no such thing can be expected to occur is a land home to a people of such a quality that they have absolutely no need of a paternal state, no matter how ideal its function.

We do not punish the murderer by giving to him our weapons in expectation of his self-flagellation therewith. Why, then, is it insisted upon that we support the monopolisation of our most vital services in the hands of those who have most scrupulously ascended a system which selects in accordance with mediocrity and immorality of character, and must from this expect that these figures will use this bestowed power solely to those ends contrary to the natures of their distinguishing traits?

The state conservative appears to presuppose a national government free from the potential of manipulation towards private ends. He is also free to suppose a pleasure which knows no ephemerality, this latter demand being no more unnatural than the former. If anything is clear from the long history of force, it is that coercion yields more bounty for he who wields it to the end of the enrichment of self than for the enrichment of all. If men of evil are destined to take the reins of a society of liberty through means of appeals to the misplaced wants of free man, how much more destructive potential does he become exposed to by the cleaving open of positions of power wherein the abuser may do away with the obstacle of persuasion altogether?

And to secure his grip on the chariot of coercion he need not even strike a bargain with foolish man by using his own assets as collateral - in his new position, a position which we are to believe, contrary to all experience and sense, is to be used for our own enrichment, this man, he who rises unjustly to the top in a society wherein men make their own choices, becomes free to promise two men one another's treasure, and then confiscate them for his own ends. Are we truly to believe that a people, too stupid to make decisions for their own benefit, too short-sighted not to voluntarily give itself up to the devil, is to be expected to, under the very same free choice, except subject to an order of magnitude more temptation than in its former predicament, and now with a whole nation's well-being to calculate rather than merely its own personal health; are we truly to simply have faith that our pre-supposed vicious fools are to succeed where Saint Peter thrice failed, and conjure up the virtue to stand fast to Good which we consider them incapable of identifying? The proposition is this: the people are incapable of seating men in positions of limited power; to remedy this, let them elevate men to positions of unlimited power so as to prevent any erroneous elevations!

The bureaucratic structure faces the pressures of vice from above and from below. The forces from above, those strings by which the agency is directed, have already been covered. They amount to an ever-increasing domination of the entity's direction by private interests, a consequence of the fact that bureaucracies dispose not with their own funds, but with those of others. With respect to our current subject, the sector of public security, this force is most likely to manifest as the corrupt allocation of supply contracts, the bribes of criminals, or even a subversion of the entire department of policing by hostile forces. The first of these is most certain, yet least nefarious - for certain political favours, those of sufficient position within the framework may buy protective equipment from B instead of A, or data from D instead of

C. This is essentially a bribe with irregular form. The second of three manifests most often when much profit is to be made in the inactivity of the police force - members of the industry conducting the bribery may even infiltrate the police's own ranks. We see this most often regarding the prohibition of the consumption of certain substances, or crimes which involve no inherent property violations, though it is not so irregular for the policing entity to ignore grander crimes should the criminal be of enough status and should the bribe with it no unthinkable risk. Examples barely need to be stated: men have devious desires and act to satisfy them as they can. The bureaucratic entity can get away with such violations of the word of law due to their absolute independence from public satisfaction, the obfuscation and non-ownership of costs, and its own internal proximity to the structures of law creation and judgement, which themselves know no competition so as to keep them under the bounds of restraint.

The third manifestation of police corruption, absolute subversion, occurs further towards the end of the entity's lifespan, once positions of power are held exclusively by career opportunities, who excel at little other than satisfying the wants of society's recesses above those of the people from whom the entity's funds are plundered. After this inevitable point has been reached, the structure is easily mobilized to support the positions of those with most power. There are naturally those with the power to direct society without offering up anything of their own, those participants in systematic theft, the state, and systematic fraud, the cartel of central banking.

If an entity possesses the unchallenged power to secure and direct resources not owned by itself, it eventually comes to own and to direct all. This force, a monopoly on coercion, is known as the state, by which we here mean not merely the formal and visible employment of the taxman, but, additionally, those pseudo-private entities which have brushed against the state's core so often in exchanging favours that the two have melded together into an amalgamation of institutionalised coercion which escapes any of the simplistic categorisations of present-day political discourse. Characteristic of these orbiter entities is that their vitality, to the degree of the closeness of their orbit, is provided through the existence of the core state principle. This latter understanding of the state better captures those hostile forces who inevitably direct stolen funds in a developed statist society, but also better explains the rise of pseudo-state organs of theft, various forms of state monopolies, most noticeably with respect to banking and currency.

An entity will tend to ideologically subvert public-facing structures to the degree that it possesses command over the society's organs of plunder, through which it can create continuous flows of costless expenditure. The subsequent direction of the bureaucratic entity can take forms as varied as can the human will itself. They may be directed towards enhancing the power of those licensed plunderers or enforcing those parties' ideological vision. The entities who hold this power desire little more than an obfuscation of their identities, such that anyone wishing to observe any such explicit, high-level corruption is bound to experience a degree of confusion when examining the behaviour of the corrupted entities: such entities, both 'private' and public, appear to systematically make decisions outside of their own best interests; they do not capitalise on innovative possibilities, the invest resources into ideological endeavours which carry with them no apparent monetary boon, support their own regulatory restriction, and so on. An invasive force plants its roots in the host and turns it into a husk with only an outside appearance of individual autonomy; when analysed under the presumption that it is attempting to aggrandise itself, its behaviour seems inexplicable. When seen merely as an exhaustible instrument of a centralised, higher cause with mandate to plunder, its actions begin to make more sense. As the statist system develops, this limitless entity, the highest peak of the coercive structure, will dissolve the vital individualising forces of a larger number of a nation's most prominent entities, from public police services to private clothing retail units. All infected entities will cease to act towards the purpose of their establishment, and work instead, in unison, towards the ideological principles of the caste best disposed to climbing the bureaucratic structures of the core coercive power.

The forces from below which act to deviate the behaviour of public security from the public good are less grandly nefarious in their nature. These phenomena derive more directly from the entity's lack of reliance on price data, rather than the fact that, as such, the entity must instead be reliant on the aforementioned plunderers. Such forces generally contain the defects brought on by a lack of innovation and the continuous transformation of the entity according to the eternal desire of each individual to maximise result sat minimal expenditure, a force which, in a bureaucracy, manifests itself in behaviour working increasingly towards the letter of the position's demands, rather than to the position's original spirit.

To better demonstrate these principles as forces continuously at work in the bureaucratic elements of our own society, it would be instructive to trace the necessary degeneration of a public service bureau which, at our point of departure, quite properly and respectfully lives up to its name. This entity, to a large degree, is serving the public's needs with little fault. It operates rather efficiently, its workers reporting little time wasted, and its relative employment of labours for the filing of assorted bureaucratic paperwork is kept to a minimum. It fulfils the public's key needs; stolen property is, where possible, restored to its rightful owner, the judgements of its courts are just, and the nation's streets are only rarely disorderly. Officers-on-duty are often seen, and always respected. The few misdeeds of the entity have prompted swift and genuine apology, and a punishment of those responsible. The police force offers advice and actively seeks to ensure the security of the property of the people. Most importantly, the service embodies the prime Peelian principle of policing: its members are of the public, and for the public. They tend to serve the public body as the public body would, in its soberest moments, desire its own conscience to direct it, and are tethered to the judgements of the public by their strong sense of respect and duty towards their countrymen, as well as by the relative efficiency of any local electoral mechanisms couples with a high public visibility of the entity's actions. In many ways, the knowledge of the public about the intimacies of the police force's inner workings is larger than the knowledge of the police force about the private affairs of the public.

It seems rather idyllic. Even if a better system could be hypothesised, a strong argument could be made for leaving the structure as it stands. After all, while a truly Utopian police force may save us some pennies, or more quickly catch some small number of criminals, or work more closely with the victims thereof, we may only obtain this if we are absolutely correct in our theorising, irrespective of our belief therein. Yet the vast majority of convinced men have turned out to be ardent defenders of the phantasmal, and, taking a single wrong turn, have crafted a doctrine which, while at first glance sound, would bring about, when implemented, a grand departure from the standards of goodness. As theorisers of a better society, and critics of an apparently worse, we may, in the ignorance to which we are always blind, run the risk of eliminating a fine societal framework which will prove quite impossible to rebuild.

Regardless of the fortuity of the matter, time must always continue to flow. The world will develop; man will act. Both occur in accordance with eternal laws. Unfortunately for our well-protected society, its protector must travel along the tracks upon which it has been set. The incentive structure of the bureaucracy will play itself out, and the guardian whose weight is barely felt will become an expensive and oppressive behemoth, a tool handled by vice and funded by victim.

Our depiction of descent begins with something quite excusable and free of ill-intent: a gradual departure away from the most proper use of scarce resources. Whenever a junction is met, a wrong choice can be made. In making a wrong choice, the suitability of the current use of one's means drifts further into unreason. If one is lacking certain relevant information, one will more surely find oneself drifting from any original solid ground. In our dynamic world, junctions frequently make themselves unavoidable. More precisely, every possible action is one such junction.

An official has new resources at his disposal. He may hire an additional officer, better improve the equipment of current employees, or perhaps invest in additional training. Further, the scenery of crime has come to change: more assaults than normal are predicted in his Northern district, and robberies in his East district are also on the rise. The official may well calculate his alternatives with fantastic precision; an investment in patrol personnel in North will have the increase of assaults, while training of current personnel can be accurately expected to be instrumental in the prevention of almost all new robberies in East. What is to be done? Further, what is the benefit of a correct decision, and what of the detriment arising from an incorrect one?

To better frame this dilemma, we will contrast it to the ideal alternative: the system in which the ultimate incentive of each actor is equal to the highest moral good. In this system, each actor would be rewarded in proportion to the degree to which his actions benefit the public. Since decision-making power in society must be limited and allocated, each actor will also receive an increase in decision-making power in proportion to his benefit of the public weal. Given that we live amongst men and not amongst Gods, we must, additionally, have a system whereby this degree of public benefit is established and judged - that is, there must, in casting societal judgement, already exist allocations of decision-making power, themselves decided according to this very process, and so on ad infinitum. This is not the best imaginable system; it is instead the best possible system.

The degree to which any decision-making system has access to the sum of information flowing from this incremental and decentralised organism, the teleonomy, is the degree to which it will have a positively developing tendency relative to the highest potentialities of the individuals from which the system is built, and the degree to which it will have valid information upon which to base its calculations of public benefit or detriment. To draw analogy from a field wherein this principle's effects have already been largely excavated, we cannot condemn the fact that those with the most purchasing power control the flow of investments in the free economy on the grounds that a poor and inexperienced man may well have the foresight to predict the explosive increase in the price of a penny stock which escaped the eyes of seasoned billionaires. To hold such an opinion expresses blatant ignorance of the need for a regression of decision-making - who is best equipped to decide who is best equipped to decide.

The poor man may well, hypothetically speaking, make a better decision than a rich man, yet upon which circumstances has the latter obtained his decision-making power, or, with respect to the economy alone, as far as we can make this distinction, how has he obtained his money? From those prior set of decision-makers whose historically successful values he had appealed to. This makes up the only structure of decision-making capable of universal employment. It is also synonymous with the traditional principle as opposed to the rationalist principle, and solves, and exposes, the grand egalitarian failures of democracy which inevitably destroys tradition, insofar as its principles are active, given that its essence lies in an erasure of prior regressions of decision-making power and a fraudulent aggrandization of those thereby least endowed, amounting to a proportional extinction of all genuinely valuable knowledge.

Should we universalise the rationalist principle, the principle for the enforced enrichment of our penny-stock investor, the principle of the democrat, and, as shall be shown, the principle of the state bureaucracy as such, we must allow the poor man to plunder the rich in order to invest the latter's his resources, for this is what a full denial of the value of the historical regression amounts to. Additionally, should the plunderer indeed prove astute in his investments, we should once more allow the formerly rich to replunder his funds should he be convinced enough of the truth of his individual principles, and in the falsity of those of his plunderer. Anyone may, and simultaneously may not, trespass upon everything, and, simultaneously, nothing, and nothing remains sacred. This is not the worst imaginable system; it is instead the worst possible system. Insofar as we deviate from the best possible principle towards the worst, we approach hell as well as man can make it. Any half-way point between these principles is mere epistemological confusion. To allow certain people to sometimes erase the regression sequence of decision-making power is a simultaneous endorsement of rationalism, for oneself and a select few, as well as traditionalism, for those who I, as rationalist, deem in need of rule.

The foregoing meander was necessary in order to properly demonstrate the inefficiency present in any of the bureaucrat's choices: the lack of voluntary exchange for services means that the regression has been interrupted in favour of the bureaucratic officer's rationalism. He may take the correct choice, but in doing so he acts to bypass the pre-existing allocation of legitimate decision-making power and, most importantly, makes the correct allocation on insufficient grounds. Similarly, one may successfully avoid a plane crash by travelling via car rather than aeroplane, a decision prompted by the grounds that one could easily call to mind many deadly plane tragedies, but only few recent car crashes. Despite the success of the action, this development in no way acts as an endorsement of the decision to travel by car, nor of future use of cars over planes. The correct decision was an accident, against the current of reason.

This point of the matter will be later elaborated upon, where its expounding will not wholly overshadow a topic already being discussed.

Aside from this epistemological failure of the statist action, necessarily counter-traditional, which pertains to the actions-as-such, independent of their results, there exists a further instrument of corruption which acts with respect to the consequences of the statist action. This is the inability of the bureaucracy to be properly cleansed from without.

Every entity will make mistakes. Error is more characteristic of the human condition than is success. As mentioned briefly, what makes life bearable is the power to transmute failure, as such, into success. Similarly, this power is what makes any entity bearable for its societal substrate. Let us presume that our officer chose training over an expansion of employment, and, doing so, succeeded in his material objectives - robberies were indeed prevented. Independent of whether or not the officer possessed remotely enough knowledge to make an informed decision on this matter of allocation, drastically simplified as we have made it, posing two alternatives at a single point of time rather than an unknowable number of alternatives over an indefinite amount of time, let us grand that his endeavour was also, from the perspective of consequentialist morality, rather good. Not perfect, no human allocation ever has been, nor will be. As such, his action partakes in both good and bad. Justice and practicality would prescribe that the decision be met with reward and punishment in proportion to its participation in each of these qualities. Yet, in this case, this is not what occurs. The entity's decision-making power in the future is highly independent of the successes or failures of the actions in the present. This can be measured by the grand distance lying between the efficient satisfaction of society's requirements and an expansion of the entity's ability to command resources in the future. Ignoring for now the election process, the entity receives its expansion, or reduction of decision-making power *before* it produces its supposed benefits, which means that an absolute failure to produce any such benefits results in a net nil difference in decision-making power vis-a-vis the results accruing from the perfect allocation. In the best imaginable world, this power reallocation would occur simultaneously with every productive action of the entity, every satisfaction of morality, and in exact proportion to this satisfaction.

As an aside, the fact that bureaucracies are, to some unknown degree, hypothetically subject to the democratic ballot is a point relied upon far more than it ought to be, given the reality of the matter. Not only does this claim ignore the fact that the knowledge required for the successful running of a bureaucratic entity lies almost wholly within that bureaucracy's own ranks, and, therefore, the demands of public majority are entirely unfit to reform its accumulated inefficiencies, but the claim also pays no heed to the fact that the electoral process can have no representative measurement of cost associated with each possible ballot option. Once more, the ideal, which simultaneously trades influence for actual public benefit, can only support those entities, be they friends, family, corporations, and so on, who give away less power in the creation of their benefits than is obtained in the exchange of that produced benefit, or its accumulation by its chosen recipients.

This supposed saving grace of the bureaucracy, that it is 'subject to the democratic will', in fact exposes a flaw grander than that which it attempts to cover up - for while the measurement of the utility of the service provided is extremely difficult when there is no mechanism of feedback at the point of final production, it is nonetheless remotely visible to the general eye of scrutiny: idle police are worse than active police, cleanliness is better than filth. The position with respect to costs is much more dire. A man may come to judge that, when looking out of his living room window, the repairs carried out to his immediate road proved quite the improvement. He is probably right, if not with respect to magnitude, at least with respect to the general positivity of the repairs themselves. What he does not and cannot cross his mind is the list of things which might have otherwise come to fruition, should the resources hereby used have been elsewhere allocated. Relative to the knowledge required for such a judgement, the knowledge of the public voter is pathetically limited. Even worse, the democratic system, anti-traditional in its essence, ensures that the best voter receives no more decision-making power in the next election than does the worst voter, so it is necessarily impossible for this position of ineptitude to ever improve.

Now, the officer has made his seemingly good decision. It partakes in both good and in bad, yet his position, and that of his entity, remain unchanged. This necessitates, *ceteris paribus*, an irreparable future societal loss: having made a good decision, the entity's ability to rule does not grow. As a consequence, *this decision-making power is left at the disposal of an entity less capable of its good disposal*. Therefore, even the present successes of the bureaucratic entity cause a future loss, vis-a-vis an equal action from an entity of liberty, due to the independence of the former from any form of feedback mechanism linked to moral truth. Over time, the successful entity does not grow as much as it ought, and so it drifts from the position justly assigned to it given its proven competence or lack thereof.

From the fact that no adaptation of our entity's size occurs in relation to its effects on our shared goals, another matter of import comes into view: that the successes of the officer from the perspective of his superiors is itself a grand distance from his true effect on society. The successful hierarchy improves itself not only by growing in total mass, but also by properly rearranging its internal ranks such that better future decisions may be made. Insofar as the entity has at its disposal information regarding the productivity of one of its employees, its reallocations will turn out correct. As such, the bureaucracy will tend to exhibit rather abhorrent decision-making with respect to the structuring of its own ranks. The ability to manage and to promote one's subordinates being decisions which have an ultimate effect on societal good, it must follow that entities which receive no direct impulse from the spring of moral values are destined to undergo a continuous decline in decision-making ability.

Man's limited position is such that all must measure goodness by historically established standards. All such sets of standards, which posit that some physical phenomenon or manifestation of action is good, or another bad, leave exposed 'blind spots' of morality, due to the fact that morality and the good are related to the acts of men, not the instruments thereby employed. Acts can merely be inferred; they are not wholly sensible phenomena.

For reasons previously laid out, we have good reason to believe that the bureaucracy, which banishes itself from the points of nearest contact with moral information, leaves itself with a remarkably large, and continuously expanding, self-reinforcing blind spot. The nature of blind spots is such that all which they encompass may be sacrificed to that which lies without, to the approval of the decision maker. This sacrifice may well be a good-natured and innocent one, an ignorance of the blind spot, or something more devious, a sacrifice of the good occasioned by a knowledge of the blind spot. Naturally, individuals who participate in the latter category of action are more consistent in their sacrifice of the good, for it is the mode, rather than accident, of the act. The more intentionally and successfully exploitative an actor is of a blind spot, the more of an advantage he has of gaining decision-making power vis-a-vis the honest man.

It never came to the attention of our officer that his received report, that robberies had been successfully held to target rates of occurrence in the country's Eastern district without thereby occasioning an unbearable rise in cases of murder in district North, may not indicate quite as successful an execution of policy as he had thereby been led to believe. Indeed, in understanding that this exercise was highly important to his officer, a subordinate made the decision to abandon for a time the task of patrolling the region of a cluster of local shops, so that he may instead be present more often at a scrapping facility. He knew that the latter attracted a higher frequency of thefts than the former and acted accordingly with much success. He caught five petty thieves of scrap and waste as a consequence of this decision. It also happened that, during this time, a thief broke into a jeweller's shop and procured for himself a very grand plunder.

Such possibilities lay in the blind spot of the officer's criteria for good results, and, as such, went unnoticed. For his instrumentality in successfully exhibiting the utility of the unit's new training investments, the patrolling policeman may receive a comfortable new position of increased influence.

But let our judging officer have a much keener eye. He spots, with the help of his moral intuition, that there was in fact no proof of the success of his chosen directive. The time comes for his own performance evaluation. What are his options? As already elaborated, the structure of hierarchy is such that information must be condensed, and some therefore lost, to be fed up the chain for higher-level decision-making. The officer has manually spotted something which would normally, by the accepted metrics of performance in his position, be lost to him. He can choose to report his failures to management, to the benefit of the structural integrity of the whole entity, or he can avoid its mention. The latter is remarkably easy for him: another layer of condensation means that higher management is quite unlikely to discover faults at ground level which are not grandly consequential. Further, should the fault indeed be detected, serious blame can be easily avoided as the error in question lay outside of the officer's employed metrics of success, that is, outside of the due responsibilities of his position assigned to him by his seniors. Such behaviour is only possible insofar as a system has blind spots.

We must presume grand levels of wisdom and selflessness to be presiding in our run-of-the-mill state-conservative police officer for our model system not to already be slipping into the quagmire. A society abundant with such great men would seemingly have no need for the paternal rule of the state. But what is a slave of duty to do when his faculties, part-blinded by his position, tell his sense of duty that a wrong can be undergone in order to avoid a greater evil? Either he or his colleague will soon be chosen to fill a vacant management position. He believes that he has reason to suppose that his colleague is exploiting the blind spots around him for selfish gain. Being blind spots, this claim cannot be proven through any available documentation. In this case, does the former secure the ascension of a moral inferior by reporting his own extraordinary, well-spotted failures and prevent the corruption of the entity? His own failures were accidents of chance, entirely independent of the principles of his actions, which, as he leads himself to believe, were executed as well as was possible with the resources at hand.

Each time the officer decides to act in such a manner, so as to prevent the elevation of immoral agents, the structure of the entity's decision-making becomes further alloyed by deceit. It so happens that the core principle of the statist action, the operational presupposition of the bureaucracy itself, that the historical regression of decision-making can be interrupted by individually rationalised consequentialism, is the one which the officer employs in making such a decision. Thus, in taking such an action, he is merely affirming the rationale which justifies the existence of his function in the first place. Such behaviour will occur, then, to the degree that coercive, statist action itself is justified in any given society. We would be beyond foolish to build a society upon such foundations, and simultaneously expect these suppositions to foreign to all individuals therein.

It is part of the nature of all moral systems and structures of decision-making to have their blind spots forced open by an ever-growing series of wedges. What is vital to such structures is not only that they have a strong defence against such forces, but also that they have access to the avenues of repair and rejuvenation.

As time passes, and an entity ages and decays, a renewal becomes increasingly necessary. But, for a bureaucracy, the possibility of renewal retreats in proportion to the advance of corruption; for whatever good elements remain in the structure, their potency becomes muddled by the inevitable forces of vice, and its direction becomes increasingly set by the higher directives of selfishness. Seeing that one of his branches had become corrupt, the head of an entity tethered closely to the judgements of the teleological regression could quite painlessly sever the rotten limb in order to enlighten the whole. Yet, when our decision maker has no access to any such stream of information, he has no ability to prune. Increasingly, our officers receive, follow and create, through ill will or otherwise, criteria of success which ignore the societal good. Repatriation of property could be more effortlessly paid from our budget than by going out of the way to track down and return the stolen item; making a case appear more difficult than it in actual fact was serves only to make my efforts appear more productive; my private life could be greatly benefitted if I were to promote my patron's son ahead of another subordinate, or if I were to contract protective equipment from corporation A instead of corporation B.

There must be increasingly little restriction on such behaviour. These deviations may always be, rightly or wrongly, justified as ultimately beneficial to the entity. As information channels break down, each individual receives instruction which, if followed fully, would be increasingly ill-suited to the attainment of the overall good. As such, there comes a point when these actions, which employ individual intuition, may well be superior to those prescribed by the official regulations of the bureaucracy, which have become inhibitive rather than conducive to correct behaviour.

When the new way of life becomes settled, recommendations of genuine improvement become mere hassle for those at the reigns of power, and could nonetheless not be justified in terms of the bureaucracy's internal moral structure. True efficiency becomes taboo. To increase efficiency means not only to increase output, but also to decrease input. Why would an entity, especially once corrupt, strangle its own life source in favour of a good visible to nobody which it cannot even itself confirm? How many would fire their own subordinates, who are regardless most likely immune from such measures in a developed bureaucracy, for no remote change to one's position other than a command over a smaller division?

In a society in which decision-making power is exchanged for a product at the point of societal satisfaction, the corruption of an entity is a regrettable occurrence, but, thankfully, a minor and temporary one. Every time a fault is committed, future decision-making power gets subtracted and reallocated elsewhere, to wherever the people disappointed by these actions instead decide to take their patronage. Within the system of liberty, any failure to provide the product appropriate to one's function means that the successful provision of that product by any other entity now becomes a highly worthwhile endeavour. The retreat of the failing structure creates a proportionally sized and equally shaped vacuum.

No such process exists in state conservative structures. Resources are allocated prior to production, and as such the failure to produce entails no necessary punishment and reallocation. On the contrary, the failures and evils of the structure work only to reinforce its resistance to reformation. It is the prime interest of the entity to forbid any close competition in market spheres and to effect a legal monopolisation of its sector. In our society, this venture has reached near completion with respect to the fields of security, schooling and healthcare - if not in the de jure outlawing of 'competitor' structures per se, at least in the universal 'bureaucratizing' of industry practice, the bringing of the entire industry under the active control of coercive forces, through universal curriculums, mandatory licensing, state regulations and unionism. But even if there were no such additional laws and restrictions whatsoever, what point is there in telling a baker he is free to offer a cake for one ounce of silver to those who have already made an irrevocable down payment of two ounces of silver for a slightly inferior baked good? At this point, are the two on remotely competitive grounds? The very nature of the tax-funded position is to blockade all competition in all but the most dire of cases, cases wherein the product of the bureaucracy has fallen to such lows that its intended consumer no longer even recognises its produce to fall within the same functional category as that which the entity was originally established to provide, as in the cases of dirty drinking water, or non-preventative police. In such corrupted circumstances, we can all but guarantee that the entity has pre-empted the destructive consequences of its undermining by using its grand leverage to coax the legislative body into giving it the protections due to an endangered species. But if both of the above points are to be somehow written off as immaterial to the core matter of the discussion, these divergences instead representing merely accidental qualities, then what of the ever-observable fact that bureaucratic inefficiency leads to increased rather than to decreased societal decision-making power?

We can view this phenomenon from two angles: that of demand or that of supply. When one proves difficult to exploit, the other is likely ripe to be tapped. The produce of the tax-funded agency is free, yet both 'produce' and 'free' are subject to caveats and conditions. Quality may always be improved, and limited resources may always be given out less or more liberally. Given an input, how much, and to whom, do we delegate? Healthcare is not given out unconditionally in quantity - one cannot receive the immediate attention of one hundred doctors for a graze of the knee. Nor can these services be given out with unconditional quality - to reduce the impurities of the water supply from functionally nil to absolutely nil would require more than man is able to sacrifice. If any entity attempts to expand either its quality or its quantity of provisions far enough, without an appropriate reduction of the other, it will find that it does not have enough resources to meet society's demands.[9] Going beyond this point in a market environment is the same as incurring a loss. Resources flee following the bad decision. In a public entity, the effects of these misallocations are known as a 'lack of funding', or as 'austerity'.

This is not to suggest that a public entity cannot be genuinely resource starved, rather that the presupposition of its existence is that market allocations do not supply the good as much as it ought to be supplied. This, combined with its lack of output signal and proper mechanisms of efficiency measurement, means that there can be no visible point at which we can definitively say that an entity needs fewer funds, or, what amounts to the same thing, ought to reduce the quantity or quality of its provisions.

A public hospital increases its desired level of quality and makes its distribution less restricted. As such, it now harbours long queues of desiring patients, few of whom it can actually serve. It is likely that a few of those high priority patients who would have been admitted under a less resource-liberal regime, will, because of this decision, forego treatment, with possibility of death. Amidst the ensuing public outage, are we seriously to suppose that 'reduce quality and restrict supply' will be the voices shouting loudest most heard when the opposite motion can be put into effect with no advocate for this latter bearing a fraction of the costs of his demands? The entity was set up because the market could not supply enough medicine. Now that people are beginning to die, are we going to capitulate to market forces and 'cut essential services even further'? In a society which has admitted the principle of a public service entity, the entity has almost free reign to employ a tactic of self-induced scarcity profitable only to those in a tax-funded field. Offer everything to everyone, and, when one finds one's stocks running short of infinity, blame either the greed of other producers, or blame competition as such. If this trick proves lacklustre, the bureaucratic department always has a second means by which to fraudulently procure its supply without detection or punishment - its inevitable self-sabotage.

This self-sabotage should not be taken to indicate a unified and intentional wrecking of the productive organs by their workers. It is rather a natural by-product of the entity's ever-widening blind spot. Given that the knowledge of the entity's aims and activities lies largely within its own ranks, it is extraordinarily unlikely that any individual is in any position to document the full extent of the entity's corruptive deviations. Compare this to our ideal entity, or, a margin worse, a modern market entity. The deviations of the former become manifest as an immediate reduction of power; the deviations of the latter become documented as a lower capitalised value of the venture's assets, lower profit, lower internal reinvestment, lower future ability to direct economic resources. These streams correspond to the method described above, whereby the bureaucracy attempts to set its productive potential higher than it ought to. This demand-related process is abetted by the flows of market investment, the contribution of capital by individuals to those channels in which they estimate highest productivity to occur. These flows, the second mode of the societal measuring of efficiency, are cut off in the public entity. All that remains to it is an appeal to the treasury. An important feature of this appeal is that it, on the presumption that the market is incapable of creating the produce of the public entity, cannot rely on any of the traditional measurements of economic efficiency for its persuasive might. The presupposition of any public entity being that it would be loss-bearing if floated on the market in its current state, these loss-bearing but supposedly useful industries participate in hypothetical loss-making to an unknowable degree, and to a degree that stands in permanent flux. An entity which could function in the market one century ago may no longer be able to, and vice versa. For example, the invention of the internet has drastically altered the economics of the potential provision of education - we cannot know the quantity of this effect, but may only insinuate through our best judgements. Public sector education may, then, granting the bureaucratic premise, be less in need of its tax-funded structure. On the other hand, we may hypothesise that an expansion of the regulatory framework of a state would increase the cost of compliant policing, and therefore further remove the ability of a well-equipped service of policing to operate on market grounds alone.

Given that these economic conditions are uncountable and in a state of permanent change, the task of the treasurer, delegating the proper amount of resources to each channel, becomes supremely complex. Presuming in him a state of saintliness, a presumption which we have much reason not to grant, how is he to ever decide if the inability of some public entity to meet its demand is due to an internally imposed inefficiency or the result of something external, such as a lack of funding? From his position, he can only make sense of a small array of general figures which show him, truthfully speaking, not even a glimpse of his problem's true magnitude. He may see money going in, and, ignoring the incommensurability of the output of the bureaucracy, some order of produce going out, in addition to a paltry few internal statistics of no remote explanatory power in any wider economic sense.

When the policing entity does clamber for more resources due to the creeping vines of inefficiency, what will the treasure see, and how is he to react? This marked inability to distinguish internal inefficiencies from externally imposed financial deficiencies means that the self-inflicted failures of a state entity will seldom cause it to be treated less favourably by a treasurer, even should the latter hold a great deal of care for efficient bureaucratic management and the proper punishment of wastefulness. Further, as previously elaborated, within the treasurer position itself there exists no systemic process of refinement in accordance with the results of the treasurer's actions; this in absolute contradistinction to the fate of the corresponding class in a state of liberty, the investor, wherein one ceases to be able to participate in the class according to one's misallocations, and grows within the class according to one's well-chosen disposals.

In order to grand to the supporters of bureaucracy yet another crutch upon which to stead their cumbersome behemoths, we have been conceding that a general inclination exists for state resource allocators, such as the treasurer, to sniff out inefficiencies to the best of their abilities and to pull up their roots. This line of support, alike all others which we have laid out before in order to assist the clarity of our analysis, is, in reality, entirely fictitious. Here, too, the exact opposite is true. The oft-forgotten universal manifests itself once more:

whenever one can allocate resources which one does not own, and, as such will suffer little from any improper allocation thereof, then we must expect to witness a state wherein the losing strategy is that of honest justice, while the winning strategy is one of doing only the bare minimum required to appease the dulling public eye, and allocating the maximum to a further concentration of societal power.

One of the most dangerous paths towards irreversible and calamitous error is that of a pragmatic, present evil rationalised on the grounds that, through these ill means, one will better be able to dispense justice in the future, by propelling oneself into a position of higher power. This moral rule manifests itself in a wide range of circumstances, from revolutionary violence and battlefield cowardice, to the simple politician, bureaucrat or treasurer caught amidst the minefield of public opinion and the opportunism of rivals.

We may lament the uselessness, the duplicity, or the sheer incompetence of our supposed political representatives; yet it must be asked: why do they all, with seemingly no exception, appear to be so? As with any game, the answer is simple: the winners have in common that they've learned to make the most effective moves. Since a grand part of politics falls to, and has always fallen to, public opinion, we must conclude that the actions which capture the (temporary) support of the public body are those which appear so commonly in our political caste. Then why so much distrust? Because every lie, in a world wherein there is a faculty of truth, is eventually uncovered. And every lie is the papering over of a less preferable future for a more tolerable present. When lying becomes the norm, as it must tend to do when it has been allowed to become a reliable means to success, telling the truth becomes exceedingly difficult. It amounts to destroying the established, pleasantly told story about the state of things and thereby inciting panic: given that any story will be believed, one puts oneself at a disadvantage when telling anything but the most fantastical of all plausible lies or untruths. As things now stand, this path has been followed to the extent that the lies of plenty strung by our more recent forerunners, who all the while remain undetected in their deceit, have begun to subject our present political class to an irreconcilable conundrum: the public are sedated on fantasies of abundance and will accept no other line, and yet these fantasies have become so detached from reality of the constraints thereby necessitated that any prospective politician cannot take one step towards a more proper use of the political spindle without hopelessly tangling himself in any number of its prior spun threads.

The grand intoxication of our time is brought on by a glorious presentation of the results of some proposed decision, coupled with a deep fog enveloping all notion of this decision's relative cost. The exact opposite of Bastiat's wish has come true; the public act increasingly more based solely upon what is seen, and ever less through a consideration of that which is not seen. It is rather impossible to see exactly what one's tax money will be exchanged for, where it will be allocated, and what might've been produced in this action's stead. One may, perhaps, attempt to find the portion of the public purse allocated to each of his endeavours and, in some muddled way, try to calculate one's tax contribution thereto, yet whatever small result occurs from this cannot begin to explain the marginal benefit incurred by one's own taxes, or of increasing the resources allocated to x by y. Further, the median member of the electorate bears upon himself a tax burden significantly lower than the mean burden of the population. As a result, quantitative, popular voice lies with those whims associated with spending funds which are not one's own, commanding benefits which are often not one's to keep. Given that political power adheres to the voices of the masses in all but the most essential activities of the state, we can expect the allocations made to government entities to consistently deviate from the aristocratic and traditionalist regression of decision-making - to be egalitarian in nature and against nature, and to always be be exorbitant - for the only way in which the public can, with the legitimisation of society, directly consume the wealth of the historically successful is through the direction of state coercion. The political class will be happy to plunder the historical successes of the nation, against the best interests of the whole society, for the benefit of its own present-day mediocrities. Despite these defects, this picture presumes a very knowledgeable voting class, capable of expertly calculating the personal costs and short-run benefits to be accrued by using the state in its own favour. Yet the public are not quite omniscient, and in their ignorance grow susceptible to false promises. The majority has never known, and likely will never come to understand, that an increase in hospitals facilitates a reduction in, say, houses, in food, in entertainment or in leisure. And, on an individual basis, they have little to lose by being wrong - the primary victim of their ignorance is society.

It is remarkable case of muddle-headedness that the economist proposes this mechanism as a means towards the reduction of the problem of 'external effects', whereby a certain mode of action is excessively undertaken due to the fact that the detriments thereof are accrued to some entity other than the actor himself. The economist asks us to simply suppose the problem already solved with respect to the choices of the voting body, and then asks the voting body to cement this removal through their vote, thereby restricting others, who are also voters, from behaving in such detrimental manners.

If the treasurer is led astray by being bound to the successes of a public playing darts with mite-sized board, how much more foolish will he, 'servant of the people', be required to behave when a second dimension of choice is added, the very nature of which leads to the temptation of deceit? We here talk about the aspect of time, of savings versus consumption. It must first be mentioned that all traditions, even all virtues, fall under the teleological category of savings. They can be done away with for present pleasure, that is, consumed. Civilisation is built upon the repression of this consumption.

Instead of plucking from man's present to fund his allocations, the state can instead pluck from the future. The advantages of this for him are rather obvious: his reign is one of prosperity and abundance for many. Instead of feeling the pinch during the reign of the lavish, it will be instead felt in the reign of his successors. To draw this causal connection in practice is something which very few men are capable of. They do not exist, and never can exist, accurate statistics about how taxes-now-harvested would have otherwise been saved or spent. And since the measuring of tax funded production yields unmeasurable results, we cannot expect much by the way of a measurement of the savings ratio of the state.

The 'savings-cost' of state activity being invisible, extremely few possessing the insight to draw causal connections in keeping with rudimentary economic theory even should such things be visible, people granting legitimacy to those who appear to bring them prosperity, and with politics gradually coming to be inhabited by those who most masterfully bring the public body to a state of near-rapture, we may only conclude a general tendency for bureaucratic entities to be unjustly funded by the future wealth of mankind - and, indeed, one need only look around to see such a state of things pushed close to its limit.

If the consumptive tendency of state activity is to become visible to the naked eye, it will do so when tax funds themselves are no longer sufficient to allow for a grinding down of enough capital to ensure a satisfactory momentary high. When this moment is reached, the politicians, knowing that the populace will not stomach any further tax increases, begin to succeed through alternative means: by taxing those who cannot vote. In a developed democracy, this class contains both the very young and the unborn. Selling the future labour of these demographics to those savers 'investing' in state bonds, the state undertakes to directly siphon from the national investment fund for consumptive purposes. Those funds aiming to purchase bonds are entirely investment-oriented: in being willing to forego consumption and hold a bond asset, the investor provides resources which may instead be invested to the benefit of future productivity. In order to not make a loss, the bond's issuer would have to invest the funds at a rate of profit higher than the interest rate agreed upon with the lender. If he simply consumes the lent money, he is punished in due proportion. With state bonds, however, investment need not occur. When its bonds mature, the state may simply tax its citizens or debase their currency. The ability of the state to pay its debts, then, is entirely independent of its utilisation of the funds initially received therefrom. The state issues state bonds, and, in doing so, carves for itself a part of the total investment funds of its citizens. It consumes these funds immediately through deficit spending, in some form of stimulus package or through a number of new, exciting programmes for social mobility. The buyers of state bonds, then, are allowed to have their cake and eat it too. They accrue yearly interest gains, as if they were saving, and receive the immediate pleasures of deficit spending, as if they were consuming. All the while, the coming generation is deprived of those capital stocks which would have otherwise been made available to them, these have instead been consumed by their parents. The state is generous, however, and for this gift of deprivation only asks that the new generation foot the bill.

At such a point, like an addict suffering from the removal of a drug which now only serves to make him feel 'normal', the voter will angrily scorn anyone who actually reduces the extent to which his present highs are to be paid for by unborn children, or, perhaps, immigrant labour. Should this siphon be removed, the addicted populace will surely blame the one putting a stop to their craze rather than he who sold it to them in the first place. Through this we see the winning move in the game of 'the politics of public legitimacy' We see no good men in politics because the public do not want them.

In condemning democratic decision-making, we do not mean to exclude other statist systems from scrutiny, or to offer them as preferable alternatives. Indeed, that iron contraption of the 20th century, the fascist state, suffers from its own array of necessarily degenerative tendencies in the domain of high-level resource allocation. We have seen and must see in all such one-party states the emergence of a new form of politics: the intra-party politics. Ignoring for now the matter of the initial establishment of the fascistic framework, be it the election to end all elections or a true and bloody putsch, the one-party state must not be mistaken for a one-opinion state. Precedent would show that the rivalries of intra-party conflict in a one-party state are far more volatile and socially disruptive than the baton passing of representative democracy. We would likely be furnished with a grander array of examples of this phenomenon if only such regimes were robust enough to reliably withstand the passing of their pioneer or his immediate heir.

When there are no explicit fights or quarrels in the fascistic state, the regular games of politics continue to be played. Its fundamentals undergo no change, merely the means of scoring points. Instead of being led by the tune of the public electorate, one plays to the whims of the party electorate - personal appeasement, promises and deceit, and so on. Is the fascist politician likely to categorically refuse to partake in the employment of deceit for the greater good when his entire system rests on the subjugation of personal to collective rights? In fact, the fascist system of internal hierarchical organisation is, in many ways, a universalised version of the modern democratic state.

The ideal fascist system contains no official mode of public election or individual mobility whatsoever. Once part of a caste, one is, in almost all instances, well and truly set by the force of coercion. This enforced rigidity spans from its roots to its highest reaches. In the developed democratic society, on the other hand, there exists *one* mode of caste mobility - the election of some part of the democratic mass of clay to the political caste, and the sinking of some part of the political caste back into clay. Within the clay, one's rank is set by the actions of the political caste, who represent the clay. Within the political class, one's actions are dictated by the wills of the highest class, to which, like in the fascist society, entry is seldom if ever granted. Holding the spirit of the people constant, the difference between the democratic and the fascistic society is, once both are settled, only a footnote.

In terms of inherent decision-making 'mass', the two systems are far more alike than disparate. What truly matters is scope. The miniature fascist state is more tolerable than the presence of a gargantuan democratic spirit, while a slight democratic whim is less decadent than the wholly totalitarian fascistic superstructure. Our modern democracies support a caste of unelected, plunder-fed decision-makers far more numerous, and more bountifully fed, than that of any of the early fascistic nations. Truly, as a fraction of the total amount of decision-making made within current society, *both* the democratic and fascistic elements are larger than many early 20th century progressive and fascist theorists could have ever theorised. If both have grown, then what has shrunken? Liberty!

To predict the course of the state authoritarian system at its pinnacle, one needs only to apply the general principles of bureaucracy previously laid out. By doing this, it becomes clear that the fascistic structure contains, in its deviations from the free regression, only degenerative tendencies. It will tend towards an unmonitored state, free from censure or any tethering to the good, a vehicle for personal gain or a tool for nefarious private entities. For, in the long run, a system incapable of taking in the revitalising waters of the moral spring will only be traversable by the vicious. In times of revolution (and some do, still, propose statist revolution) this tendency is hastened. The moral structure of society is upturned and recast, and nothing is easier than to open up blind spots in an untraversed, liquid moral structure. We do not need to look very far back in order to recall what has been justified by attempts to satisfy the official norms of revolutionary societies as they drift further away from the roots of moral truth.

Our shining example of state security, whether it be nested within the fascistic or democratic society, must eventually succumb to its destiny: a secession of innovation, an exaltation of failure, a subservience to vice, a revocation of its reimbursive function, an expansion of its cost, an irreversible damaging of the moral fabric of society, and a general transformation into an instrument of the forces embedded above the commonplace democratic structure. For this not to occur over a long enough period would be a miracle in the strictest sense of the word. One who denies this has no ground to stand on when he criticises the supposedly degenerative tendencies of liberty, for both our argument and that of the anti-libertarian attempt to root themselves within the fundamental claim. The attack on liberty, however, rests on claims spurious from the outset, mistaking the accidental for the inherent and suffering from ill vision - as we shall soon address. It needs little stressing that the degenerative tendencies of state security apply also to all other institutions within the tax-funded realm. These entities all travel a similar path. State schools, for example, will educate less; then they will not educate at all; and then they will anti-educate. They will do this at a cost increasing in proportion to their own degeneration.

With this we may end the critique of the largely *economic* decision-making structures of the state. It is to be hoped that the repetition employed in the foregoing chapter did not prove too blunt for the general reader. It is more to be fretted, however, that an excess of swiftness in these matters would have left some grain of faith in the deeply embedded notion that the alternative to liberty is a mere willing-into-being of the solution to our woes through the omnipotent, benevolent state. As long as this notion stands to any degree as a presupposition of political discourse, and injection of liberty into the public debate is sure to miscarriage.

# 9

## FRAUDULENT AUTHORITY

Statist authoritarianism may be roughly defined as the system wherein resources are redirected from the productive classes in order to fund agencies which act to ensure the enforcement of the social norms selected by a sovereign power. Insofar as this principle is endorsed, one's political lens is a brand of statist authoritarianism. There are many such brands, differing in their "why's" but united in their "how's". As we share many of the higher ends of the state conservative, we restrict our critique of his proposals to be exclusively applicable to the means which he seeks to employ. This completed, we will attempt to reconcile the libertarian and the traditionalist with respect to both means and to ends.

In accordance with our definition of statist authoritarianism, a separation of our analysis into four essential parts will prove useful: the coercive redirection of resources, the agencies funded thereby, the enforcement of social norms thereby, and the sovereign power which chooses. In the preceding chapter we dealt with the second of these factors, and further back we disposed with the fourth. It still remains to discuss the first and the third; taxation as such, along with its parent, coercion as such.

The redirection of resources from private to public, occasioned by the breaking of the chain of rightful property rights, consists of two halves: taxation, the breaking of the chain, the seizure as such; and spending, the harnessing of this force for some particular purpose. While the former appears to always occasion the latter, these phenomena are nonetheless separable categories, each of which sets into motion its own combination of socially pernicious effects. A pure taxation, from which no spending results, would be the mere destruction of some entity's purchasing power, without any particular increase thereby incurred by the agent of taxation. A pure spending would be the increase in purchasing power without the direct destruction of any other individual's purchasing power other than insofar as such power is displaced or diluted by this fabrication of purchasing power itself. We outline this so as to better combat the myth that taxation is the evil necessity of the bounties of spending, a thesis held often even by those who hold that the bounties are not large enough to justify the seizures. As shall be shown, this belief is the opposite of true. The spending-side of state activity is inherently *more* destructive than the taxation instrumental therein.

Put roughly, taxation is legal plunder, an oxymoron under private law and a necessity under public law. Its essence lies in its severing of the decision-making regression within the field of the monetary, that is, with respect to the 'purely economic'. Mentioned towards the beginning of this work was the fact that there exists no coherent, categorical division between economy and teleonomy - not because they are the same, but because the former is a mythical entity, which attempts to balance the objective upon strictly subjective underpinnings. Conceptually speaking, the economy sits illegitimately within the confines of the teleonomy. 'Monetary taxation' being strictly economic, it runs into similar problems. It suffices to say that tax is to the economy as force is to the teleonomy. Once more, this realm of incongruence arises from spurious attempts to define in physical terms some subcategory of functional reality.

The effect of taxation as such is a reduction in the personal benefit accrued by activities deemed useful by the decision-making regression. A prime example, income tax, reduces the benefit of activities which generate income - all non-illegal work undertaken within the region of the sovereign's borders. Working becomes less beneficial to those who previously worked, and a shift occurs towards those activities not punished by the tax - from leisure to tax avoidance to black market activity. Strictly speaking, this does not mean that the effort going towards the taxed activities will immediately decrease, though in the long run this is likely to occur. It may be claimed that those in fields affected by a tax increase may work even harder than before in order to ensure that they do not experience some fall in income. This is half-true. The total fraction of purchasing power within the economy which accrues to those engaging in the taxed sectors will decrease. Given that this taxation is mere destruction of purchasing power, of money, and given that all societal resources exist under someone's command, it follows that this loss is gained directly by those whose economic power is not accrued by means of the taxed behaviours, to the degree that they have any such power. In terms of activities within the whole social body, the taxed activity is repressed, while other activities are propagated in proportion to their usefulness.

This is the immediate effect of taxation. Effects follow from this as ripples in a body of water. They decrease in magnitude in proportion to their distance from the initial taxed event, which manifests itself immediately in the reduction of the power of the taxed and an enhancement of the non-taxed. An increase in capital gains tax, for example, would immediately punish investment and increase the purchasing power of non-investors. This will at first manifest itself through a higher demand for, say, entertainment, and a lower demand for capital. From this, the entertainment industry will exercise a higher proportion of economic power than it had prior, while creators of capital will have less. As a result of these changes, both of these parties exercise some effect upon their own customers, and so on.

It may be claimed that the principle universally inhibited by taxation, the appeal to the judgements of the regression of economic decision-making, is itself the cause of much societal deterioration, and as such taxation may be a force for good. We must answer that for whatever historical flaws such a mode of decision-making has demonstrated, we must resist the temptation of comparing a history limited by man's imperfection with a post-revolutionary of man's unlimited perfection, and through these condemnations attempting to establish something resembling the latter. Secondly, such a critic must first provide a proper answer to the following questions with respect to his revolutionary urges: given that almost all men hold some notions regarding the inadequacy of their given society, and given that the notions of one man stand in stark contrast to that of another, by which mechanism are we to choose which social revolution to embark upon? Clearly, 'belief in the truth' is here an invalid criterion, for all believe in their own truths. Further, with which power ought a revolutionary enact his changes? Ought he have the sum of societal power at his command, or only what he can muster freely? Lastly, what right does he have, as a subject, to subordinate to his own plants the desires of competing revolutionary sects?

Regardless, by inhibiting the force of the regression, the sum of all past decisions made under the conditions of liberty, we simply ensure the propagation of all activities which mankind has hitherto judged to be more harmful than alternative courses of action. In which epistemological position does an individual rationality stand such that it can with certainty endorse the enactment of a judgement which denies and deforms this process? Such a claim, which belongs to the mindset of a permanent revolution, requires an admittance that the general tendency of man in his natural state is one of all-around decline: decline of the intellect, of memory, of action and of judgement; that man has no faculty of truth nor of memory nor of regret, that man has no participation in anything higher than matter. Supposing the nature of man to be so destitute, one wonders how the revolutionary, himself man, plans to mould such useless fodder into the form of his ideals?

With taxation briefly discussed, we move onto its counterpart - spending. In spending, the state employs monetary purchasing power granted to it through some coercive means, be these direct taxation or indirect fraud. Since purchasing power refers to the ability to obtain a certain fraction of society's resources, it is clear that this relative enlargement acts to decrease the purchasing power of all other agents, as total resources are not increased by this increase in state power. This reduction of purchasing power negatively affects non-state entities in proportion to their value as allotted to them by the processes of freedom. If the state exercises a hitherto unaccounted for ability to purchase ten percent of society's resources, the vast majority of these will be taken from the hands of the classes of highest wealth. As such, spending is destructive of the traditionalist principle of decision-making and of natural economic hierarchies.

In the place of traditionalist decision-making, state spending allocates society's economic resources according to methods unbacked by the economic regression, the consequences of this being that, since these decisions contain no internal feedback mechanisms, and are instead the spawn of desires unrestrained by the constraints of the totality of historical values, all spending rooted in coercion is necessarily and permanently revolutionary. Secondly, it breaks with a fundamental principle of economic activity and the inherent purposes of currency and of purchasing power. In a state of freedom, or adherence to the totality of prior and just allocations of property, one obtains future expendable economic decision-making power in proportion to the work which one does within the economy. The reason why this purchasing power is accepted as such, that is, has any *power* at all, is because it is backed by this added value. In obtaining purchasing power without having been judged as a value-adding entity in some due proportion thereto, state spending debases economic decision-making as such. It is, in essence, fiat power. Fiat power bears an exact relation with fiat currency, this latter being a category of the former. This is best demonstrated through an examination of fiat currency.

Insofar as currency is of fraudulent origin, it will, in the natural state of things, lose its universal acceptance and become functionless. Only when imposed upon a people by force will a highly fraudulent currency remain in use. A one-hundred percent fraudulent currency ceases to be a currency and is as such a contradiction in terms. For in a wholly fraudulent currency system, all actors can produce currency without incurring any cost. When the currency gains any value, fraudulent actors will compete to claim the value latent in the currency with an immediate expansion of the currency supply, until the value of the currency falls once more to nil.

An economy governed wholly by fiat decision-making, then, ceases to be an economy. In such a system all purchasing power allocated by the traditionalist and voluntary regression would become instantly debased upon being acquired. In fact, it would be impossible to acquire any power through these means whatsoever. As such, acting in society's economic interest would be an endeavour of zero material reward. The system would become absolutely worthless for all within, first for those who generate wealth, who would consequently cease to produce, and then for those who plunder, who would have nothing left to steal. In such a catastrophic scenario, the only beneficial choice is an attempt to re-establish a consciousness of some theory of property justice whereby an immutable thread of decision-making can once again be spun. Such a rebuilding is bound to be arduous, for the knowledge contained within the previous economy's decision-making regression will have become irreversibly lost. Investments are no longer to be made by proven investors, capital will not be owned and known by those who can best make work of it, and labour has been expunged from channels of proven use, instead adapting itself to uselessness. All within this economy lacks historical precedent and is as such undeveloped.

In brief, then, the immediate reallocations engendered by taxation as such flow from the taxed to the untaxed. Those resources thereby flowing into different uses do so according to the judgements of the untaxed in proportion to the historical sanction. Yet, with respect to taxation, the vast majority of the immediate benefit of the action accrues not to that individual conducting the taxation, but rather to all of those who have not been taxed. While this indeed causes a degeneration of society, not least in the form of those behaviours which society adopts in order to avoid taxation, the effect is, *ceteris paribus*, less than that of a coercive spending of an equivalent amount. For, in the case of spending, the immediate benefit of the deviation accrues entirely to the wrong-doer, and as such the effects of the unjust action undergo absolutely no redirection according to the proportions of historically sanctioned hierarchies. When compared to spending, the taxation acts on a hierarchy like light through a prism, such that some element of the original nature of the structure remains manifest in the action's effects. Legitimisation of the spending function opens up a

permanently parasitical class above society, which, according to foregoing analysis, will fester until it engulfs all that society still has to offer.

Our justification for this severing of taxation and spending is not
solely for the purpose of analytical clarity, but also to better understand the consequence of state action which leads to either a predominance of taxation or a predominance of spending, budget surpluses
and budget deficits.

In times more dated, such splitting of the redistributive state action may well have had limited use. Deficits rarely created a fraudulent
purchasing power unlinked to any particular tax, and surpluses did
not result in a destruction of currency. This was due to the relative fixity of money and a degree of separation between state and mint. A surplus was reflected by a physical increase in the treasury's coffers, and a
deficit with a decrease in these coffers or an increase in the state's outstanding debts. These debts themselves were bound to the projected
deficits and surpluses of the state's wallets. It was still somewhat possible for the state to become insolvent, and so the state could not rely
on the guarantee of an endless stream of debt. Insofar as this form of
fiscal management is active within a state, the act of taxation becomes
rather inseparable from that of spending. A surplus now leads to the
ability of the state to fund a deficit in the future, excess taxation leads
to an excess of spending, and vice versa. The relative inseparability of
the phenomena does not mean that the preceding analysis loses its applicability; both effects are rather set into motion within the initial
action of the confiscation for private money, or the promises of future
confiscation by which state debt is backed.

In our more modern state of affairs, the situation is rather different. Having entirely engulfed the mint, the coercive class has alloyed
the fiscal foundations of its treasury with the function of the monetary. There are no longer any coffers to be spoken of, as such a contrap-

tion lost its function with the rise of the central bank as a lender of last resort, and increasingly of first resort, which may provide the treasury with a seemingly never-ending stock of emergency capital funds.

At first glance, the mechanism of the central bank may not appear to change the fundamental natures of state finance laid out above. Yet, given the necessary ties between the state and an entity granted by its laws an advantageous monopoly mandate, the central bank and the treasury are linked by inseparable mutual interest so as to act, in essence, as a legally bound unit. This relationship maintains the appearance of one of relative independence through a mutual understanding of the tact required in avoiding suspicions of explicit corruption.[10] Make no mistake - the central banking interest of a powerful nation will not permit the bankruptcy of the source and mandate of its existence. This is obvious, and the market understands this. This is why private interests no longer pay any attention to the tremendous levels of debt maintained by the modern nation-state. For this is not true debt. All inabilities to meet obligations will be compensated for at the printing press. This is why, in essence, the modern state partakes in an almost pure form of spending. The sums of debt, of historical deficits, will never be recuperated by future tax-funded surpluses.

As a consequence of this, both public and academic opinion regarding the state budget deficit has undergone a shift. Previously, both camps understood that, due to the implausibility of continuous deficit spending, any deficit spending should be taken cautiously and only when merited by genuinely pressing and extraordinary current events. Spending no longer bound to taxation, both parties seem unphased at the prospect of a debt which only grows. Both prior and now, men have held to the notion that spending is the fruit of the toil of taxation. This being so, a leniency towards the modern deficit is only natural. From this claim also stems the understanding that spending financed through a state bond provides to the economy a 'stimulus' that will, unfortunately, need to be paid back. These critics say that If we as a nation were to declare our bankruptcy on a national level, we would lose out only by our inability to attract cheap credit in the future. This difficulty in attracting future creditors aside, the whole act of incurring state debt, enacting a 'stimulus injection' and then enacting a default would be beneficial to the economy.

From our analysis of spending as such it should be quite clear that these so-called positives, the initial effects of the bond sale and of the unconditional granting of 'credit' by the central bank, act merely to swell the proportion of resources in the economy allocated by revolutionary forces, with no historical precedent, destroying immediately part of the fabric which allows for the proper functioning of a society in which one man's labours produce fruits not just for himself, but for society at large. These actions contain a necessary attack upon the natural aristocracy, be it manifest or otherwise[II], establishing in its place a fiat aristocracy, a hegemony of pirates distinguished and possessed by the general bureaucratic traits we have already examined.

The so-called positives of these debasements of the natural order are nothing less than the remnants of a deformed retribution. In a voluntary economy, a debt obligation is a call from society: justify yourself! If one borrows two hundred ounces of gold and must the year thereafter fulfil one's obligation to return two hundred and ten, society is requiring justification for its temporary abdication of its own purchasing power. The debtor received the funds as he was freely deemed most capable of nurturing society's capital stock into a multiplication. If he fails to do so, judgement will punish him. As such, to view the spending sprees of false credit as a good, and the subsequent repayments of credit as a bad, is simply to view the world through the archetypal sinner - the immediate pleasures accruing to myself are the Good, and the inevitable retribution of moral law is the Evil. In his ludicrous position, however, the proponent of state spending does not even reap the pleasures of the sin which he stands to defend. He reserves this primarily for the new castes of career criminals and parasites born through his wishes yet offers up his own neck to the blade of judgement, so as to take the blow for any of these castes' ill deeds!

One further note must be made regarding the effects of spending insofar as it is funded by genuine credit, one day to be repaid with interest. In our times, the repayment of debt has begun to form a not insignificant part of the state's yearly expenses. The existence of these to-be-redeemed obligations must raise alarms to anyone with pretensions towards traditionalism and against an ever-encroaching monetization of intimate society. Insofar as these obligations exist, future man is bound towards activity within the monetary sphere above and beyond the voluntary and natural inclinations of that society to participate in monetary interactions. A debt-heavy state thus leads towards a society which is incapable of reverting to a state of affairs desired by the person of traditional leanings - unless, of course, there occurs the miracle, to this day never once witnessed, of a properly traditionalist revolution.

Despite the aversion of certain conservative strains to ever-expanding state spending, these points regarding the particularly noxious effects of modern means of state resource allocation remain nonetheless relevant in our critique of state conservative means due to the natural harmony existing between the explicitly fascist or totalitarian aspects of conservative thought and the system of economic beliefs which we may summarise as being Keynesian. Prior to the Second World War, this conceptual harmony was mirrored by a very real ideological oneness within the academic field. For quite some time, both the existence of a national central bank and some form of grand state industrial planning were simply the economic manifestations of that strain of thought which, culturally speaking, raised its banner in favour of coercive eugenics and of fascism in general. These ideas rest upon an identical epistemological position and arose as a result of the infusion of the revolutionary temperaments of the socialists into the dogmas of a less overtly political, 19th-century conservative-liberalism.

Regardless, the more totalitarian strains of thought are consistent in wishing for the state to control the means by which current national governments define themselves fiscally, the central bank. Additionally, as follows from our preceding chapters on the workings of the state apparatus, we can expect these means to naturally come into the possession of the government of a society which permits coercive rule and denies the sanctity of property rights and of the allocations passed down to the present through the economic regression, for this power tends towards a permanent expansion.

The positions of power opened up by this modern form of financing are so dire for society not merely because they, in part, condemn man to an intractable servitude reaching indefinitely into the future, but also because this entity partakes relatively little in the properties of bureaucracies which lead to internal inefficiency. Owing to the wholly destructive nature of the fraudulent central bank, any such tendency towards inefficiency would be for us a welcome gift. The entity for the creation of money and finance has no particular product by which its 'produce' can even begin to be evaluated, however. As a consequence, it is rather minute with respect to the scope of its bureaucratic verticality and staffs few people in relation to its ultimate power. Further, it is self-funding, self-renewing and knows absolutely no competitor. For these reasons, in addition to all of those already addressed, a position of absolute monetary domination must never be allowed even the slightest possibility of entrance into the good society. If man cannot be trusted to accrue to himself a just benefit when selling his wares in daylight, how much less are we to trust him to benefit society when he can enrich himself through an invisible plunder?

It remains to ascend to the highest universal of state action and to discuss the consequences of force as such. Before beginning, it must be remembered that, as a species of force, economic taxation and spending must be seen to possess the inevitable consequences below in addition to those already allotted to them above.

To begin with, we must do away with the notion that force, being the severing of the chain of teleological power allocations, is in any way hierarchical in the traditionalist or natural sense of the word. Naturally, force, as a category of action, presupposes an immediate hierarchy, an actor and an acted upon. Nevertheless, such a hierarchy, taken in isolation, bears no essential resemblance to the ultimate hierarchy of morality in any normative sense, whereby good and bad, superior and inferior, are sorted into degrees of being and not-being, of above and below, of power and powerlessness. If coercion were truly conducive to the creation of hierarchy in such a sense, it would, having run its course of natural effect, tend to organize society such that the bad sinks and that the good rises. Contrary tendencies to this, whereby the good ceases to rise and the bad ceases to fall, may properly be called either forces of absolute egalitarianism or forces of degeneration. Let it here be noted that a society based upon these latter tendencies could only come into being given that there exists in no action therein any reference to the goodness or badness of any previous action.

One such anti-hierarchical effect of force is the societal levelling inherent in any universal application of a negative principle, a thou-shalt-not. This application need not be universal in the formal, legal sense of the word. Rather, we refer to the universal principles from which some coercive action is spawned, or, what is the same, the set of imaginable circumstances under which the action of coercion will occur. As such we may properly speak of the negative principles behind the actions of both the highwayman and the manufacturer of state legislation, regardless of the generally more moral intentions of one than the other, a contingency perhaps open to some doubt. This universal may be quite limited, as in the case of the former, who, due to his lack of power, may employ force against those travelling a certain road on weekday evenings, and only against those who look particularly weak and vulnerable. The universal may also be quite large, as in the case of the manufacturer of legislation, who may restrict all men, everywhere, from the consumption of any liquid with an alcoholic content. What binds all such universals is that they act to halt a certain category of behaviour without any reference to the natures of its particular manifestations. Further, such universals can only be based upon objective phenomena, as opposed to the individuating, subjective qualities pertaining to those on the receiving end of the force. No object is inherently good or bad, since all permit an indefinite number of functions, and since morality refers to the functional.

Each rule of coercion is defined in objective terms independent of actual functional use of the prohibited objects. Thus, the rule is independent of the quality of the prohibited action as such. Therefore, the application of any such rule forbids both good and bad actions and applies to them equal punishment or restriction.[12] This, naturally, applies to both the rule of the highwayman and of the legislative branch to some varying degree.

It is true that the above applies equally to non-coercive rule, through those conditions which one must satisfy in order to use another's property, as well as of coercive rule, through those conditions under which one is forbidden to employ one's property in a manner not conducive to the coercion of another.

The universal principle of coercion is physical intervention which prohibits an action through which another wishes to employ his property. In more detail, the coercive action is one which denies what man has been permitted to do by historical allocations of societal decision-making power. It is useful to bring into view an inverse of coercion, the sum total of all permitted actions, as this concept allows us to see more easily what it is that must be denied by coercion.

Any act of coercion leads to a reduction in the benefit accrued in following those voluntary paths of action which lead to free power. This occurs for two reasons. Firstly, the voluntary actions themselves lose use for the actor as their fruits are reallocated into the hands of the coercive. Secondly, there opens up a new path in society, a competitor to the power of the free action: coercive power. If the doors to this path do not slam shut behind its latest entrant, as they seldom do, it is sure to attract more followers. There follows from this a sort of coercive 'tipping-point', analogous to the bank runs inspired by fraudulent money multiplication in a half-fiat monetary system. At this tipping point, the general benefit of voluntary action falls below that of the coercive act. Should this occur, a society becomes irreversibly one of universal and tyrannical coercive domination and ceases to be, properly speaking, a civilisation. The best that can be said of such societies is that the plunderers and their assistants inevitably run out of genuine productivity which may be stolen, and starve along with their victims. Such magnificent displays of the human spirit have indeed been made manifest multiple times throughout the revolutionary century, within the totalitarian regimes wherein coercion became so omnipresent that it appeared prudent to common man to feed his family to the dogs, irrespective of the truth of his indictments, in order to avoid his own immediate destruction; and wherein genuine accrual of free societal power led to assured extermination. Any who could flee, did flee, while the rest were barred from any such freedom by new rules prohibiting emigration and personal movement. Such collapses of societal fabric demonstrate again the parallels linking voluntary society and coercion to sound money and fiat currency. Every unpunished act of coercion leads us one step closer to our very own societal bank run; as the analogy suggests, however, the date of this event is not predictable in advance.

Additionally, force, insofar as it is expected, leads to attempts to avoid the losses thereby incurred. Man will employ means of preventing force until the point where the cost of these means outweighs the impact of the force's might. It follows from this that force, independent of its own ultimate goals or effects, casts a shadow of itself upon society which is nought but an absolute waste of resources, vis-a-vis the non-coercive society. The entire sector of security is but a fragment of this shadow.

Now, the authoritarian opponents of modern decadence are naturally averse to a system of unrestrained coercion open to all. In fact, they often claim that their proposals would act to avoid the state of unrestrained violence and coercion towards which they believe, without much injustice, modern society is directed. They instead advocate for the force of a sovereign few or one. For the sake of the following analysis of sovereign force, we will take the sovereign to be a single entity, independent of how many individuals it may be made up of, or whether or not its advocates desire their statehead to be made up of one, few, or many men. It will exhibit a trait about which all defenders of the state agree: that it is an entity which established enforced norms universally applicable to all those within its active jurisdiction, the borders of the sovereign agent. Any deviation from this principle would ultimately separate the unity of the sovereign. Additionally, the sovereign force, in making universal rules, may amend its laws with any number of clauses and caveats. No matter how many of these caveats it creates, its law will nonetheless be fixedly universal, since none but the sovereign force may make any form of incremental amendment to these laws without the sovereign thereby ceasing to be sovereign.

As demonstrated towards the beginning of this work, we must expect the rules of the sovereign to be far broader than the incremental norms which we encounter in our daily interactions with the voluntary segment of society. The main reasons for this, not yet explored with any real proximity to force as a category, is the fact that rules applied coercively must be applied to what is not under one's full possession, and, therefore, there must exist a chasm between the results of the behaviour as accruing to the owner of the property to which the rule is applied, and the effect of these results upon the rule setter himself. If the full benefit, to all involved, could accrue to the enforcer, then he would benefit from his action enough to be able to conduct the whole operation on a wholly voluntary basis - provided that his action was genuinely good

The above being so, we can see great incentive towards exploitative, or ultimately negative law forming when laws may be forged with exact preciseness, such as in accordance with geographical location, personal status, and so on. The more specific the laws of the state become, the more potential there exists for the drafting of wholly reformatory laws and judgements according to some immediate and transient whim or personal distaste, laws which have little effect upon the lawmaker himself. The fact that these gulfs exist between consequence for society and consequence for lawmaker when law-making becomes particularised means that, in any remotely healthy society, the levers of law creation lie as far as possible from the whims of taste. Its laws will be as highly categorical as possible, with respect to both the prohibited and to its resulting punishment. The laws of legislature will resemble the laws of physics in their necessity and impersonality. This distance being established and alloyed by a system of laws-for-lawmakers, be these formed by precedent or constitution, one may hope to uphold a legislative body freer from manipulation towards the end of individual gain. Such barricades, however, may only ever provide limited and temporary respite against the tyranny of unbridled coercion - for in order to rule, the sovereign must be able to decide; in order to decide, it must be able to, whensoever it wishes, occasion some effect and restrain another. The branch of legislation ultimately rests under the sovereign's primary command, else it ceases to be sovereign. Thus, any such barricades or king-binding customs must themselves rely on the continuously dutiful behaviour of the sovereign forces. Man refuses to learn that the de jure is not almighty. Whatever their respective merits, both the constitution of the Americans and the common law of the British are powerless to govern a settlement of apes.

For the time being, then, we will examine the effects of those coercive measures which are most often suggested by the state conservative as a remedy for decadence: universal behavioural norms from on-high.

The emergence of the national, sovereign form of legislative norm creation announces with it the onset of two trends relevant to this chapter. The first of these is the weakening of sub-sovereign decision-making units. These may be of concentrated regional power, such as Lords, Mayors or city councils, or be they more diluted and widespread constituents of societal fabric, such as the command a remote religious authority, or of an ideology, or simply the various everyday processes of decision-making, including those norms of the family or of the local community. The second notable consequence of higher-level sovereignty is its tendency to equalise the populace independent of their merits, by applying one universal judgement to an extraordinarily wide set of actions.

We begin with an elaboration of the former consequence, the disintegration of the sub-sovereign. To a degree, the effects which follow from such an event are quite obvious. Yet, for whatever reason, the necessary effect of the sovereign state on these lesser powers seems to pass most by fairly unnoticed. In our interventionist and statist age, there is much clamour about the apparently universal necessity of some intricate 'balance of powers' within the state system, which any society must possess lest it fall into immediate tyranny. Any such popular discussion rests upon a fraudulent supposition, or, at best, a mere glimpse at the true matter of the question at hand. The modern discussion boils down to this: it must not be so that the central state can change its mode of governance at will without the tacit assent of, or correct disposition towards, its own constituent parts. As such a notion of balance has come into being, the line dividing man from state has grown ever starker. Indeed, as this line grew, so did the distance dividing those state departments whose powers it is apparently our task to 'balance'. Missing in the modern discussion is the balance of utmost importance: that between the sovereign power and its subjects! This state of opinion has occasioned, and been occasioned by, a decline of all of those powers bridging the lowest and the highest, the absolute federalisation - the absolute nationalisation - of modern authority and sovereignty.

These intermediate authorities, separating individual from the absolute whims of the so-called 'balanced powers', have served two grand purposes for man. These institutions, from all of which only some silhouette of the family really remains, provided both a positive function and a negative function. The former refers to a set of norms tailored to the self, and a self-tailored to these norms. The latter function refers to the role that these institutions play in shielding the individual from the club of the state, which has, since the disappearance of these defences, spared him no trauma. As with much else of importance in society, the function of this shielding fabric is no consequence of grand intentional design, but rather more like the shelter of a great and rounded cave - each rock suspended above man, refusing to impact into his skull not from some benevolence of stone, but because of the particular dimensions and forces of each other bit of the cave's walls. Dislodge a segment to mould the cave into some more perfect shape, and another, now free of its restraints, will feel few regrets in ending the thoughts of even its inspired architect and inhabitant. This natural state constitutes the true balance of power, one in which every individual plays a part, and upon which every action has an effect.

Now, any of these decentralised forces and institutions, along with their ability to influence societal behaviour, will become diminished in strength should any other issuer of norms come to possess a larger influence within the former's realm. The raising of any institution to absolute sovereign, then, immediately destroys a large portion of the remaining forces, who may no longer affirm where sovereign now denies. Additionally, any commandment of the sovereign encroaches further upon all of these lesser areas, independent of their particular contents and spheres, inspiring doubt in their authority and inspiring certainty with respect to the might of the central state. From this, we see the beginnings of the joint traditionalist-libertarian case against the central absolute sovereign as such.

Let us suppose that a youth understands that all of the rules which he follows, both casual and legal, are ultimately issued by the highest and most abstracted national body. What authority remains for him in the edicts of his family or of his community if he sees no explicit state sanction behind them? Once more, we need only to cast a glance back towards our own revolutionary upheavals of natural balances in order to have this question answered. He begins to sell his family for credit with the party.

Tangential to this we arrive at a brief analysis of the nationalist claim. It must come to be understood that the nationalist argument, which justly asserts that national norms are inseparably bound to those peoples around which they have taken form, must in fact prove its own undoing. This argument, if true of nations, is equally true of the regions from which these nations are built, whatever size they may be, and to whatever extent they may overlap. In fact, the true spirit of this nationalist argument, expressed in slightly modified form earlier in this work the current work in an analysis of the effects of the democratic spirit, applies more to the subdivisions of a nation than to the nation itself. For the unnatural and absolute divisions presented by the national border are in fact far closer in spirit and in content to the fretted borderless world of the 'globalist' position than the so-called borderless world of the traditionalist libertarian. Unable to think beyond the categories of the modernist politic, degenerate in essence, the nationalist is merely the runt of his kind, who, affirming all of those notions which make the one-world state a beneficial inevitability, refuses to take the final step only due to his reactionary dullness. That type of world which springs from liberty, 'borderless' though the nationalist may call it, contains within it the only borders which genuinely merit the name, unless we wish to strip the term of any of its natural and meritorious qualities. The borders of the modern nation-state are simply weak and failing images of this higher type. True borders are not those which sew an absolute divide between the lands of Germany and France while categorically unifying Kaliningrad and Kamchatka. True borders are encountered in every one of our interactions, the combined incremental might of the sum total of all human norms, insofar as these norms are a product of freedom.

Naturally, the sovereign centres and borders of the supra-national 'customs unions' are closer in spirit to the global state than are those national states, but are so not in contradistinction to the principle of the nation-state, but rather through an extrapolation of this principle. Authentic and incremental borders, destroyed by the processes of the nationalisation of sovereignty, have provided general man with his highest and most precious senses of belonging and unification of being. In irony, it is the self-proclaimed nationalist who seems more than most others to feel the pain occasioned by this stripping bare of the social nexus. He seeks to restore it by further and forever concentrating power at the disposal of the artificial central state amalgamation. In doing so, he is truly lost. It is not the state which differentiates one people from another, and it is not the state which defends one nation from its absorption by a super-nation. Rather, it is those borders which arise from a decentralised liberty which defend the nation from the super-nation, by providing a true and natural distinction between land and land. In this sense, it is the nationalist idea itself, which champions the liquidation of natural borders into a 'national unity', which has allowed its lands to be so easily entranced by the call of the nation-state's natural heir, the world state.

So much for the deracinating effects of federalisation; we move on towards the effects of the sort of law which the sovereign decision-maker is bound to introduce - the absolutely impersonal law which respects no borders but the national. It was briefly mentioned that these national norms serve, in a horizontally minded manner, to direct the ruled region away from genuine hierarchy and towards the degeneration of its people. These consequences arise from two unavoidable features of sovereign rule - especially the form of rule suggested by the state conservative - its objectivity and its grandness of scope. By the former is meant that such laws condemn object rather than action, for example through the prohibition of certain drugs, of certain symbols or of words, or of weaponry. Ultimately, however, this mode of condemnation is at variance with the actual merit of the object in question, for such merit is determined not by the object's apparent physical properties, but rather by the purpose for which the object is to be employed, or its functionality. Since any object can be employed towards an undefined number of functions or ends, it follows that the objective mode of condemnation runs the very real risk of prohibiting genuinely advantageous behaviours.

Naturally, when critiquing the limits of the objective condemnation, we do not mean to purport such condemnation to be entirely useless or to have no place within society. The mode of judgement is itself a tool to be praised or condemned according to the contexts of its employment - as already mentioned, 'personal' and highly contextual judgements flowing from the level of a national sovereign would, due to the lack of any sort of functional feedback mechanism for the quality of such judgements, and the immense hoards of knowledge required in the execution of a judgement so broad and so deep, guarantee a swift descent into both tyranny and error. What is rather said here is that the forced concentration of decision-making power into a sovereign will serve to make a society increasingly bind to moral context in its judgements, and therefore ensures that the society's governing structures, coercive or otherwise, will punish a greater number of positive behaviours as a necessary by-product of its chosen means to the prevention of negative behaviours. By doing so, the society ensures that those individuals of a higher quality, capable of using commonly dangerous objects to positive effect, are refused their natural ascent in the societal hierarchy, thus making the future social fabric increasingly egalitarian.

This being admitted, however, it does not immediately follow that such sovereign and objective rules are *essentially* egalitarian. Of course, the rules serve also to punish incorrect behaviours, presumably at a rate far greater than that at which they punish correct behaviours. Does this punishment, lowering the status of the bad, not serve to more than offset the above-mentioned flaws?

The answer is certainly 'yes'; but only partially. To fully judge this mode of judgement, we must first compare it to its alternatives. Compared to an alternative of absolute lack of judgement, we would indeed hope that such sovereign rules, in the short run at least, come to our aid. Let this be admitted. This is the point of comparison most often drawn by advocates of the norms manufactured sovereignly, and it rests on the implicit position that without centralised state order, there can be no order at all. For now, we will make our position to the contrary quite clear, and leave a full defence of our position for a later chapter: the voluntary society makes up for in localized, non-monopolised, incremental normative structures that which it cannot reach in terms of sovereign universality. Such norms are moulded to the intricacies of the regions in which they come to form, or the part of the soul which they have come to govern. Indeed, before any such calls for the rule of the sovereign were thinkable, since man had not yet unlearned what it meant to behave, the primary enforcers of correct behaviour were those very institutions destroyed through the process of forced centralisation which is now offered to us as a solution.

It needn't be said that the current form of the state, even when not centralising itself (which it does so unceasingly due to its monopoly of coercion) acts as a continuous prohibition against the formation of any form of serious sub-sovereign authority. Additionally, even if the modern state were an instrument comparable in quality to the tailored natural authority which it works to undermine, it would nonetheless be of an inferior quality with respect to its ability to enforce norms in a manner which does not impede virtue and genius, for norms formed regionally adhere to a more contextual, function-oriented methodology of judgement.

Our final point on sovereign centralism is one more long-sighted in approach and has more to do with the principle of enforced paternity and its particular ideals. As in preceding discussions on the centralisation of norms, we again take as our subject something not exclusive to force, but rather a societal element exaggerated through its employment. In particular, the following regards a certain intent behind the employment of force, an intent which lies at the heart of the state conservative doctrine and most often distinguishes this type of ideology from the ideologies of other advocates of state coercion.

In brief, the political aims of force can be categorised as redistributive ~ correction towards a perceived state of natural justice ~ or preventative. The former type, independent of its particular conceptions of justice and precepts of choice, be these the reimbursement of stolen property or the institution or a state of equality, is distinguished in that its aim, as such, is rather to correct an unjust action rather than to prevent an immoral action. These wishes are often entangled: the desire to enact justice upon an unjustly enriched soul is often coupled with the aim of the elimination of the creation of the unjust state, but, as evidenced by egalitarian redistributionism, the ultimate goal is the correction of a particular unjust allocation. The egalitarian is not particularly outraged that an 'unjust' inequality of wealth has been generated, *provided* that there exists a mechanism in society which redistributes some sum of this wealth to society's poorer peoples. If given the option to avoid use of such a redistributive mechanism and to simply ensure that the rich man did not act to generate wealth in the first place, the egalitarian would react indifferently at best, provided that the ad hoc mechanism itself required no resources. Similarly, the defender of natural rights would prefer twenty acts of theft to occur and be subsequently rectified in full, than for the objects of one plunder to go eternally unrestored ~ again ignoring the direct costs of the redistributive acts themselves.

It is otherwise with the preventative use of force. The aim of this strain is not necessarily the punishment of unlawful deeds already enacted. Again, the two desires often appear to coincide in practice: the paternal lawmaker prefers rule breakers to be punished, but the ultimate motive for such punishment is the prevention of future ill deeds, not the correction of an until-then unrectified societal injustice. This latter type of force is often marked by a sentiment on behalf of the rule-maker that he would prefer not to have to resort to a display of his power, but must do so in order to prevent his authority from falling into disrepute. No such sentiment is present in the redistributive will as such.

It is the sovereign enlargement of the preventative branch of force, proposed by the state conservative as a means to ensuring proper behaviour and hierarchy, at which we now take aim. In particular, we wish to look at the goal of such legislation, independent of whether or not this goal can be reasonably achieved with minimal cost over an extended period of time. Practically, any attempt to enforce such laws will be subject to all of the hitherto discussed degenerative tendencies particular to bureaucratic and coercive measures resulting in a paternalistic power both incompetent and misguided. It is worth mentioning that any failures and inefficiencies of authoritarian means do not necessarily result in a better state of affairs for the libertarian traditionalist vis-a-vis a hypothetical success, even when we consider the active principle of state action to be wholly negative. The failures of the state may make the consequences of its ill-conceived goals even more disastrous for the fine society; the laxity of authority, occasioned by the empty threats to which the state police inevitably degenerate in matters actually conducive to the public good, serves only to invoke in the public spirit a general disregard for authority as such. Additionally, the tendency towards ill-judged or positively malicious legislation, a breakdown of the state's manufactory of norms, can only further dislodge the natural direction of society away from the principles of a sound morality.

To begin with, we must have a coherent idea of the aims of conservative paternalism. The following summary should suffice: left to his own voluntary whims, the standards to which man is held are too weak to deter him sufficiently from vice and to direct him instead towards virtue. As such, all men under the ultimate sovereign ought to be subject to coercive measures which, through sufficient threat of punishment, cause man to follow an alternative path of action. Under such rule, man will go through life having made decisions to his ultimate wellbeing rather than having behaved according to his immediate pleasures and long-term detriment.

It should be noted that this summary intentionally excludes those behaviours which, while uncoercive, negatively affect the lives of those other than the actor himself.Strictly speaking, the prevention of such behaviours, of excessive public loudness or drug usage, for example, is not a consequence of the paternalistic and preventative will here critiqued, but is rather reimbursive or redistributive in nature, resting on the notion that one person has unjustly wronged another. This exclusion serves not to avoid the discussion of such important matters; they will be written of at length in this work's final segment. Rather, they are here severed and excluded so that the paternalistic state will as such can be discussed and disposed without the need to address innumerable caveats and tangents. We address here exclusively the coercion of man for his own long-term betterment.

The sound moral prescription must secure not the immediate wellbeing of one man, but rather have as its aim the ultimate well-being of all men, irrespective of time. Modern times are marked by a diseased morality, or absolute lack thereof, which sacrifices the latter for the former. This state of affairs is the object of highest odium to those of a genuinely conservative sentiment. By virtue of being the sole popular voice against many of the prominent causes and symptoms of decadence, the conservative movement seldom has its arguments examined on an instrumental level, for their ability to ultimately secure their desired ends. Being scrutinised entirely from without, any declamation against the proposed conservative remedy has attacked it on the grounds of its incongruity with progressive egalitarianism. Should debate penetrate beyond the useless level of discourse which results from such conflicts, it arrives only at the auxiliary and logistical features of the matter at hand: whether or not outlawing certain behaviours is detrimental to the treasury's budget; whether or not this particular activity is, in fact, on average, when appropriately regulated, minorly beneficial or slightly detrimental to some section of society; or perhaps, breaking through to some shaky ethical foundation, whether or not there exists some unconditional right to behave in this or that particular behaviour. As interesting as these matters may be, and however much their discussion adds to our lives instead of merely serving to further the intellectual's own sense of moral and speculative superiority, they are entirely subservient to and derivative from the question never posited: whether or not a hierarchical society can be crafted, or ultimately strengthened, through the implementation of universal sovereign rules categorically dominant over private rules wherever the two conflict.

This work began with a proposed equivalence between the function of entities within the monetary nexus and of the social workings external thereto. This notion may be further elaborated upon in answering the above-posited question.

Universal rules of conduct, generated by the state, must weaken society in precisely the same way that such prescriptions for the fiscal activities of business would damage the formal economy. The kernel of the economic critique of state guidance of business is as follows: the epistemological position of the state ruler is inferior to that of the business owner with respect to the regulated activities; such proposals restrict innovation; such proposals inhibit the process whereby bad decision makers lose power; the creator of such rules is not proportionally affected in accordance with their successes and their failures. All of these points stand equally strong against cultural paternalism as they do against economic paternalism. One may not support one and ignore the other. Despite the simplicity of this, an exposition of a number of these points will here be necessary in order to numb any reaction occasioned by the unfamiliarity or outlandishness of the claim in question, and to answer a number of likely misconceptions. Having already discussed at length the first point, which tackles the relative knowledge contained within the state, we will below give space enough to fully address the latter three.

Any law, however framed, universally prohibits certain objective interactions. As such, it attempts to bestow universal matter-of-fact value on an object independent of its function. Since, however, the ultimate utility or usefulness of an object is dependent solely on its particular function, it follows that all such laws must eliminate potential positive usage of the outlawed object. This much is widely understood. The necessary consequence of this is that paternal laws must tend to benefit those incapable of properly interacting with the world, and be detrimental to those who in that same respect are most adept. Let us take the substance of alcohol as an example: for the best of men, its intoxication effects, like the effects of any part of reality, may be turned into a productive tool, allowing them to temporarily navigate the world in a way beneficial to themselves which may have otherwise been outside of their capabilities. There are also those who use alcohol to their absolute detriment, as a means to temporarily ignore life at a high physical, moral and fiscal cost.

Left to their natural courses, the consequences of these facts of life are the elevation of the virtuous man, who is capable of using the world as a tool against itself, and the decline of the vicious man, who uses the world as a weapon against himself. Over time, the course of nature will be to proliferate the former type of man and to diminish the frequency of the latter. To ban the substance inhibits this selective process. Regardless of whether or not the above 'Darwinism' is 'inhumane', it is the case that without this very process, man would never have become anything remotely resembling the sort of higher being that he has now become. This very argument, and any objection thereto, could never have come into being without the proportional decline of the failure and the proportional reward of the competent. These processes cannot be begotten without a certain measure of suffering being experienced by the former *individuals*. As a counterweight, this course of events ensures that groups doomed to cause such sufferings diminish relative to those groups fated to cause great joys. Who now laments the pains of the failures of distant pasts?

The faculty of reason itself is, and even more so used to be, detrimental to many of those upon whom it has been bestowed. Many would have had longer and more pleasant lives if they had merely followed the habits of their forebearers. The overwhelming majority of beliefs are erroneous, whereas successful tradition, if imperfect, has at least shown itself undeadly. Ought we, then, consider banning reason?

The elevation of the weak serves to make the future one of enhanced pain and failure. Prevented from one fall, mankind will have additional capacity to fail in his future endeavours, and fewer means with which he may succeed. The degree to which the paternalistic force bans a man from failing is the precise degree to which the man of the future is bound to be the behavioural descendant of the less advanced man. The proposer of paternalistic law must answer this: if one is willing to inhibit proportionate inequality and the self-selection occurring through man's interactions with nature in the present day, why should one refrain from wishing that the same had been done with respect to man's more ancient exploits - in his first ventures away from the lands of his evolutionary origin, for example, given that such journeys into the unknown would have ended the lives of so many men?

In addition, and perhaps more importantly, the matter of innovation must be addressed, defined as the discovery in some object of some previously unknown usage. In banning an object for perceived negative function, man not only loses his ability to adapt to become this particular function's master, but also loses any potential to form the item to himself through the creation of a new functionality. It is impossible to confirm that the array of functionality for any object has been exhausted, and, thus, impossible to confirm that any object does not have hidden within it a novel functionality which fully justifies its utilisation.

Every function of every object was at one point unknown to man, both as an individual and as a species. They were therefore unthinkable to him. As such, all known functionality in the world has come as a consequence of the permissibility of interaction with objects independent of their currently known functions. Much, if not all, of those objects which are of utmost importance are functional also to our detriment if interacted with improperly. This is true of all from art to iron. It so happens that creative interaction with a potentially important means may initially unearth a highly detrimental function far in advance of the discovery of eventual beneficial use. To eliminate interaction with the substance would eternally forfeit the uncovering of the positive function. Being consistent in the application of his principle, then, the paternalist would have to find it preferable to forbid all interaction with all objects for which a negative function was early discovered, being deterred in the scope of his legislation only by the hypothetical logistical costs of their enforcement. Since all that is at odds with a peoples' present way of being must be considered dangerous by those inculcated within that culture, and since essentially every aspect of our current culture (and of any idealised culture of the past) was at some point at odds with the ways of our human ancestors, the paternalist must consistently support a hypothetical, perennial outlawing of those cultural traits which he most cherishes, crushing their energies before they could intrude and inflict pain upon a more ancient culture to which they were originally antithetical.

The paternalist must also take into consideration the transparency of ruling powers and the effect of this transparency on his groove-lodged peoples. The presumption of the paternalism in question is that without the presence of the state's guiding hand, man would often encounter his own disadvantage. So be it. Yet, as we have seen, such prescriptions create a tendency towards the *ceteris paribus* elevation of the weak relative to the strong. A consequence of this is that an ever-growing caste of men will come into being which owes its existence to the explicit and continued legislative dictates of the state. The state becomes a sort of moral dam. No longer weeded out through internal considerations and the ever-active sieve of nature, the behavioural traits barricaded by the state do not simply die away. They instead become latent. The general ability of man to naturally behave will begin to fade, since authentically successful behaviour becomes less necessary in the procurement of worldly success. Consequently, the state must erect further dams and barricades, or else the weakened society will be once more faced with the effects of its growing failures.

For as long as the state remains fully competent at deterring the banned behaviours and erecting new dams, the core problem at hand remains unmanifest. Yet the state's dams must one day give way. This event may be caused by any one of the factors already addressed in this work, the inability of increasingly degenerated populace to understand and to therefore to properly support the function of a growing list of sovereign laws[13], or, instead, simply through some one of the chance events of time. Regardless, the fall will occur. Unlike cultures, which fade slowly and often perceptibly, rigid state structures resemble landslides in their collapses. At this point, the degeneration of the people will be all at once laid bare. All positive modes of interaction with the previously outlawed parts of reality will now be unknown and will be impracticable. Those traits will have wholly disappeared which made possible any successful neutering of the danger posited by those outlawed objects. Face to face with nature's equilibrium once again, man will be woefully unprepared. Those fatty castes spared by the benevolence of paternalism will have swollen in number. Upon this collapse, each of their members will face a backlash more swift and more cruel than that from which the statist wished to hide them. As a consequence of past short-sightedness, some part of the population which would have otherwise been competent enough to safely traverse this landscape will have been replaced by members of the doomed castes, born only to experience failure. The voluntary society, on the other hand, will face no such trauma.

Turning away from matters of the soul, we address now the matter of responsibility and feedback in proportion to the merits of one's decisions. As previously addressed, the hierarchical society, and the ideal society, must yield reward to some member in proportion to that individual's total contributions. The ideal system of rule creation, then, would cause the effectiveness of any given rule to have a direct relation to the prosperity of the rule marker. Yet within the paternalist structure, this is demonstrably not the case.

On the contrary, the paternalist rule-maker is wholly detached from the ultimate effect of his rules. Whether he creates a universal norm which immediately assists man, or instead one which acts to man's immediate and absolute detriment, is irrelevant to his position. This is a problem of grand import to the actual practicality of any suggestion for paternalistic lawgiving, for it removes any tendency towards the gradual refinement of this time of statesman. Further to this, we have previously addressed in our chapters a significant number of tendencies to the contrary, tendencies towards vice and corruption. All of those points are also valid here, proving the notion of a benevolent, paternalistic behaviour-tinker to be a mere fantasy, an intellectual crutch for those idealisers of the past who, despite their well-disposed wishes, make use only of the opposition's instruments when constructing some proposed pathways to a better world.

In light of the above, it would be more fitting to characterise the enforced paternalistic will as a manifestation of egalitarianism than as one of hierarchy. Fundamentally, the egalitarian drive wishes to destroy the inequality engendered by the variability of man's character, ultimately by equalising man himself. The hierarchical will wishes to perfectly reflect this inherent variability in due accord with the virtues or vices of each man. Further, the egalitarian wishes the existence of a society as a means for the development of the individual. The hierarchical will asks of man his duty to the whole. How else, then, are we to characterise the will which works exclusively towards halting the segregation of virtuous choice from vicious choice, for the sake of the immediate well-being of the vicious individual, paying no heed to the strength of the people ten generations hence?

It is the lack of serious ideological alternative to the assorted proponents of modern progress - the individualist rationalists, the liberal economists, the thorough egalitarians and the neutered Trotskyites of modern party politics - which has led to a state of powerlessness and intellectual fragility within the traditionalist-leaning camps of today. This lack of thoroughgoing ideology is, it must be admitted, a partial spawn of the very anti-rationalist essence of traditionalism. This super-rationalism, however, applies only to the static part of the traditionalist idea, the part which affirms that the value of a received norm is not to be judged according to the continual rationalisations of the present-day individual. The dynamic segment, whereby a traditionalist society rejuvenates itself in accordance with the movements of man and nature, concedes itself to rational critique. It is this dynamic traditionalism which must be brought under unity if the discontent of the anti-moderns is ever to put its whole force behind one single thrust. Despite any of their claims to the contrary, all of the above modern sects are united by a oneness of foundational structure. Their doctrines are all founded upon, and thus cannot critique, egalitarianism, materialism, and rationalism. This unification has allowed these sects to continue unhalting in their permanent march, despite any disagreements on matters of means. When such small ruptures occur, they are often swiftly resolved through resort to the analytical toolkit which they share in common. The continued lack of such an equivalent factor of unification underpinning their detractors may soon prove fatal. Having now completed the disassembly of the patchwork solutions of state conservatism, which, if truly instated, must only act to hasten a departure from all things resembling natural hierarchy and tradition, we now move on to the construction of a positive alternative - the society of natural voluntarism, the free teleonomy.

# Part Three: Teleonomy

# 10

# A UNIFICATION OF ECONOMY AND CULTURE

The inconsistencies of contemporary economics stem from an attempt to divide reality into a sum of economic and non-economic objects, which hold their essential characteristics within themselves and independent of man. This practice of the economist is much further away from the truth of the matter than would be suggested by the formal definition of economics under which he claims to operate. Most such definitions differ little from "the science of the allocation of scarce resources with alternative uses". While imperfect, this definition offers no reason to suggest that reality may be, though this science's pursual, strictly divided into the economic object and the non-economic object.

The cause of this division is partially historical and partially ontological in basis. The science was first furnished with the aim of procuring practical, material benefit. It attempted to discover any potential laws which may be residing within the activities of commerce and business. Being a practical science, far detached from any purely philosophical heights, its theorists felt little need to examine the limits of the science itself under the philosophic lens. As such, the enduring restriction of economics-in-practice to the science of the commercial is partially a matter of habit and inertia. This conception of economics has been rather solidified by the academic prevalence of the belief in the notion that the subdivisions of phenomenological reality occur as such along definitive, objective lines, observable reality ultimately consisting of objects-in-themselves, with properties independent of time and of man. This understanding persists despite the supposed attempts of twentieth-century economists to integrate the subjectivist buds of Menger into their frameworks. Economists may have taken enjoyment in some proofs and conclusions of these works of Menger and of others, but habitual and continuous application of subjectivist foundational presuppositions remains entirely scant.

With the objective classification of reality, selected phenomena may be deemed similar according to the lack of distance between themselves and some apparently common factors. Under such suppositions, a cat is objectively similar to a dog because both are animals. A Labrador is more similar to a Pitbull than is a cat, as while all three are animals, the former two are grouped by being dogs, a particular species of animal.

Given this framework, it is difficult to find any universal grounds for the economic science. Are we to treat the family as much as we treat the commodity? Surely a distant star is no object of economics. Understanding the categorisation of things to be ultimately objective, and already possessing, from its historical roots and practical applications, a seemingly comprehensive common factor of economic goods in the form of money, the science has remained running along its own grooves. This restriction of subject matter, and the happenstance of the intrinsically quantitative nature of money, resulted in an academic science which, if enshrined and made a tool of statecraft, could seriously threaten a permanent eclipse of the 'non-economic' functions of life. Such an enshrinement has indeed occurred, and, as shown in this work's first part, dire consequences must follow from this.

A satisfactory basis to the economic science must eliminate the field's conceptual inconsistencies, as well as ensuring that the conclusions of the science are of inherent rather than contingent usefulness.

The field's conceptual inconsistencies are as follows. Primarily, it attempts to classify in objective terms that which is ultimately subjective and functional. Secondarily, it has attempted to universalise around money, hereby running into a number of problems: first, if economic refers to things of monetary commerce, then a barter economy is a manifest contradiction in terms. The field has hitherto leaped over this point by simply transplanting onto a barter economy the array of commodity goods currently accountable into the dollar. It then seems satisfied in its claim that trading a one's bucket of milk for a neighbour's pound of flour is economic, whereas the division of labour between man and woman within the household is somehow categorically uneconomic. The second problem of its monetary fixation is the child of the science's first two overarching methodological flaws: its attempts to understand money as an object rather than as a function. The prime manifestation of this is its belief that, when excluding the miscalculations of man which may result from this, it is possible to expand the 'amount of money' in an economy. It treats an increase in total dollars from fifty million to one hundred million as a doubling of money as such. Defined functionally, however, it is nonsense to speak of an increase in money in any sense similar to how one may speak of experiencing an increase in pliers should a pair of pliers fabricate it-self up from the soil.

Yet money is ultimately a functional category, and any similarity between moneys must be drawn on functional grounds. Should money lose its functionality, it follows that the economy, defined as the nexus of things which may be traded for money, may entirely evaporate sim-ply because of a change in man's subjective disposition, simply because money has fallen out of favour with man - that is, the objective (so de-fined) may change itself without changing, and some object be simul-taneously economic and non-economic. Naturally, this objectification of economic phenomena is strictly nonsense.

The third problem of economics is its lack of universal grounds upon which to rest its claim to usefulness for the human race. Con-straining itself to an analysis of one subset of that with which man comes to interact, it may only attain for itself undoubted utility if it proves either that its schemas for the maximisation of economic can-not cause a reduction in the production of the non-economic, or that the non-economic is of no value. While these notions have some num-ber of adherents, both implicit axioms are increasingly subject to a just scrutiny. Should either of these claims become wholly accepted, consequences for human society will be immeasurably dire.

If, then, an economic science is to exist which may never have its utility doubted, and which may be certain of its own foundations, it must be wholly functional in its ontological classification of reality, and, under this banner of functionalism, utilise an apparatus which treats, as such, that which man values, such that any remote moral claim may be analysed underneath its scope. Its purpose, then, will be to draft the rules of the maximisation of the moral in society, the moral as made manifest through human action.

# I I

# VALUE AND TIME

In attempting to cover the essential properties of the whole of man's valued world, it would first be highly prudent to briefly address certain characteristics of value as such. Foremost: what does it mean for something to be valued?[14]

For something to be valued, it must be deemed by a subject to be a proper instrument to the attainment of a goal or an end. This definition appears to run circular to itself in presupposing the existence of ends. This problem may be solved by understanding any phenomenological end to itself e a mere means of closer apparent causal connection to the absolute imperative of action: to achieve the perfect state of being. If man acts, he does so with a purpose - he aims to improve his position in his own terms. It necessarily follows that all action aims at perfection. Value is man's understood causal nexus of perfection. Action presupposes interaction with a valuable reality.

There exists an empiricist and nihilistic perspective which claims that value is without foundation as, if one follows one's value hierarchy towards its apex, one must find that there is ultimately nothing there. Therefore, life is without absolute meaning. This approach is another attempt of man to locate the thing-in-itself within phenomenological reality. Man has previously used the same approach to prove the absurdity of the concepts of space, of time, and of causation. If there is time, it must be limited or infinite. If it is limited, by what is it preceded. How could it have begun if not from a different state? If it is infinite, then an infinity of time has passed up to the present, which means that infinity, which permits no limitation, is limited by the present. Additionally, if time exists independent of man, as a thing-in-itself, it must be possible, or at least cannot be rendered strictly impossible, for man to come into contact with something outside of time. Yet this is clearly a manifest absurdity.

The solution to the problems of space, time, causation, and value, considered as things-in-themselves, is for all four categories the same. They are not things to be sought and verified within phenomena, but rather are preconditions of phenomenological reality. As with time, value is a precondition of experience as such. To argue the contrary point would require interaction with reality, which requires an aim and some instrumentally valued means. To look for a valueless object is, itself, a contradiction in terms, for the chosen 'valueless' object was selected for its function of purported 'valuelessness'. Further, the shape of man's individual reality, that realm with which he interacts, is 'matter' moulded to his own array of functional forms, an array which makes up the essence of his being. To look at a chair (that is, to recognise an object) is to affirm the value of its functional form of chairness. And indeed, it is absurd to suggest that the 'valueless' object exists 'underneath' the valued functional reality. To give any example of such an existence is impossible - more clearly so under the empiricist epistemology which affirms the world's ultimate meaninglessness in the first place. It is impossible because this isolation of an object from the observer must, to be consistent with its own suppositions, also abstract from its object participation in space and time. As such, the nihilist's claim is this: an inconceivable non-entity may be value-less. Perhaps! But the inconceivable may not be expressed, while all that may be expressed, and all that with which one may interact, and all that may be conceived - these things all hold value. To arrive at the heart of the matter, one cannot look at the particulars of experience, or even towards their limits; but must instead examine their presup-positions, the fabric upon which experience must rest.

One further consideration on the fundamentals of value: the per-fection at which man must aim, as demanded by phenomenological reality, cannot become manifest therein. Perfection and valuelessness share that they are entirely incompatible with the existence of phe-nomena. Herein lies the asymptotic equivalence between the aims of the 'life-denying' philosophies and their 'life-affirming' equivalents. If man could cease to desire, or could instantaneously achieve all that he desired, he would cease to participate within anything resembling our reality of space, time, causation, and value. To avoid digressing too much from our subject matter, this area cannot be much more discussed. In short: these notions of perfection must be considered to represent more the walls or boundaries of that in which we act, rather than things which may be taken in and fully understood from within reality. That something by which all particular values are up-held, which when subject to a scrutinous eye appears to become noth-ing, is simply a limit. It is not established by asking 'why?'

From all this, it must be understood that the nihilist asserts noth-ing. Life goes on within and without him; he continues to act accord-ing to the imperative towards perfection. Using his beliefs - which he denies by existing - as a non-existent wall in order to hide from the true demands of Being, he comes to be one of the archetypal fools.

Having drafted a general understanding of value, such that all with which man may ever interact may be said to have value, it follows that any categories or principles of action as such are universally applicable, in some way or another, to each part of the reality inhabited by man. Therefore, should there exist any principles which further elucidate upon any aspect of the imperative of action as such, these principles must be considered absolutely valuable insofar as they provide the impetus for any given action, or insofar as one's being is aligned therewith. Conversely, any deviation from such principles would of necessity become absolutely incorrect actions. That being so, it is imperative that we examine the possibility of the existence of universal laws of functional reality.

The best starting point for this endeavour is that which has already been proven: man is; he acts; he interacts; he interacts with valued means; he interacts with valued means with an established conception of their functional causality, and in doing so has a predefined notion of success.

Man does not perfectly know the future, as there are no a priori grounds upon which the positive content of the future may be deduced from the past. Further, to come to full knowledge about some future event would necessitate knowing how one reacts to the knowledge gained through this learning. Knowing the contents of this response, however, supposes that one already knows what it is that one is responding to. With every newly gained piece of knowledge, a hitherto unthinkable possibility becomes ponderable. Thus, to arrive at perfect knowledge from a state of ignorance is an impossibility. Perfect understanding necessitates perfect action, yet our reality as such is inhabited exclusively by beings of imperfect knowledge. As such, the future develops itself such that each of man's actions proves itself to have been a success or a failure. The eventual distance of a man's action from absolute success, or the perfect act, is synonymous with the degree to which man incorrectly valued reality at the point of his action.

This introduces our first absolute ought: that man ought to act such that his actions never stem from an incorrect valuation of reality, that is, from a misunderstanding of the causal nexus of reality.

Having arrived at these basic principles, we now understand enough about the framework of reality so as to posit universally meaningful concepts of that which lies within reality. Mimicking the groundwork of the science of economics, we will attempt to justify our claim of rectifying the science by transfiguring the constituent categories of 'economic produce' into the reality of functional causality.

In accepted usage, the products of economic activity are created by combinations of land, labour, and capital. Land is understood to mean that value which exists independent of man's intervention; labour being that value generated from the efforts of man; capital being the merging of the two. These conceptions are more-or-less correct. Where the economist goes wrong is in his presupposition that land and labour exist within reality and that pure examples thereof can be given. As such, the beauty of a mountain is to him land value, while the talents of the opera singer or the dancer are pure labour.

The error of this conception that it fails to operate on the basis that all phenomenological reality exists as a relation between oneself and the other. As such, all value is caused jointly by man and by nature. For each supposed 'pure land value', something added by man may be taken away to render the 'thing' less valuable or wholly without value. We may demonstrate this with the beauty of a mountain, the most plausible example of pure land value. What value exists in this domain once all assistance of man's faculties is excluded? The value of the mountain's beauty requires the mountain as much as it does the eye through which the mountain is brought to man. Further, it requires a particularly crafted set of values within man capable of appreciating the mountain's form.

The fundamental origination of labour, on the other hand, is the part the subject plays in the generation of value. All of his actions require something other than himself, something acted upon or something which acts upon him. In considering labour to be the causal relation of the subject to the object, it becomes obvious that the recognition of some value as being derived from labour requires that one consider this source to be an ethical unit like oneself, that is, to be subject and to have will.

One may not ever be witness to land or to labour. All valued objects are capital. We may talk of land or labour only because the existence of phenomena, or of capital, supposes some relation of land (object) and labour (subject).

Since man may only come into conscious contact with capital (embodied value), a greater understanding of the nature of capital will necessarily give us an insight into the nature of man's reality.

We have said that the value of that with which man interacts, of capital, is determined by the degree to which man understands the object to be capable of bettering his position, bringing him closer to perfection. One concept included in action, then, is the notion of a future self, of one's continued existence. Since causation takes place within time, it is impossible for man to act without the notion of his own continuation through time. What also is contained within an action is the belief that the valued things which one seeks to bring about through interaction with some chosen means will themselves come to occur within time.

Man cannot fathom the infinitely distant, so he cannot act for the purpose of an infinitely distant benefit. On the contrary, for any given benefit, man, existing at a certain point, must wish for any benefit to occur at this certain point, ceteris paribus. If this were not the case, it would be possible for imperfect man to act in contrary manners under the exact same circumstances: suppose man postpones the consumption of some benefit for the sole sake of postponement, with no change occurring in himself or the desired object in the duration between postponement and eventual consumption. In this case, he must be absolutely indifferent to consumption at any given point in time, and, the confrontation being unchanged, he would postpone benefit in any hypothetically equivalent confrontation. This means that he does not wish for the benefit to occur at any point in time - which is absurd, since he would be valuing nothingness. The logic of action therefore contains a universal element of preference for the immanent, preference for some equivalent thing to occur at this point rather than at any other.

While all sensation supposes duration, it does not follow that all sensation is of an equal duration. Similarly, while a preference for the immanent is a factor in all action, it does not follow that this preference exhibits an equal weight in all action. As with magnitudes of time, there exist also varying intensities of preference for the immediate expressed in every action.

Conventionally, this trait of action is known as time preference. The Austrian School of Economics has done its science a great service in elucidating matters in this area, paving the methodological path for the unearthing of such categories, and providing much of the intellectual vigour required to bring the notion to a satisfactory state. Despite this, the notion of time preference employed by the theorists of this school is in a number of ways lacking and has to this day failed to properly universalise itself. This is of no small importance, for the proper universalisation of this fundamental aspect of action serves towards the integration of a proper interpersonal ethical imperative into the axiom of action itself. The interpersonal nature which may be uncovered through an analysis of this aspect of action has been made entirely inaccessible by the fixation of the Austrian theorists on the dimension of time alone. To properly demonstrate this, a number of the failings of the theory of pure time preference must be addressed.

Suppose a man chooses to consume some appetising dressed poison but is terrified of death. After a short while, he comes to recognise his action has his most fatal mistake. This seems to be an exhibition of an extremely high time preference, a preference for the immediate pleasure of consuming the appetising object that is so large that it outweighs the prospect of certain death at some point in the near future. Yet, through an understanding of the values displayed through this action, what exactly may we attribute to time preference alone? An absolutely unknowable amount, and thus no determinate, positive effect can be attributed to time preference in any action. The poison-consuming individual may have been demonstrating an extraordinary level of time independence in his action, his action demonstrating only his lack of understanding of the qualities of the object.

This being so, what possibilities exist for the usage of the underlying categories of time preference in any positive or quantitative sense, such that some particular action may be identified as being occasioned by an abnormal desire for immediate gratification.

To be able to identify a particular act as being influenced to any understandable degree by time preference, we must identify a factor in action both necessary to all actions and variable in its magnitude. If time preference is both necessary in content and variable in magnitude, then, in order to avoid contradiction, some part of the impetus for some subjective action must be ascribable to time preference alone. The actor must be able to consider an isolation of time preference in his hypothetical structure of values - that is, he must be able to isolate time preference as existing *within* his understanding of the functional causal nexus. The contradiction which arises should this isolation prove impossible is that an equal understanding of the functional causal nexus, one's understanding of the ability of reality to generate the perfect state, an understanding which is the sufficient and complete cause of action, may inspire a multiplicity of actions due to a difference in time preference. Thus, identical causes would result in non-identical outcomes, which is absurd. As such, what is commonly called time preference must lie in, and be some part of, the actor's understanding of the functional nature of reality, which is his understanding of the consequences of his actions. The form of this understanding is this: the degree of being which the actor recognises the states influenced by his action to possess.

Time preference is a consequence of the fact that man may only act to the benefit of a state insofar as he understands it to be an ethical reality.

Man's conception of ethical reality must be the degree of its equivalence to the present, the present being the point of subjective Being. Man must recognise himself as an immanent ethical reality. If he did not do so, he could have no values and would cease to be. This recognition is a requisite for, or component part of, the framework of reality. Further, there must exist in acting man the conception of other ethical realities than the present. This is necessitated in that he acts *for* something, and that the consequences of his action must take place in time. The strength of this conception of the other ethical reality, however, is entirely variable in nature, just as how the spatiality of experience, while categorically necessary, is entirely variable in scope in any given object. Man acts with reference to 'another time' insofar as he considers there to exist an ethical reality ultimately equal to that of the present: the present, prerequisite of action, is the yardstick by which all other ethical realities are to be understood. The concept of other ethical reality, without which man could not place value on any action or object, must be derived from our particular moment of Being - now. A number of conclusions from this: it is impossible for man to act for something which he understands to contain no ethical reality. I cannot act for the sake of the benefit of a stone tomorrow unless I consider it to ultimately partake in ethical reality so as to experience the effects of my action. In the exact same way, I cannot act for my future self if I consider myself to be at that point dead, to not exist, to never experience the effects of my action.

A second consequence of this is that 'time preference', taken as a universal trait of action, is a misnomer. There is no inherent preference in terms of minutes of calendar months, nor any notion of time that can be meted out by any phenomenological categorisation. Rather, there is simply a necessity that the value man ascribes to an object in action is derived from his understanding that it causes an effect on something with ethical weight. The existence of "time preference" as such has a minor a priori justification and a major empirical component. The present is universally preferred to the future, while future time periods of closer proximity to the present are generally recognised as having greater degrees of ethical reality due to our subjective understanding of the continuance of our being and the increased intensity with which we may relate to a version of ourselves which has been subject to little change, that is, is closer to the present.

An error of the *a priori* doctrine of time preference is its inability to explain interpersonal ethical behaviour in a way that would not equally eliminate the necessity of time preference. In examining an action motivated by a reward to be reaped years from now, this doctrine claims that man, *ceteris paribus*, would prefer to take less of the item but receive his reward tomorrow, given that the understanding of the good remains unchanged. Let it be so. Yet in theorising the factors at play in valuing benefit accruing to another person in ten years, this theory posits the essence of the action to be entirely independent of the 'distance' of the affected subject from oneself. Should one appear indifferent between benefiting some unknown, never-to-be-met man now, or instead some other man one hundred years hence, this theory can only explain such an action by claiming that the whole value of the action lay entirely rooted in immediate, present effect, which exists through both actions; namely, the moral pleasure gained by doing what one believes is good. Ultimately, then, the driving-force of the action is the moral pleasure, rather than the effects themselves, since it is the effect of the driving-force of any action which is supposedly discounted by time preference.

This denies the possibility of action with essential reference to another being or individuality, which raises the question: why admit the possibility of action with essential reference to another time? Could the essential spur of such an action not equally be 'because of the pleasure which one feels when doing something which one thinks will be to one's ultimate benefit", and does this line of reasoning not deprive us of any function of time preference in practice?

A second error: the notion of time preference supposes that an equal subject must value an equal object less of its effect occurs more distantly. Yet if no change occurs to the subject's understanding of the object's effects, how can different actions result? So the change in time, contrary to the definition of time preference, requires a change in the perception of the effect, such that the 'good' affected by a change in time preference is no longer homogenous with the 'good' valued according to the initial rate of time preference. Thus the "object modified by time preference" is no longer equal to itself, and the conditions for the existence of time preference cannot be met.

As such, the only way to rectify the doctrine, incidentally expanding its explanatory power and the scope of its potential usage, is by replacing the linear conception of an intrinsic preference. This conception is to be replaced with a notion of effect, in the understanding of the actor, which consists of an understanding of not only the object acted with, but also the subjects thereby influenced, for only in relations between the two may reality be conceptualised. From this it follows that man acts according to his understanding of the effects of his actions on the whole teleonomy - on the totality of experience.

A fundamental factor of other intrinsic aspects of experience, action and Being is that they are comprehensible as wholly indefinite concepts which partake in neither zero nor infinity. This applies, as we have mentioned, to time and to space. Both must be present for experience to occur, but neither can be conceptualised as being infinite without contradiction. The same is also true of the will to improve one's condition, or of value. One may not be wholly without will and yet still participate in phenomenological reality, in time and in space. Equally true, one here may not be perfect. What, then, of the understanding of ethical reality, our ability to properly perceive the teleonomy as a whole? It is presupposed in action, and it, too, may not be infinite. For then the totality of experience would be conceptualized as being equal to, or contained within, the present, and the present, no longer participant in time, would cease to be 'the present'. Under these conditions, action, and thus any conceptualizable reality, would be impossible. Any being which could contain within itself the totality of ethical reality would become the One or the absolute.

It must be of interest to us, then, in what exactly a recognition of a subject may consist. What are its limits, what defines it, and how may this recognition vary in intensity? Finally, we must address an all-important point: how can we know that something is, in fact, an ethical reality?

The recognition of external reality derives from the belief that there exists outside of the immanent reality of the present something which shares the latter's essence - its being, at some point, immanent. To act with relation to an understanding of such an entity - to demonstrate a belief therein - requires an understanding that one may, through the causal nexus of which one's action is a part, have an effect on that other reality. As we have said, action as such presupposes a belief in this other ethical reality. Despite this, no specific further content is given to this affected other through this presupposition.

Therefore, the other reality need not be understood to be a future 'I', a continuation of the existence of the immediate personality. Nonetheless, it is clear that this conception of the future self is the one most often arrived at, most often acted for, and most wholly understood, of all possible other realities or objects of action.

The primary source of this understanding lies in the memory. The habit of directing one's present behaviour to consider its effect on a future reality identified with oneself is one bolstered by a recognition of memories as being reflections of the causal antecedents of the present. Such an interpretation of memories is not logically necessary. Despite this, man is not capable of an absolute rejection of this interpretation, the limit of this rejection being set by the fact that any attempted rejection of this interpretation utilises means of action understood to be effective due to a particular understanding of causal history. When subject to his memories, he rejects their utility because past memories have taught him that memories are useful - by learning this lesson, he affirms the contrary. This much aside, a complete rejection of memories seems like an ill-advised approach, for should memories be useless for guiding action, then all responses to them are equally valid. Should they be useful, then an ignorance of them leads to error and decline.

When memories are understood as being reflections of one's own past, involving one's own behaviours, one begins to understand the consequences of past decisions and their effects on the present self. From this comes the idea that, should one face a similar state of affairs in the present, one might be able to enact some change upon one's future, as one had done in the past. This needn't ever be concluded. It is a matter of faith, and always remains so. Once this path has been chosen, however, it naturally tends towards a solidification and reinforcement, for those who succeed through time will be those capable of learning from memories as if they were indeed reflections of a very real past. Further, the initiation of such learned behaviour will inevitably result in its expansion over time, as its consistent applier must ever more come to believe in its utility as a technique of action.

Insofar as one comes to understand this matter, that one's actions may be augmented by knowledge of one's past in order to benefit one's future, one becomes more habituated to acting for the benefit of other ethical realities, and one crafts a strong notion of one's persistence through time. Yet, for multiple reasons, this understanding of future ethical reality through personal identity remains generally more complete according to the temporal proximity of the imagined future state. Primarily, learning from the past is easier according to the lack of complexity involved in drawing a useful connection between that past and the present. "I just put my hand in fire, I am now in pain". This connection is easy to draw as there appears to be little difference between now and ten seconds prior other than one's hand entering the fire and the sudden feeling of pain. "I put my hand in fire twenty years ago - I am now in pain". Naturally, much happening in these twenty years other than putting one's hand in fire and feeling pain, this conclusion is much more difficult to draw. The former memory being more useful, it will more often become the material for the active striving for one's own future benefit. Since the lessons learned from such memories refer to shorter chains of causation, the individual will tend to have a higher degree of consciousness for those future states closer to the present. One will, through utilising a reflection on the past, be inspired less often towards those actions which take into consideration more distant ethical realities. It is this lesser learned certainty which allows us to deceive ourselves so easily to sacrifice the future for the present, or to forget the future altogether.

This, in rough, is how the notion of ethical reality can be transfigured from an immediate present into the conception of the future self. Through this transposition, one must believe that one will come to live that affected future - that is, that it will at some point be an immanent reality in the same way that the present now is. What remains to be asked is to what else, if anything, this status of true ethical reality may be applied.

Having generated a belief of the continuance of identical ethical reality through time, which allowed him to employ the concept of immanent reality to that which differs from the present, man must, should he expand such a concept any further, seek to apply it on the level of space - to apply the concept to that which differs from *here*. To do this, he must first have an understanding of a concept brought to his awareness by his notion of existence of the identical self persisting through time and through change.

If things change, yet the I remains, then there comes to man the notion of the not-I within space. The exact boundaries of I and not-I need not be absolutely understood for this division to take place. One may recognise a cup as being not-I without being able to define the exact limits of I. Indeed, the empirical grounds which cause one to recognise oneself within the world are far broader than the conceptual grounds contained within the idea of the time-independent individuality as such. Fundamentally, prior to his recognition of any other spatial thing as subject, man crafts his I from what may be generally called the intersection of the relatively permanent and the relatively willable. As such, man quickly recognises the faculty of sight, and its objective manifestation, the eye, to be part of himself. He has likely been with them through his whole life, and can easily distinguish his ability to will his sight towards his chosen ends: to turn or to close his eyes, or to look at something. In short, man tends towards an identification of himself with the permanent tool. This is primarily the biological body, but not exclusively so. Eventually, man comes to identify himself more with his tools for the communication of meaning, his words, and his thoughts.

Having learned to divide the world into I and other, through recognition of phenomena rather than through pure reason, man puts himself in a position to see himself in the other. That is, to see clusters of phenomena which remind him of his constructed idea of self, which, nonetheless, may not necessarily be him. The more another thing seems to him to possess the most fundamental parts of his identity, the more he will consider them similar to himself - to be as another individual. Naturally, the most core parts of man's identity of self are those permanent and most willable. These will tend to be the mental faculties which are presupposed in any entity capable of creating concepts, as well as any physical reactions thereto or displays thereof. Thus, it is clear that man comes to relate himself empirically to other realities, to phenomena, by varying degrees. The step from this position to one of recognition of the Other as an ethical entity is the same as that made when presuming or extending one's continuance in time - while empirical, it is also a matter of absolute faith. The attribution by man of this subject-substance to the other is a result of two underlying understandings: the degree of likeness between the other and the self, and the degree to which one understands the dynamics of the world to be governed by will rather than by matter, by the laws of freedom rather than the laws of nature.

As with a multitude of other concepts here explored, the form of this division of concepts is as follows: in order to exist as a subject, man must believe in both the law of freedom and the law of nature. He must believe in his own freedom and must interact with the world on the basis that it reacts to his force. He cannot believe in a reality of no freedom nor of no nature, but he may choose any point in between.

Whatever range man leaves for the explanations of change in terms of natural causality, the remainder must be attributed to direct acts of will. This must be so, as no other conceptions of causality can be arrived at given the ingredients of being. As such, in a world with little understanding of things as part of an interconnected casual-material nexus, we will see that the threshold point is remarkably low at which point man assigns to a thing a status of subject in accordance to its resemblance of himself. One may expect to find in history times of spirituality under which almost all change, especially novel and chaotic change, is understood as being imbued with spirit. Certain categories of empirical events will be designated their own principal spirit, God, or will-cause.

To avoid further detailing these current elaborations away from the central thesis of this chapter, and diverting instead into a matter more appropriate for the history of philosophy, it would suffice to posit that, given that this initial understanding of the causality of the world through various wills comes from a projection of one's empirically conditioned sense of self, rather than from a philosophical evaluation of the limits of freedom and of nature. Additionally, it must be understood that the patterns of the empirical may all be explained in terms of their natural antecedents, man may find himself subject to, or creator of, a wholly materialist of naturalist understanding of phenomena that entirely destroys the explanatory power of the world of the will within nature. Like a rising tide, this materialist metaphysic will slowly submerge all of the causative notions man has naively built upon his projection of his own understood freedom onto the world itself. The manifold gods, flag-bearers of will-in-the-world, will shrivel in importance under ever-growing knowledge of natural laws.

This transformation of the world from will to nature need not be negative for man, but despite its own conceptual innocence, we see that man has likely engineered his own existential undoing in the formative stages of the creation of his initial notions of self and ethical-other. For in drawing and developing an ethical equivalence between himself and human-as-phenomenon (his experiences of other human beings *within* phenomenological reality) he must, being consistent, attribute to himself all that he comes to learn about these other men as phenomena. From observation of nature, he comes to understand two grave things, and comes to increasingly take them for granted as the naturalist metaphysic takes stronger grip: the extinguishing of life at the expiration of the body, and the ability for all of his behaviour to be explained by antecedent natural causality, destroying the last flame of freedom in the self. Indeed, this misunderstanding may become such a conviction to man that he will attempt to force himself to believe that the whole of his being is an illusion "generated" by a natural material-ist causation of dead matter occurring temporally anterior to all that he perceives or is.

This is the unfortunate state into which advancing man is likely to fall. While a reconciliatory medicine has no place here, the example serves to demonstrate the flexibility of man's 'spiritualising' of the world - imbuing it with the status of ethical entity. What, then, be-comes clear from the above is the exact identity of the sources of the notions of future self (time-continuous self) and external other? This identity requires further examination before moving on, for its impor-tance to the framework of morality is of a magnitude not immediately obvious. As such, we will strip both aspects of being down to their conceptual minimums.

All things considered to be ethical subjects need share only one property - subjecthood itself. This notion, lying inherent in all notions of self which man can project forward in time or outwards in space, contains within it all those things which may be said to be valid of one's own existence as such. It is this quality, and none other, which causes man to adjust his actions such that they consider the fact that some given entities will thereby be influenced. For proof of this, we need only to analyse man's behaviour with respect to his future self.

As previously elaborated, man will tend to have a greater concep-tion of his least distant future states, primarily due to the fact that man's disposition towards the world is highly habitual, or, in other words, the result of training and learning. Further, man more often considers the near future in his actions due to the relative ease of such calculations vis-a-vis more distant ones, as well as the fact that, generally speaking, man is more able to adjust himself now to an immediate future than to one more distant. For example, it is generally more prudent to act now with respect to an event occurring in an hour and to act in three hours with respect to an event occurring in four hours than vice versa.

Now, despite the fact that man will tend towards a greater conception of the near self on these bases, these considerations make no claim towards determining the *limit* of man's ability to recognise other times of real experience or ethical realities. It is also the case that, when acting for the future, man places no *necessary* constraint on the conditioned similarity of future being with his own particular characteristics. There is no reason why man may not, in an action, come to understand that his actions will affect a 'him' one million years from the present, who shares absolutely none of those properties which constitute the particular personality of the present self, the totality of accidental properties of one's being-as-such. Included within this list of accidents is the fact of memory of self, recognition by the future being of the fact that he 'used to be' the actor in question. Yet, despite this absolute dissimilarity of personhood, the final cause of the action in question remains, as with actions directed towards oneself in the immediate future, the strength of the understanding itself of the existence of the other entity.

What, then, exists to separate action for a 'future self' and the action for 'another person'? To answer this, we must remind ourselves of the core concept which furnishes both of these ideas: it is the abstracted, identityless immanent Being at the core of our own existence. In essence, both the future self and the other are defined by their participation in this category. Yet we have seen that the sole cause of action for a future self is a present understanding of its ethical reality, that is, its participation in the very same thing which constitutes the other! As a consequence, we may no longer draw any qualitative distinction between the impetus of actions to the benefit of our future selves, and those which act with respect to others. The difference becomes simply one of degree, wholly quantitative in nature.

The obvious point of objection to this claim is the intuitive notion that there must be something essential which separates the conceptions of future self and other, and, therefore, acts for oneself and those for another. We must make an attempt to locate any such difference. Before examination, it seems natural that there exists a duality of concepts with respect to the existence of other ethical realities. One concept for oneself, continuous through time; one for the other, not part of our own ultimate field of experience. Any attempt to properly define the essence of this other under such a condition, however, must turn out quite nonsensical. For the fundamental concept of Being, which we must derive from ourselves, is merely that which is experienced. There is no concept herein of some phenomena being experienced *by* anything in particular. This *by* is something with which man never comes into contact, never experiences, and therefore can never derive from experience; he cannot conceptualise this concept. Furthermore, this unthinkable modification of Being attempts to distance itself so far from the only true source of the conception of Being such that it essentially denies that which set the ground for its own supposition - it attempts to modify the nature of a concept derived from immanent experience to create a particular experience real and yet incapable of being experienced (in terms of the concept of 'experienced' presupposed by this very conception).

Given this conclusion, the following must be admitted: *all that we understand to ever be experienced, will be experienced in precisely the same way, with precisely the same essence, as that experience of the immanent present.*

It follows from this that the only division that can be made between real individuals is the accidental property of individuality, rather than the essential property of subjecthood. This being so, the ceasing of the individuality, through death or otherwise, cannot be understood to occasion the ceasing of one's being. Essential Being ceases upon individual death exactly as much as it would cease should any individual come to live long enough that every single one of his accidental characteristics, from his memory to his body to his personality, would undergo complete change and revolution - that is, it does not cease at all.

With more exact relevance to our surveying of the imperatives of action, the upshot of the above is twofold: if we admit incorrectly judged actions with respect to ourselves to be error, then we may no longer talk of a morality distinguished from error. Secondly, man's knowledge of the practical consequences of his actions is pathetically limited. The first point should already be rather clear: if acting for "another" is the same as acting for oneself, then, as with the purely 'selfish' action, the incorrect action must arise from either a misunderstanding of the natural causation latent in the object acted upon, or from an incorrect estimation of the existences of the totality of ethical others. In the case of the 'selfish' act, this later is a misestimation of the totality of one's individuality. This misestimation is what causes time preference. The rational act, then, is the moral act, and the moral act is supremely rational.

The second point requires clarification. Under the orthodox conception of rational behaviour, man had merely to act with a full consideration of his own life span in order to be capable of directing the best possible action. According to the imperative of a fully integrated Being, man must, to avoid error, understand the totality of experience. If this were a learnable matter, the case for man would be dire but improvable. As we have seen, however, the existence of other ethical entities is a matter of complete faith. This is additionally true of those realities outside of our approximate individuality. Since there is no single dynamic of the phenomenological world which requires the concept of freedom, or from which freedom must follow, man may be a solipsist. Similarly, man may attribute to all phenomena the status of ethical Being, allowing all change within nature to become the consequence of the active will of a supra-sensible soul alike his own. This being said, that the current work is one particularly "political" presupposes certain conceptions of ethical reality or unreality. Namely, the general participation of the biological human being in the ethical sphere. Without this, the political effort could, even in the extraordinarily unlikely event that any such work has any lasting effect on human society, amount to nothing more than an intellectual pastime. It is doubtful that anyone with a serious interest in the general topic of this work denies the ethical reality of all other men, and so we will continue with the employment of this supposition whenever the matter is of any conceptual importance.

It is relevant to note that despite the faith-based nature of the matter at hand, we do not hereby lose all means to critique the actions of others (or ourselves) with respect to the other-orientedness of their actions. Under certain circumstances wherein the cognitive faculties are temporarily impeded, all men experience the temporary dissipation of their recognition of the true existence of the future. To act in such a manner cannot, as such, be condemned for its lack of foresight. What may be said, however, is that such an action may be rationally reprimanded in terms rational and provable to the actor himself insofar as this state of mind comes to fade and man's awareness of the ethical reasserts itself. From this new perspective, under the given beliefs of the actor, his previous actions caused his unfortunate current state. Essentially speaking one may critique a position on this matter insofar as it is internally inconsistent. Additionally and similarly, man must aim at all times to act such that his behaviour provides an honest reflection of his genuine ethical understandings, unimpeded by any momentary allure. Being destined to experience in due proportion the totality of the effects for each of his actions, it is of utmost importance for man to properly examine the contents of these eventualities when organising his own life.

# 12

# POWER AND PROFIT

Having analysed how man comes to act, with what and for what, it remains to be described how actions are to be qualitatively differentiated. At the beginning of this part was introduced the concept of success. Success, being a concept inherent in purposeful action, may be defined as the alignment of the consequences of the action with the action's purpose. Since all actions conform to a hierarchy of purposes, each subsidiary aim having value insofar as it secures the aim above it, and all aims having value insofar as they secure perfection, all actions each conform also to a hierarchy of successes. The highest success, in proportion to which all others may truly be called successful, in addition to the highest good, the alleviation of imperfection or limitation. As time passes, any given cause becomes instrumental in the creation of a larger number of effects. In fact, once enacted, no past event ever exhausts its importance within time, the specifics of each present moment being only possible through the continued development of prior chains of causation. As such, each action may be continually re-evaluated with respect to its ultimate success, its goodness, even if its immediate success has become a solidified matter of fact. The quality of the perfect action is that it demonstrates a perfect understanding of both the object acted upon and the ethical realities thereby affected. The sum of these real effects, that is, particular effects on particular ethical realities, may be called an action's teleonomic effect.

From this may be drawn a proper concept of profit. It is regrettable that the common and academic usages of this word have in modern times deviated further away from the sense which it had in older times conveyed. The earlier usage of the word, describing little more than that which was ultimately to man's general benefit, lay much closer to what we wish to convey than does the more contemporary usage, which has muddled the concept with money-grubbing, social decay and despicability of character. It is along the former line that we will seek to work.

Profit will here be used to mean any individual instance of gain accruing to a person at any given moment. To clarify this, an understanding must be formed of what it means for gain to accrue to something. And the ways through which this may occur. All aims of man fall under the supremacy of his will in the direction of ultimate perfection. As such, all gains accruing to man must participate in a furtherance of this goal and be highest according thereto. From this it follows that profit may be considered to be an increase in the value of man's means. We must here restate that since all which man does, or comes into contact with, derives its ultimate value from his understanding that it alleviates his imperfect state, we consider all imaginable, particular ends to be themselves means of varying degrees of proximity to man's ultimate, transcendent aim. There is therefore no contradiction in our definition to be found through the fact that man profits also from an increased joy arising from those things misleadingly called ends-in-themselves, such as a contemplation of the arts.

Before proceeding further, a more obvious objection to our conception of profit must be addressed. If profit is an increase in our means, then loss must represent a decrease of means. What, then, of those circumstances whereby man is brought into immediate discomfort about which he previously had no active conception? For example, in receiving a headache, how does man lose means? This objection rests on an error of thinking whereby the identity of means remains ultimately material rather than functional. A means is ultimately a condition whereby man partakes in a desired state of affairs. All other usages of the term refer to means only in a potential state - things which derive the label of "means" from the fact that one expects them to become means in action.

Now, a state of discomfort, such as a headache, must, definitionally, come into being if man lacks the means to prevent it. Therefore, for it to occur, man must lose the means to its prevention. We here unearth an additional error, that of considering means as being only valid when employed with a particular sensation of struggle. Would we say that man lacks the means not to fall to his death merely because the floor underneath him is 'passive' in his actions? Certainly not, for then he would be falling.

From the above elaboration, it may be sensed that means as such are in fact identical to power. Like 'profit', power is a term subject to much modern malign. This malign, however, must be seen as being entirely unjust. As with profit, we will attempt to cleanse power through a proper, universal conception. In fact, a cleansing of the former needs must purify the latter, following from the fact that any conception of power in human action as such must be seen as an increase of means, that is, an increase of power.

The function of power within the modern ideology is primarily to be a general cause of a society's injustices. One person having power over another is understood to be at the very least distasteful, and, when talking with relation to the general mechanisms of a given society, the notion of a 'power structure' serves only to be a synonym of a "system of oppression", A proper account of the spiritual grounds of the development of this approach towards power would merit its own distinct work. On the other hand, a clarification of the concept itself may be completed quite succinctly.

The modern conception of power may be defined as 'the ability to exert force upon something' - societal power, 'the ability to exert force upon people'. In contrast, aided by the discussion of means, we define power as 'the ability of man to procure the ends of his will#. The key distinction between this conception, purposefully materialist in implication, and the alternative for which we argue, is the former's lack of after-the-fact re-evaluation of the supposed power-display. In short, the former is static, matter of fact; the alternative is dynamic, matter of value. For, as we have seen, all given means or values of man derive their value from man's understanding of the road to the highest good.

Therefore, should his understanding be incorrect, his values must also have been incorrect on their own terms. Properly speaking, means cease to be means when they are shown incapable of procuring their originally intended ends. Take a berry that is understood to be, at the point of its utilisation in action, a means of procuring its end - in this case, the satiation of hunger. Should it be revealed to us afterwards that these berries cause only nausea and vomiting, we must understand that they cease to be means at all in the strict sense of the word - for the item was only a means insofar as it was capable of satiating the man.

In not having the causal relation first esteemed of them, an item or an action may be re-evaluated as worthless, or worse than worthless, insofar as they are incapable of producing satiation (and insofar as that chain of values, connecting satiation to the perfect state or highest good, itself remained unchanged between the period of action and the moment of revaluation). Now, given that all means point ultimately to the same end, it follows that historically considered means cease to have been means as such insofar as they in actual truth procure perfection less than was originally supposed. We have identified means and power to be one and the same concept, so we must see power only as that which genuinely brings man towards perfection. It is ludicrous to posit that a man has demonstrated power whose actions have been diverted from their ultimate ends by something external to his will-as-such.

Power having intrinsic reference to virtue, the moral inculpability of power can be demonstrated through an understanding of that which constitutes perfection, or a movement in its direction, for any given being. It has been proven that man must act in accordance with his understanding of the totality of the ethical effects of his actions. If he has a greater conception of the future of another than of the future of his own individuality, he must value more the effects of his actions upon the former than upon the latter. We may frame this subjective imperative of action against the absolutely best action - the one for which the totality of beneficial teleonomic effect is highest. This perfect action must be embarked upon given a perfect harmony of subjective understanding with truth. It here becomes clear that the difference between the actions of man in actuality differ only from what they ought to be insofar as man's understanding is in error. As such, power at no point becomes introduced into the concept of immorality. Moreover, power becomes entirely antithetical to immorality. Since both the will and power, as such, are incapable of being the cause of any deviation from the Good, it follows that the concept of 'intentional evil' disappears as an absurdity. Any reference to a chasm between the moral action and the rationally selfish action is ultimately misguided. The only claim which may be made to the irrationality of moral action is this: that the inherent epistemological position of man is such that all belief in any ethical reality other than the immanent is ultimately a matter of faith - neither observable empirically nor inferable through the employment of any of those categories which necessarily underlie being. Since belief in a non-immanent reality is a prerequisite of action, it follows that all action is possibly only through faith - or, in other terms, is incapable of sufficient rationalisation. This faith or irrationality is one in which all men, as immanent ethical subjects, must partake, for the intellectual conception of any Being, the understanding that one *is* an immanent reality, is only possible through the framework of action - namely, that to even bother contemplating one's own existence entails the supposition that attempting such a contemplation would *cause* a preferable state of affairs which one does not currently possess. Doing so requires acting for something other than the immanent, and, as such, requires faith. One without this faith does not exist.

Unfortunately for man, his position entails that he will never be able to know with certainty the degree to which any of his actions is participant in the perfect action - for while there exists a sum total of all ethical realities, man has no way of knowing the distance between his currently understood ethical realities and this absolutely exhaustive list. The irrationality of morality, then, when properly understood, is not a practical irrationality - that the moral act is an error, to one's own detriment - but rather an irrationality of knowledge - the epistemological rootlessness of (moral) action as such.

Power being the ability of man to meet the ultimate end of his will, and the ultimate end of man's will being the most positive teleonomic effect, we must also admit that the state of highest power for man is that which considers all true ethical realities. A conflicting opinion may argue, for example, that while the whole of ethical reality may be much greater than a single human lifespan, a man, given an unchanging ability to correctly satisfy recognised and understood ethical realities, has nothing to gain by an increase in his correctness of his knowledge with respect to those ethical realities which exist outside of his individuality. Living in ignorance of their existence, man may make the perfect actions with respect to his own correctly estimated lifespan and, subjectively speaking, be meeting the ultimate ends of his will - the maximisation of teleonomic reality. His power in this way may be absolute. Yet, in not considering others to be real, his absolute power may hurt other ethical realities. Therefore, the power of one may be the (incidental) cause of the wronging of another. Such a line of reasoning may be levied at man's treatment of animals, for example. Should we imagine man to act perfectly with respect to the betterment of mankind, but to be ignorant of the ethical reality of some higher species of animal, which we for the sake of our example presume to exist (this matter being beyond the scope of these writings), then the power of man, used to the benefit of man alone, may come at the expense of some number of animals.

Despite the fact that this conception still leaves a far greater respect for power than afforded by modern times[15], it still affords too little. The error of this proposition is occasioned by a misunderstanding of the essential concept of ethical reality, already partially addressed. Let it be repeated - the substratum of all ethical realities is identical, Being as such. The concept of I, rather than he, can only ever enter into the understanding with respect to the personality as recognised through empirical phenomena. It is only through the blindness caused by an adaptation to the dazzling lights of the world of the senses that this quality of separation is carried over to Being itself; and it is only through Being itself that this Other has the status of ethical reality at all. The 'continuance' of oneself is a belief occasioned empirically, insofar as we speak of our memories, our body, our habits, our identity and so forth. It is a consequence of a belief in the past.

This 'going forth' of our bodies and personalities would be meaningless to us were it severed from the continuance of ourselves as an ethical reality, as subject. If 'we' were to continue onwards, but never to observe the fact, the point of this departure would be nothing less than death. It is the quality of subject-as-such, derived only from the substrate of immanent reality, which furnishes all belief in, and therefore action towards, both one's future self and all others. Insofar as one acts for one's future self, one must believe this self to one day be experienced - independent of whatever memories, body, habits, or identity this future self may have. Insofar as one acts for another, one must, alike, and in precisely the same way, believe this action to be experienced. The question 'by whom?' is a meaningless one - for it attempts to elevate the accidental properties of an individual existence to the level of substrate of phenomenological existence as such. All that we may answer to the question of 'by what are the realities of another individual experienced' is this: by one and the same thing - by that which experiences. The only positable 'thing which experiences' is the 'I' of immanent reality.

This being understood, we may see how the critique above is fundamentally misled. In presuming that other ethical realities exist outside of the recognition of some given human being, and that the human in question is an ethical reality, it should now be clear that all of his misunderstandings which cause a loss to the other, unknown realities must be experienced by that which experiences - that which experiences the giving of the action must also experience its receipt. All benefit or loss, ethical terms, must accrue to an ethical reality. As such, these misguided actions must be considered less powerful than they would have been given a more correct understanding of the totality of ethical reality - for in presuming that he ignores, and pains, something real, we say that that which seeks to gain causes unforeseen loss. It causes this loss in precisely the same way in which it through its action sought to gain.

This is the principle of eternal justice: that no erroneous deed ever goes unpunished, that no virtuous deed ever remains unrequited. All that one effects will be effected upon oneself, and all that one receives from another will have been given through one's own will - the only will which may be comprehended.

If the cause of one's pain or happiness is not understood to possess this bridging quality, then we cannot admit the effect to be the result of action, and we cannot admit the 'actor' to be ethically real - the 'actor' is instead the product of nature's own mechanisms, no different than stone or dust. There is little more foolish than the wish to exact retribution upon some mound of dust.

As such, we may now readily admit that the absolute goal of all action and of all society is the maximisation of total power, of the ability to bring into being the ultimate ends of the will. We may also therefore say that the ultimate goal of all action is the highest profit. At this point, the question may be raised by some as to why, exactly, we would insist on using this term 'profit' given its exact replaceability with 'increase of power', since the former term has to its disadvantage an overwhelming amount of prejudice and negative public sentiment.

It must be admitted that an insistence on the use of 'profit' in our analysis may evoke an implicit prejudice against our own argument, and that use of this now-muddled term may simply pervert to some readers the clarity of the arguments at hand. Despite this, we shall continue to employ this term due to the damage done to liberty by the continued reign of that false King of Orthodox Economics which bears its name. For as long as the word 'profit' retains its current inseparable ties to both liberty and money, effect of the first and cause of the second, it should be clear that the opinion of the former shall continue to be smeared by the flaws of the latter, to which it in actual fact bears no conceptual relation. This economic science, wishing to give universal value to its apparent laws drawing inseparable connections between liberty and 'economic growth', has in doing so has ascribed all the flaws of economic growth to the bill of innocent liberty. In attempting to rectify 'profit', rather than adopting a new jargon of our own, it can only be hoped that the profit of the orthodox economist will be eliminated completely from the minds of those interested in these matters, instead of being allowed to glide beside our true profit as its own independently striving concept.

Further, in using the same term, we better capture the essential aim of this work - not a destruction of economics in favour of some conservatism, but rather a critique of the fundamental grounds of economics to show that it is, in fact, an inherent ally of the conservative cause.

# 13

## POWER AND JUSTICE

Having outlined the forms under which action must take place, the ends according to which the acts and societies of man must ultimately be scrutinised, and having clarified certain notions regarding time and selflessness, we may now attempt to give this form some practical application in finding, should they exist, principles of means - particular modes of action which necessarily lead to our ultimate end, or, instead, further distance us therefrom.

The simplest form of action, to which the fewest caveats and clauses should need to be amended, is that of man alone with himself. In our passage on the contradictions of nihilism, it was asserted that there are at least two necessary facts of Being - that there exists the subject of this being, and that there exists his desire. All action of man moves towards the satisfaction of desire, a closing of the distance between what man is and what he wishes to be. In achieving this movement, there exist two fundamental and strictly oppositional modes which man may follow: he may move himself, or he may move his desire. All theories of personal ethics fall into either advising one of these extremes, or to advising some combination of the two. At a certain level of abstraction, all approaches on this line are of equal correctness, for one may treat man as being nothing but pure will. As such, the denialists, most spectacularly embodied through the simplicity of the Stoic and esoteric Hindu doctrines, and the affirmists, most seriously embodied by the extremes of "Zarathustrian" Dionysius-worship, may both easily covert readers, or even the very same reader, into a belief in the absolute correctness of their ideals. Yet, while we remain men, it must be obvious that neither extreme alone may suffice. Both ultimately rest on the claim most succinctly condensed as "faith may move mountains" - that is, roughly speaking, the absolute reliance of the will on the intellectual 'belief'. Yet once we discard this notion, and understand man to be something between nothingness and true Being, it becomes clear that man must seek a path between that of the removal of all desire and the immediate obtaining of the object of all desire. Simply put, because man must try to advance towards one of these extremes, he meets some form of internal resistance - and every time this resistance is met, the question must be raised: in this case, perhaps the other path might be correct. The cases in which one approach is superior to the other cannot be known *a priori*. From this it is clear how naivety ethical monism, both affirmist and denialist, must be washed away as soon as one admits that self-knowledge is possible, for it is only in categorically denying the possibility of self-knowledge that one may advocate for a categorical affirmation or denial of desire as the correct path to perfection. As such, we may be secure in affirming self-knowledge to be the first virtue of man.

This granted, we may now give definite substance to those forms of action which we are to consider necessarily positive. In the first place, an action is positive insofar as it inspires in others[16] the correctness of desire. Secondly, insofar as it provides for others the means to the procurement of a desire (insofar as that desire is ultimately correct). By happenstance, this junction serves quite well to demonstrate the moral failures of contemporary economics and its alliance with thoroughgoing egalitarianism or quantitarianism. For it is only the second of these beneficial forms of action which orthodox economics has ever recognised. The division indeed lies deeper, rooting itself in a confused materialist and objective analytical framework. Under such a framework, the procurement of the second category of benefit is much more easily recognisable - it is easier to quantify an increase in the production of food than the education of an individual towards more tempered desires. Further, it is a consequence of this depiction of an economic good as being that object which satisfies the existing desires of a person, whatever they may be, which has led to a grand ignorance of the former category of benefits, which, in rough, we may call culture. This trait, in combination with the general modern-day conviction that all desires are of equal merit (unless they 'hurt' someone), clarifies the antithesis between conservatism and economics as it stands. Indeed, this antithesis is becoming more absolute due to the reaction of conservative thought against the matter of economics, such that, repulsed by the effects of the purely monetary society, the conservative increasingly wishes to admit that it is *only* culture which carries value, and that the benefits of an efficient economy are entirely illusory. We hope to properly demonstrate the necessity of both.

The matter of economic efficiency may be swiftly dealt with, for it is one of relative simplicity and one about which most tend to have a roughly clear understanding. As we have said, an action benefits from material efficiency insofar as it provides others with the means to the alleviation of imperfection when holding their desires constant. Hence, given that, for example, the alleviation of hunger is a good, then an action which has the effect of alleviating hunger is to this degree good. Quite obviously, the complete lack of any ability to satisfy desires would lead to a completely hopeless existence for mankind.

Yet this produced efficiency is not to be confused as interchangeable with the material good as qualified by orthodox economists. The error of the economist lies in that moral efficiency may not be defined in material terms, but is rather wholly functional. A functional definition of efficiency may genuinely entertain the notion that an increase in the number of *material* goods may well be negative for man solely in terms of satisfying his current desires. The orthodox economist, on the other hand, must use his materialist conception of 'economic good' to affirm that any increase in the efficiency of machines or the swiftness of human hands must be good for man. This conception is what leads him to a full ennobling of the economic aggregate statistic, which measures not the quantity of *subjective* goods (these being immeasurable), but rather the quantity of *objective material.*

More important for our current purpose, however, is that category of action which is conducive to wisdom or a refinement of the faculty of desire. Wisdom, far more than efficiency, is subject to inhibition and ultimate destruction due to its absolute exclusion from orthodox analysis.

Fundamentally, the effects of wisdom change man rather than his world insofar as a separation of these may be permitted. As a consequence of this, they tend more often to be excluded by economics since they are only rarely valued *prior to their consumption* by those who they affect, since they are not direct means to any of the established, particular desires of the affected man. As with a child affected by a proper education, the affected person is in no position to properly judge the value of that which is to have an effect upon him before that very effect has run its course. As such, these effects can only rarely constitute a 'good' in any economic sense. Despite the fact that only the conservative branches of thought appear to explicitly place value on this category of good, which is fundamentally discriminatory and hierarchical, some level of implicit recognition must be afforded to the objects of wisdom by all theorists regardless of their intellectual disposition. Even the most anti-hierarchy dogma must grant preferability to the system of values in man best conducive to his ideal, thus the importance given by egalitarian sects to a regime of uniform and compulsory education. Indeed, an inherent hierarchy of value structures may be nowhere as fervently affirmed than in the very doctrines of some thinker like Foucault, whose prime means to the betterment of society consists in the universal domination of the value structures of his opponents, and of all men, by his personal convictions. In wishing to pull man away from the latent 'violence' of established culture, one would of course have to establish a hierarchical system of norms through which dissenters may be punished and excluded.

From the phenomenological perspective, the class of goods of wisdom are those to which exposure has the foremost effect of a change of belief rather than the satisfaction of a wish. These are the things which must be shown as best procurable through liberty if the libertarian is to be reconciled with the conservative - that a free society will best produce those effects which temper mankind to fit the shapes of virtue. This asks far more of liberty than is asked of it when proving that it procures a boon of mere efficiency, since, as we have mentioned, the effects of efficiency are more likely to be valued and actively sought by the free individual than are those effects which work to refine his judgement.

Prior to attempting such a justification, however, we must create a framework of the voluntary society by applying our precepts of action to actors within a nexus of ethical interaction - first to man alone, and thereafter to man in union with his fellows.

Should man be alone, the value of his action is determined by the totality of effect which some given action has upon his future, independent of whether or not he is aware of being the cause of his present state. Should he understand a present powerlessness to be the consequence of his past actions, he will adjust his future action, through an amendment of his values, wherever he understands there to be some equality between the grounds for the past error and those of his current situation. In properly adjusting his actions in such a manner, he will be better disposed to capturing the Good, however he understands it. Thus, the man's life is inherently and inexhaustibly meaningful should he only have the courage to examine himself. This also shows an inherent tendency in man to discard the bad and to foster the god - to update his value structures in the light of new information about reality.

We must also note that, in terms of conviction in the moral truth of his action as such, the latter man is in the exact same qualitative position as the former, that is, true belief is categorically inseparable from false belief in terms of emotional and psychological content and its demonstration in action. This reveals to us a *ceteris paribus* advantage, of indefinite magnitude, of the naturally developed moral notion over some radically new, external proposition to its contrary. If we know nothing of a man other than that he at one former point in time believed it best to plant his crops in August, and at some point later believed it better to plant in October, we must concede the point in favour of October crop sewing. While neither claim, in isolation, stands superior to the other when independent of relevant empirical information, the fact that the later belief necessarily took form through a process of the natural refinement of knowledge inherent in rational beings as such means that we must give it some measure of preference.

Naturally, this preference is not absolute. Any other relevant information, changes occurring in either the subject or object of belief during the timespan in question, calls the superiority of the later developed position to a due measure of scrutiny. Nonetheless, we are bound to retain this predisposition in favour of the tried-and-tested as a stone on the scales of judgement. The weight of this stone is to be determined *a posteriori*, given introspection and experience regarding the external effects in question.

Man's subjective power may be changed through the activities of two faculties: intuition and perception. By the former is meant the effect of a thing on man, insofar as this effect is determined by his own nature, in determining the relationships which create his immanent reality. By the latter is meant the effect of the man upon some thing in determining these same relationships. Jointly, these two faculties determine the relation of subject-as-such and object-as-such which is made manifest in phenomenological reality. All studies of the relationship of these faculties in determining sense-data are bound to fall short of the procurement of any certain knowledge, for these faculties are empirically inseparable yet presupposed in the very concept of sensation. This joining marks the point at which value and matter of fact necessarily clash with one another when man begins, as he must, to create abstractions of his world. This point is also intimately related to the essential incommunicability of the strictly private experience. In appearing to suffer more than another from a particularly harsh winter, one often asks another: are you naturally more resistant to the cold than I am, or are you just used to tolerating it? Similarly, an abnormal ability to discern distant shapes as words may be due to either the receptivity of the eye or a high perceptive value placed on certain words or letters.

While we may at times estimate this relative relation, we may never be precise, for preciseness here requires a congruent evaluation of two incongruent realities.

As it is with the evaluation of the object of sense-data, it is also with the value of sense-data. The existence of art, and the social evaluation of the artist, lies in the ability of the artist to create for others those objects which carry with them intuitive value. More precisely, the artistic object increases the value of the reality of its contemplator, the artist being appraised in his ability to create objects in a manner which most skilfully predicts the particular perceptive faculties of the art's audience. It is the novel prediction of the values of the other per se, rather than the creation of the object in which these predictions might be made manifest, that strictly qualifies this particular function's greatness. In predicting the perceptive faculties of his audience, the artist can most skilfully create a cherished work which requires no strain on behalf of its contemplator. Its beauty seems natural. The artist himself, on the other hand, in the moment of his inspiration, undergoes a subjective alteration of perception in understanding a new function for that object displayed to his intuition. The reason this change may not be 'forced', and why this change has often been seen as miraculous or divinely inspired, is because neither pure intuition nor pure perception may themselves be sensed, such that the case of a change in one of these two can never be traced into the past through the application of known phenomenological laws, which can only apply to that which arises from the mixing of intuition and perception; that is, to phenomena. Thus, a change in perception as such, or intuition as such cannot be the subject of a science. Should any such moment of inspiration happen, attempting to find its direct causal antecedent is an impossible task.

This diagnosis of the artist, according to the rules set above, refers to the recognition of the artist within the judgements of the teleonomy, or from all who ever receive his works, rather than his inherent artistry, insofar as such a difference may be stated. We may clarify this difference as follows. If a man were to somehow fathom a single and spectacular chord of a lyre, hitherto unknown, to be the apex of earthly art, the hearing of which would correctly elevate man's consciousness to its highest reaches, we may speak of the artistic merit of this discovery through two distinct modes. The first, its status as art according to its eventual recognition as such, is that which we have above laid out. Of course, we do not by these means seek to posit that art is simply whatever one wishes to call art. Instead, this mode of quantifying art states only that a particular action comes to be a great artistic act insofar as the totality of its effect works to raise the consciousnesses of the totality of men through an intuition of the modified object. Thus, if it comes to be that many men are profoundly influenced by the resonance of aforementioned man's singular lyre chord, we may consider the action a great work of art from the perspective of the teleonomy. On the other hand, we may attempt to diagnose the merit of a work of art entirely independent from whether or not it resonates with anyone at all. Yet this is the task of particular judgement, which lies outside of the scope of our present survey. In this teleonomic study, we seek not what things are independent of men, but rather the rules categories according to which man comes to interact with his world, and the movements which necessarily follow from these causal interactions. As such, we here consider what it means for man to consider something particular to be true, rather than diagnosing what it is in particular that he ought to be believing. Similarly, in this present context, we consider what it means for man to consider something to be a work of art, and what it means for man to consider some man to be an artist, rather than examining the particulars of what he ought to consider to be art, or who he ought to consider to be an artist.

The generation of art is but one human endeavour classifiable under the category of an increase in the power of perception. This category may be more properly universalised under the name of genius. This latter word, however, contains a qualitative element in that it is primarily used to refer to extraordinarily large increases in percep-

250 - JOSEPH KEANE

tive power. It is this attribute, perceptual virtue, through which man increases that portion of his power which lies solely within himself, rather than being dependent upon the accidents of his environment. Insofar as the value within his life is dependent upon the purely intuitive faculty, his power is, strictly speaking, not his own. This is precisely what is posited by the initiative schools of alchemy.

The important principles of action within lone personality being thus, we can now move to an analysis of the behaviours of man around other men. This analysis must be considerate of a pair of states possible in any interaction of true people: action where the other is not recognised as part of the ethical totality, and action where he is. Naturally, that which is true of action conducted under an absolutely correct ethical understanding will be true with respect to any particular, concrete action to the degree to which the particular action is conducted under a sound ethical understanding.

A wholly correct understanding of ethical totality will first be dealt with, for the reason that under such principles social action becomes rather simple for all political theorists. The political question ceases to be. For man to come together with other men, the other must be recognised as valuable. This is true independent of the former's recognition of the other's status as an ethical being. Other man must be recognised as being instrumental in directing the ethical totality to perfection, either strictly as a means, as with a hammer or an axe, or as part of the ethical totality, himself to be led to perfection. In a society of proper ethical understanding, the only way in which man may be detrimental to the whole is through an ignorance of the laws of nature - of the natural, material consequences of his actions.

The prime question with which almost all sects of political theory have hitherto been concerned is that of property and rightful ownership. Properly speaking, this concerns the recognition of man, through his actions, that certain means are reserved for direct use by certain individuals. That which is useful must be put to some end, and yet multiple men may have dissimilar ideas regarding the usage of some scarce object. Naturally, it is likely that the singular objective means may not be utilised towards both ends simultaneously. To have the thing put to best use, then, certain allocations by certain individuals must be made not to occur.

Alternative uses may be prevented in one of two ways. The first is through a suspension of judgement when faced with an object which is considered to be the property of some other individual. Through this, the individual, when confronted with an object which is not his to meddle with, negates or rescinds his own particular judgement regarding the best utilisation for the object. In doing so, he considers the way that things have hitherto been ordained to take categorical precedent over his own fallible judgement, regardless of how superior he believes his preferred alternative to in fact be. This relation is inseparably related with the generation and recognition of the sacred.

When a populace refuses to suspend judgement in the face of just property, the property must instead be secured by an expectation on behalf of the would-be dissenter that breaking the given rules of property would simply not be of value for him. In this case, the negation of his will occurs on the level of the particular, rather than the categorical. His alternative utilisation of the object is weighed directly against the particular demerits incurred by violating the societal norm, rather than being subordinated due to the existence of the norm as such.

Theories of property occupy one of two opposed strains. They posit property as either an ethical absolute or, otherwise, a result of practical considerations of utility. Before expounding our own notions on the matter, the claims of a particular school of property thought must be thoroughly critiqued so as to justify our distance therefrom.

The theory of absolute private property rights, popularised in explicit academic form through Locke and brought to its necessary conclusion through Rothbard, in which much sentiment in favour of liberty once has its birth, is today dominant among the more radical theorists of liberty. This is unsurprising. Radicalism is demanded by its absolute claims which permit no practical compromise. Anyone who holds such suppositions and does not end up an anarchist is simply muddle-headed.

Its dominance notwithstanding, this school is here singled out for critique for a number of reasons. Firstly, of all the absolutist schools, it is the only one which may not be proven to be immediately contradictory through its very own particular presuppositions. Secondly, it is likely to be the choice theory of a large part of this work's proper audience. Thirdly, as a result of its claims to absolute value, the practical claims hereafter elaborated upon will be irrelevant unless certain claims of the school be subject to dismissal and due reform. Fourthly, these claims to the absolute overshadow the necessary relation of liberty as being the shepherd of traditionalism

We begin at the roots: the notion of value- and function-independent ethics is itself nonsense. Their defender must posit one of two things: either they are outside considerations of regular morality, or lie within and stand at the top. The former demands from us the potentiality of the unethical moral action and the immoral ethical action. Should ethics demand an ought, then we must admit the possibility that man ought to do that which he oughtn't do. If not, then the ethical claim is not worth considering. It is valueless in the strictest sense of the term and has no place in the discussion of the justification for particular human actions, for, if the ethical dictate could not demand an ought, then any moral consideration whatsoever would take priority over the ethical claim, and the latter's scope would be nil. Should the ethical claim be within morality but necessarily of a higher magnitude than all other considerations, we nonetheless create a two-storied system of 'morality', which must permit such absurdities as the preferability of protecting an infinitesimal unit of objective property from violation than the original creation of all of the world's property, including that part which later demands the sacrifice of its own cause. And, as shall be seen, the most common demonstrations of such absolute ethics result in a system which contains no reference to quantity or magnitude, and therefore must adhere to the former, more strictly absurd category of absolute ethics, from which position it may be easily forced to concede that its only possible function is the justification of the morally unjustifiable.

It is curious that the proponents of these ideas continue in their task of expounding succinct (and, as far as we are concerned, correct) practical arguments in favour of liberty given that the matter is supposedly wholly settled independent of consequence and on absolute, object-oriented grounds. Either these writers have little faith in their own theories of ethics, or they are intentionally engaging in tactics of deceit to convince their readers on grounds which they themselves consider irrelevant to the discussion at hand. It would not be disproportionate to here add to our four reasons for the reformation of this doctrine a fifth: that, insofar as these notions are genuinely believed, intellectual endeavour towards the application and refinement of practical defences of liberty will be stifled. This is a secondary reasoning, a justification of the removal of some aspects of this doctrine should they indeed prove false.

Theories of property may seek their rules of appropriation through grounds either objective or subjective, or through a synthesis of the two. The proponents of the ideas in question are keen to approach the issue on wholly objective grounds, partially due to their desire for definiteness in answer, though primarily due to the relative ease of positing absolute and necessary ethical structures on a base of the material - for the theory can then be more easily defined in rigidly mechanistic terms independent of anything which might occur after the mechanistic action binding man to property has originally taken place. Take the most well-known line of this strain of theory, Locke's 'mixing of labour' with the object, positing hereby a change in the material substance of the object which offers absolute grounds for the binding of some property to the labourer. To transplant this theory point-for-point onto a framework of subjectivity would make for a world so tyrannical and unworkable that the moral instinct of the political theorist forbids him from seriously entertaining the idea. Such a theory would posit that any thing which ever enters the mind of one man before any other's becomes absolutely his. However absurd this may appear, the logical form of this belief differs little from the objective variant: for, ultimately, perception of an object requires the mixing of the self in a creative act with the intuited supra-sensory object, and, in terms of the object, part of the essence of its totality of eventual manifestation is dependent upon the perception of it by that which may perceive. As such, the existence of the perceiver works to modify the perceived object. The only difference between this and the objective claim is that here the product may never become the object of another (for that which is added to it subjectively may not be yielded to another individual): but the change is nonetheless dependent upon a mixing of the owned with the unowned.

The highly objective approach of the private property absolutists, however, exposes a spot of vulnerability. It appears that the theorists in question are to some degree aware of the extent of this weakness, since they appear in their writings wholly reluctant to address this topic which, so it seems to us, arises naturally in any discussion of property and appropriation: in any act of 'mixing labour', what, exactly, are the boundaries of that with which one is mixing? What defines it as an object?

In Locke and in Rothbard, and in those theorists who came between, it is to be marvelled that this topic has never met with anything approaching an appropriate level of attention. An examination of this topic, however, is utmost imperative - not only so as to expose the weaknesses of a theory of ethics which, if false, may bear grave moral consequences should it be put to practice, but, more importantly, to open an avenue towards the proper reformation of the theory so that it may stand more properly reconciled with strict morality and justice. This problem may be outlined through the following example.

In the shade of a local and seldom trodden woods plays a town youth with little to occupy his mind. His attention is caught by a blackberry bush, from which he tries to pick his fill. Having eaten the choice fruits, and left with only the small, sour, and squashed, he seeks some other way to use those few that remain. Wandering, he comes across a grove of trees with some of their paler woods exposed by peeling bark. The child squashes the runtish berries in his palm, and smears a crude, smiling face on each of the many trees' trunks. Hungry for some food of substance, wipes his hands down and runs back home. Some of the pulp sinks deep into the tree's more porous wood, while some falls to fertilise the ground below, and the boy never returns.

A number of decades later, the forest is being cleared. The painted trees' timber, and the land around their roots, are to be used for the construction of a true cultural testament - a cathedral has been planned, conceived in the minds of the kingdom's most divine architects and to be birthed through the labours of the town's strongest. A small number may perish from the construction of such a monument, and a smaller number still will live long enough to see the project's beginning and its end. Eventually, through the miracle of man, the cathedral stands firm.

Something here has happened which causes the conservative property absolutist to pit his intellectual and moral sentiments against one another. For in the boy's actions, he appropriated some previously unowned trees - or perhaps their trunks, or perhaps only the wood directly under the painted faces? In creating his art, an act which we cannot deny to be a purposeful endeavour, he had mixed his labour with some unowned objects. Something has become his, for his own exclusive disposal, and has subsequently become destroyed - made to make way for a cathedral. The boy, now elderly, has been made the victim of an absolute injustice. He knows little of this fact until, nostalgic for his youth, he lays eyes upon one of the still-standing trees of the forest and is reminded of his bramble-picking days. He remembers the trees he played around, and, for the first time in his adult life, the faces drawn with fruit pulp, the product of his creative endeavours.

He is something of a naturalist and loathes the established religion of the land. He has a personal distaste for those developments which have affected the land since his youth. He is, however, lucky enough to be acquainted with the theory of absolute and objective property rights. In that forest stood something his, and his rights have been violated by its removal. He visits the nearest layer and pleads his case. He wishes his trees to be put back in their proper place and to receive adequate compensation for the infringement of his rights. The lawyer is initially disheartened, being quite fond of the cathedral, but, being fonder of justice, works to fight our man's cause. Justice on his side, he wins the case in swift order, finding in many of the cathedral's essential supportive beams a circular stain which could only belong to our man's blackberries. The owners of the cathedral, and a large number of locals, offer to our claimant as much as they can muster in exchange for the rights to the timber, but to no avail. The man wants what is his; nothing more or less. The beams are removed, and the cathedral collapses. Justice has been served.

In this depiction of events there is no twisting of the essential claims of the Lockean doctrine. If anything, our example is one quite lenient. What of a man who, on finding a new continent, previously trodden upon by man, pours an extraordinary amount of dye into the highest mountain spring which feeds the lands largest rivers? Any utilisation of these rivers by later-coming men would constitute some violation of property rights should even a single speck of dye be found within the used water. The dyer would have absolute leverage.

This is recognised by the most prominent figures of the absolutist doctrine, who do us the disservice of dishonesty in avoiding confrontation with the central problem underlying these dilemmas. The most glaring example is that of Rothbard himself, in a discussion regarding whether or not the claiming of Native American land by British colonists constituted a violation of property rights which would demand, according to his theories of ethics, grand, present-day redistributive justice. Should the natives have a good claim to the original land, then all that was subsequently built thereupon, in the centuries hence, would have to be given to the native population. In response to this, Rothbard simply reassures us that we are unlikely to ever find the rightful claimants for these wrongdoings, and as such there exists no real problem. This tactic has been utilised by multiple such theorists. One argument made in favour of absolute private property rights is that if one could not be sure that what one did was permitted absolutely, then one would never be able to initiate an action with any moral certainty. Yet, under this doctrine, may we claim with certainty that we have an ethical right to eat the food in front of us?

Despite its false grounds and potentially repugnant conclusions, there remains a certain correctness in the absolutist doctrine which has to our detriment been largely neglected by the dogma's methodological opposition - the utilitarian theorists of private property. This kernel of correctness within the absolutist doctrine is that it rests upon the essential ethical consequences of the subject as such within the world: the universal, but not absolute, form of justice. In truth, this form is that which has been stumbled upon and distorted by the absolutists - they have mistaken a universal truth of justice for a truth of absolute moral magnitude. It is upon the former that we build our own claims.

Theories of ethics deal with ethical beings. If the subjects of a discussion are not admitted to possess this trait and its consequences, then any effect which might hypothetically accrue to them is irrelevant to the field of ethics. As such, we have license to employ universal truth of ethical beings as a framework to which justice and ethics must adhere, insofar as these truths are relevant to this latter topic. A number of these truths have already been discussed. Ethical beings act, and are therefore causes. They are causes in a way different to mere efficient or mechanical cause, which exists as a tool for the clarity of our understanding of natural law and on wholly empirical grounds. The causation from an ethical being is teleological, a necessary form of necessary relation flowing from the manifest existence of the being rather than having grounds as a contingent explanation of nature, as does mechanical causative law. As a consequence, we may say of an event that man caused it in a way not applicable to an event of nature. We may say that a man threw a ball and also that the wind blew a ball, but we may not, knowing these facts, therefore shift these causes back in wholly equivalent and parallel fashion to antecedent events in an attempt to further explain the causative principles at hand. For we may claim that the wind was caused by the action of the sun on the Pacific sea, and that therefore the action of the sun ultimately caused the ball to move, but we have no grounds to claim that a man's position in lying in bed at night caused a specific activity of the brain which, the next day, by affecting the man's sleep, led to the ball being expelled from the arm connected to the brain. Should we attempt this regression of causes with respect to the teleological, we introduce an empirical and contingent *tool*, unprovable in its essence, anterior to and as cause of a rational and necessary presupposition. With the effect of the wind on the ball, our grounds for our connection of antecedent cause (the sun creating the wind) to descendent cause (the wind moving the ball) is already contained within the idea that the wind caused the ball to move, and so our tracing backwards of cause is entirely justified *given our original claim*. With respect to us positing that the brain *causes* human action, rather than the two simply occurring alongside one another, or the brain movements being objective manifestations of the subjective imperative, we introduce in our explanation of action, antecedent thereto, a claim which *denies the existence of that which we are attempting to explain*, namely, the teleological cause itself. Now, the teleological cause is, for all rational beings, logically anterior to the empirically established tool of causative mechanics, which has no inherent, essential grounds in reason. In *positing* any argument to the contrary, one supposes causation through purpose - namely, the purpose of denial of an axiom - before one supposes causation through universal natural law. As such, the erasure of the teleological law through a universalisation of natural law, an unprovable proposition grounded only in its utility, is a proposition which cannot be espoused without contradiction.

It is this teleological causality, present in every ethical being, upon which all possible justice rests.

Whenever we represent a free or ethical being as being through his will the cause of a valued thing, that is, changing the power of a thing, we are bound to conclude that these are his effects. This claim differs slightly to that utilised by the absolutists. There is no question of rights within this claim, merely an identity.

In contemplating the action, we assign to it some value according to the totality of its effects upon the realm of ethical beings, or the teleonomy. If we consider a man's actions good, then we must too consider the man to be good. If his actions be bad, then we must consider him to be a bad man[17]. Insofar as we do not cast this judgement upon him,, we do not consider him to be responsible for his actions - that is, we believe the effects in question to arise wholly mechanically, and deny the active presence of his will within the wild. We consider his 'actions' to be caused independent of his values.

Justice demands that good be done, in proper proportion, unto the good. We here inject no values of our own; this claim follows from moral judgement as such, which each one of us must exercise. If there is moral action, there must be some conception of justice. As a result, there must arise theories of the application or meting out of justice, and conceptions of what, exactly, constitutes the good and the bad within the world. It is a manifestation of this universal sense of justice, more an identity than a belief, that those doctrines which most deny the agency of man also deny the justice of punishment. The ultimate question of dispute is not the existence of justice, but rather the existence of freedom. If there is no justice, then there is no ethical sphere. The ethical totality becomes nil in scope.

Immediately, it follows from this that we must consider slavery to be categorically unjust. In this relationship, the effects of the enslaved moral agent are accrued entirely to the owner of the slave. Such a practice requires that the cause of a good, that is, the good cause, receive no proportional recognition thereof, and is therefore subject to injustice.

Yet it is only this far that we may follow the absolutists in the precise practical implications of our universality - for in admitting that the good must proportionally accrue to the good, we can make no definite statement regarding in what form this good consists. We know only the identity of its dispenser and recipient. It is our belief that all theories of rights or property are mere approximations or codifications of this eternal law of justice, good unto the good, and that all vulgarities of consequence of any particular codification result from a confusion between the particulars of this codification and that which it ultimately approximates, justice itself.

Matters of codification are necessarily complicated by the very nature of our reality - for the Good is functional, yet all verifiable allocations of justice in the world must be objective. Thus, should we wish to allot some reward to a man in proportion to his goodness, we must attempt to satisfy the functional dictates of justice in terms which are, ultimately, object-oriented rather than function-oriented. As such, just reward and eventual reward are incommensurable categories. We may draw a rough but insufficient metaphor through use of colour: if justice demanded that a certain action be repaid with a certain amount of the colour yellow, how could we possibly meet this reward out with any absolute certainty? How much yellow does a banana have in comparison to an early autumn leaf? And, ultimately, from some certain perspective, the yellowness of any given thing can be made to disappear completely. So it is also with respect to function.

Despite this, there are particular characteristics of man's essential nature which allow us to narrow down the array of potential answers to the questions which arise when attempting to give some fixed objective reward or punishment as the due of justice.

The two characteristics of justice which must be addressed are those of form and those of function. The question of form refers to the rules of a particular codification of justice, why one has been chosen and why another has been deemed unfit. These rules aim to provide a solution for all problems of conflict. With respect to function, we find ourselves in something of a paradox. For here we must justify adherence to a codification of justice, that is, quantify its value according to prospective consequence. That is, we must elaborate why one ought to follow the dictates of justice at all, given that the calls of consequentialist morality do not cease when questions of justice arise. Yet the essence of any adherence to justice, and a subordination of one's individual, consequentialist understandings on the matter, is an understanding of the fallibility of one's own belief in particular and contingent truths. This is the apparent paradox which must emerge in any argument in favour of the prudence of the suspension of particular judgement for those who do not already believe such a trait to be good - the argument must appeal to the very faculty of judgement which we are to wish suspended. Nonetheless, some such line for the suspension of judgement must be drawn, in any society, lest we resolve to resign those within our society to some endless combination of conflict, resentment and fear.

We treat first the forms of justice, the general laws of allocation, if indeed there are any. All forms of justice attempt towards a singular closeness with ideal justice. They must do so through means of object - for function we cannot begin to quantify. Should man turn unowned trees into a house, it is conceptually thinkable that we may allot to him something of equal function. Despite being able to think of the possible existence of such an allotment through the faculty of reason, we can never conjure up any particular functional equality through use of the faculty of imagination, for while it is possible to suggest that something may participate in the good equally to a house, any particular attempt we make to satisfy this notion is bound to fail as the functionally equal are necessarily indistinguishable.

Regardless, some approximate solution must be sought. An inability to exact justice in perfect proportion does not lessen the imperative that a society ought to be as just as possible. We must, then, search for the best possible objective approximation of justice. Given that man's good is to be matched by some proportional object of coming to his exclusive disposal, there is much reason to believe that this best approximation may be served by rewarding the good man with that object through which he has become good, that is, through which he has improved the totality of ethical reality and thereby become due some proportional reward. Naturally, this object becoming the good man's reward requires, for justice to be properly served, that justice has not hitherto ordained this object to be the rightful reward of another, previous actor. Otherwise, justice would demand its own violation. This caveat will be returned to at a later point.

A prime reason for such an allocation is man's own ignorance. Let us say man improves some previously worthless object - how are we to estimate the totality of the good springing from such an action? No man may know the particulars of this with certainty, but he may make a categorical claim: the totality of the good issuing from the improved thing will be equal to the good which man will make of it. Should a man build a house, nobody can claim to know the participation of this latter in the good. Yet the nature of this good is that it makes itself known through time. What we do not know about an object and its future relations with other things is unthinkably large. What we do know is only slight. And so we can be far more certain of the justice of our rulings should we allow those unknowns to bear upon the object's initial modifier. Let us suppose that the house was built upon unstable soil, or with poor foundations, and that the fact of this is unknown to the item's initial evaluators. Any estimation of the merit of this action of housebuilding would become highly invalid when this knowledge comes to light. By giving man the object himself, the effects of his creation will continually come to bear upon him in due time, without no deviation from justice coming to occur due to the interference of the man's own ignorance and inabilities. This mode of justice, insofar as it is practicable, allows for a profound simplification of the rules of society, a simplification which comes at very little cost: for what large percentage of society's labours would have to be allocated to the task of continuous judgement if, instead of simply allowing man to own what he has created, the merit of the created or improved object were to be continually evaluated by some department of allocation which would, as a result of its evaluations, also be tasked with the continuous enforcement of the transfer of supposedly equivalent goods? Indeed, it seems that if such a measure were taken to be the default recourse of society, rather than one to be called upon only exceptionally, mankind would have very little hope to progress in any single one of its aims.

Despite the supremacy of this direct mode of appropriation when dealing with the matter of allocating that object the goodness of which has solely sprung from a single man[18], or the matter of the dispensing of justice is not always so simple. We may imagine a case in which the modification of an unowned thing does not seem to us to justify its sole ownership by its modifier. Should a man pour a bucket of dye into a grand lake enough to slightly change the shade of every pale of water thereafter drawn ought, we cannot see it just that he may, because of his action, ban all from drinking from the lake. This remains so even should the new hue be somewhat pleasing to prospective drinkers. A proportionate justice here demands that this innovator be rewarded for his aesthetic improvements, but not for the services of the lake in which he played no part of creation. In this case, the proper enforcement of justice is incomparably more complex than would be suggested by the proponent of objective property rights. When following the prescriptions of the latter, no dispute would be allowed for unless a more original claimant were to stake his claim. Further, should this original contestant prove his claim true, the just ruling to his benefit would demand nothing more than a transfer in kind to rectify all wrongdoings. Under the proper prescriptions of justice, however, both claim and solution take on a manifold complexity when ruling the ownership of the lake.

In a case of objective rights, we need only proof of a singular fact: that man was the first cause in the changing of the thing contested. The most difficult part of this proof comes in defining this very object of dispute, one of the conceptual pitfalls of the objective doctrine. Regardless, this matter only causes genuine concern in rare cases of arbitration. Should it be proved that nobody had interacted with the lake prior to the dyer, then whole ownership over the lake would accrue to him. In judging the justice of the pool, however, multiple factors require incremental consideration such that a proportional resolution may be made. In rough, the matter must rest on the proportionate utility of created functions compared to those functions existing independent of the object's now-proclaimed owner. To best approximate justice, some effort is to be made which would compare the aesthetic utility of the dyed water to the utility to be gained by those claimant latecomers through drinking from the lake. Once a scope of knowledge has been obtained to cast a reliable judgement on the justice of the case, there comes the issue of reallocation. It is quite possible that the amendments of the actor to the object have hereby become quite inseparable from the modified thing. In such a case, and only in such a case, we must have recourse to an attempt at functionally equivalent exchange rather than exchange in kind. Instead of returning the employed dye to the dyer, or simply concentrating his dye or some small part of the lake, he will have to be given some item of compromise of roughly equal good to that which he is made to forfeit. This will result in an allocation never as final or as satisfactory as one which may be justly resolved on wholly objective terms. We may better see the problems which are bound to arise in properly resolving more complex matters of justice by analysing our example in the context of the above.

Let us first imagine the following: the spiller of dye cares no great amount for his product, but is still remotely well-disposed to the sight of a water purpled up to the horizon. A caravan of city settlers finds a position on the lake's far banks well-suited to its desires. It disembarks, and, after a preliminary survey of the surroundings, finds all in

266 - JOSEPH KEANE

good order. The local water source's hue is a remarkable but otherwise irrelevant feature of the promising land.

The settlement grows until, eventually, our dyer can no longer peer through to the horizon without perceiving the form cast by what has now become a bustling village. He visits his neighbours and finds their society to be built upon his exploitation! They quench themselves through theft. Our dyer takes the high-ground and, while forgiving their trespasses to this point, demands that they henceforth cease drinking. The settlers protest, but this matters not - what says justice on the matter?

Objective justice affirms our dyer to be wholly in the right. He owns the lake wholly, and may deny all others its thirst-quenching properties. Let it not be contested that he only owns the dye within the lake. If that route of retort is to be taken, then we must seek that man whose property utilises no electrons other than those which he himself did make. Though the issue is supposedly solved, we somehow remain in discontent. While we had hoped that possession of the dyed lake should prove just reward for the slight labours of the dyer, it appears to our moral intuition that this is not so, and that we have somewhere misstepped.

Since ownership of the whole lake grants to our man power disproportionately large to his goodness - by allowing him to capture the whole value of the lake through exchange with the settlers, leasing out rights for a function in which he had no hand - we must find a resolution which reduces his claims. Despite this, his claims are not nil - he has, however insignificantly, made something of use from the lake, and it is wholly plausible that to grant absolute drinking rights to the settlers, (and, by extension, any who wish to modify the lake) would be to treat him too harshly. A settlement must be made which either grants partial ownership to each party, in proportion to their claims, or deprives one party of its ownership in exchange for a settlement of equal value. To reiterate, it is not posited that this latter exchange of 'equal value' is practically feasible. Such a standard is rather a conceptually ideal settlement.

Both of the alternatives here listed forego the prime advantages of categorical justice, its independence from particular claims of value. Under both cases, ownership must be distributed in proportion to the apparent magnitude of value involved for each of the claimant parties. Presuming our dyer to tbe the only coloured water aesthete invoiced, his claim in dispute rests on his own reports of the importance to him of his creation. The claims of the settlers rest on the benefit they claim to receive through drinking water. While the latter desire should be well estimable by all men of flesh, the former presents to us a clear view of the problem at hand. In this case, the dyer has to gain from an exaggeration of his claims, since any such exaggeration increases his claim to the object in the eyes of the case's appointed arbiter should the lie go undetected.

Following from this, one may make a charge both true and just against the general practicality of settlements of justice. Yet if this charge is directed against our own doctrine in particular, it does not know its own proper object. The fault here lies in man's own vicious nature, not the nature of our proposal. Man still awaits that system which would make angels of beasts and virtue of vice. Any society which ever makes a decision based upon the claims of men lays itself open to manipulation by the ill-spirited. And, indeed, in a society governed by these conceptions of justice, susceptibility to the exaggerated or malicious claims remains relatively low - for should a society be built upon wholly consequentialist allocations of resources, then it would be susceptible not only to the category of lies presented above, but, additionally, containing no objectively verifiable framework of justice, opens itself up to corruption through a grand mass of libellous claims. When judging in accordance with justice, the person to be granted an object must be shown to have exercised some good which would justify his ownership of the object at hand. This good, in all cases other than the extraordinary, must manifest outside of his own individuality - that is, permit some degree of objective verification. To the degree that this clause limits justice, all consequentialist modes of allocation are to that same degree unlimited in their susceptibility to the lie. For how could it feasibly be proven in a court of law that our dyer, in fact, constructed the houses of the settlers? Under a wholly consequentialist doctrine, however, that fact which is to decide the ruling rests not in proving some construction of the houses, but instead in the relative desires of the dyer and the settlers for the houses contested. Thus, while the possibility of the lie does do damage to the practical goodness of our framework of justice, it does damage to a proportion far smaller than the equivalent degree of deception would certainly do unto the consequentialist alternative.

The possibility of the lie, however, is not to be blithely overlooked. We introduce the legal structure of partial settlement - or any legal structure at all, for that matter - as a means to the procurement of the dictates of justice. Only to the degree that this form of ruling can be conducted successfully in a society ought it be utilised. Societies of vice must always content themselves with strict and regular rules or laws when it has been made clear that any avenue for nuance or trust will be dismissed or abused. This case is no different.

It ought to be noted that the prime function of this system of ruling is not to define the rights of the late-coming party to the object in question. It is rather to define the rights which the original appropriator obtained through his free usage of the contested item. These rights are limited independent of the ruling, yet absolute ownership will, in any imaginable society, be the presume state of affairs until a claimant to the unowned makes a strong enough positive case, which reveals that our absolute judgement is in need of tempering so as to fit the mould set out for it by the authority of justice.

If our settlers have not infringed upon any of the dyer's truly acquired rights by drinking, then our judgement must be that they may henceforth draw from the lake's water with impunity and may not be made to cease doing so. Should the judgement be split, then the claimant party owes to the dyer some form of recompense for his losses in exchange for the aforementioned drinking rights. On the other hand, should drinking be considered a frivolous thing to the settlers, and should the wholeness of the dyed lake be of utmost sacrality for our creator, then it is highly plausible that the rights to drink therefrom may be denied to the settling ban, since their action, whereby they transform the lake into the satisfaction of some want, is of little effect on the totality of ethical things in proportion to the damage to the done to the justice whereby the dyer has been given his lake.

It would be prudent to briefly differentiate this position from that of the Georgist, so as to show more deftly the implications of the above doctrine. The Georgist holds that man may rightfully own capital, but not land. On a superficial level, this bears some similarity to the way in which we differ from the objective absolutists - for we deny that, from the objective effect of dyeing a lake, the dyer thereby has the right to exclusive ownership of the body of water. The Georgist would agree with us thus far. As we have said, however, land is not a phenomenologically existent category. All with which man interacts is capital. The failure of the Georgist doctrine is twofold. Firstly, an overestimation of the role of pure land. Every object has contingent value. This value is contingent upon the constitution of the valuer's body. If he cannot control the world so as to interact with some object, it cannot be valuable to him. As such, land - that which has not been 'mixed' with the constitution of man - has no inherent value. Rather, it is inherently valueless. All that may be spoken of in this regard is capital value which is the result of faculties quite common to mankind. Thus, by means of the mouth and the biological imperative towards the consumption of water, the lake acquires capital value. It follows that the categorical repudiation of the ownership of land coupled with the affirmation of the ownership of capital is a strictly untenable position. Further to this, the Georgist has a tendency, springing from his misunderstanding of the proper existence of 'pure land', to overestimate its supposed value, and to take as land that which is strictly speaking some functional good flowing from the actions of some man.

Let us, for example, take the case of the price of so-called land in a crowded city. In such environments, the price of land is relatively high, a reflection of its scarcity. According to the Georgist, any ownership of this land, and certainly any charging of rent for the land's utilisation, constitutes an injustice - for, land being land, and not capital, no man has played a role in its creation. This being so, it would be unjust to allow a single man, or some short number of men, to reap the full reward of that valuable plot which they did not create. The Georgist solution to this dilemma is to have the value of the land factor evaluated by the state, and to levee some proportionate tax upon the so-called owner of the land. The funds raised in such a manner will be used to provide services to all who live within the state.

We must make an objection to this series of propositions. It is false that the inner-city land is not a product of man's labours, even if no single man had hitherto trodden upon its soils. Excluding, for the moment, the fact that all supposed land requires some certainly constituted man to give it function in some manner which requires some prior interaction with the land so as to make it valuable to the observer, the Georgist fails to notice that any of the value accruing to this untrodden city land *is the result of those activities of labour which have been undertaken around it*. Thus, any value which this land has in excess of the value of some land situated entirely apart from civilisation has come about through the actions of some number of men who have, through working upon their environments, granted the untrodden land some increased function. Suppose that a man has built a well a short distance away from this plot, and has made its access free to all who wish to drink. In doing so, he has increased the value of the untrodden land, which has gained function insofar as it is useful as an intermediary means to the procurement of the well's supply of water. The case is the same with the construction of shops, or the proximity of the land to one's place of work, or the pleasantness of the people in the land's general vicinity. This is not value inherent in the land as such, independent of man, which nobody may therefore own. This is function imparted by man, through his labours, to an object otherwise to that degree worthless. Thus, while the Georgist would demand that this object remain unowned by all, or owned exclusively by the state, and posits that any private ownership of the good would constitute some violation of the rights of all of those who wish to use the land, we, on the other hand, state that the only injustice which may occur in such a scenario is that some individual, who has imparted some value to that unowned thing around him, has been forbidden from retrieving from his labours some justly proportional reward. Any complications which arise from this desire for a just reward, such as the matter of working to improve some object which is already owned by another individual, will be addressed at a later point.

The second failure of the Georgist doctrine lies in its confused response to its rejection of private land ownership. In most cases, it seeks to have the masses of national land resources owned wholly by the state, the value hereby raised to be distributed in some egalitarian fashion by the state apparatus, or used in order to fund the so-called essential services. This we repudiate in its entirety. Even under Georgist suppositions, it absolutely does not follow that, because land may not be kept by one man from his fellow men, the value of that land must therefore be harvested and distributed to all men equally. Such a proposition smuggles in the supposition that all land is of equal value to all men, and subject to equal potential utilisation by all men. This is simply nonsense. By way of demonstration, let us revert to our example of the lake and its dyer. In dying the lake, the man has worked to benefit the ethical totality to the degree that this action provides to him some aesthetic merit. Given that no other individual has acted by means of the lake, and therefore no other individual could be deprived by the lake's whole ownership by the dyer, allowing the man to act as if he wholly owned the lake is in strict accordance with the dictates of justice. This ownership is the best conceivable approximation to that reward due to the actor arising from his beneficial action.

Only when the settlers arrive and utilise the lake as a means of quenching thirst does the lake take on a multiplicity of function. The problem that has arisen is that sole control over the lake has revealed itself to be an unjustly large reward for the actions of the dyer. This reward is unjustly large to the degree that it allows him control of some manifest function disproportionate to that function added to the ethical totality. It is not that his control of the lake was never just - it is rather that this allocation is shown to be a faulty approximation of justice once new information comes to light. Thus, the continued sole ownership of the lake by the dyer is no general affront to mankind - it is rather an injustice to the settlers alone. At no point should the 'value of the lake' be seized by the state and reallocated to all men under the state. Instead, this matter of just distribution concerns no parties other than the dyer and the settlers. Given that the dyer is attempting to claim control over a *function* in which he played no remote part of creation (a creation which includes any bringing of the item to the attention of its eventual consumers), we consider him to be acting unjustly in exercising some coercive control over the function created by the settlers insofar as this latter utilisation does not interfere with that function created by his dyeing. As we have said, insofar as the action of drinking *does* interfere with the function created by the dyer, we must have recourse to a more complex mode of approximate settlement.

The simpler matters of form dealt with, we must now address the function of justice. Immediately, such a question seems to demand a tautological answer: we ought to prioritise justice for it is just to do so. Yet any system of laws of justice must be able to demand adherence to its rules when consequentialist morality would have otherwise. Two points arise from this statement which must be answered. Firstly, how is it possible for something to be both just and yet not moral, and how is it possible for something not directly moral to have the authority of "ought"? Secondly, how is it possible to qualify the claims of justice above moral consequentialism on grounds ultimately consequentialist? Should these questions be left without answer, justice, though it may exist, has no apparent claim to our respect.

In order to understand the authority and character of justice, it is of great assistance to call to mind the situations in which recourse to it is never sought. The first of these is within the perfect society. This society, unimaginable product of reason, is characterised by a state of perfect insight and unity within every act. As already described, the hypothetically perfect action values every immanent reality appropriately, and has a perfect understanding of the effects thereupon occasioned by any natural effect or action. In such a society, all men are in absolute unanimity with respect to the value of an object or act. Whenever a man procures something, all men agree as to how it ought to be used. As such, no recourse to justice need ever be made - yet the rules of morality continue to form the structure of each of these identical judgements.

The second case wherein justice has no proper place is one where man is wholly alone. The question of justice can never arise as there can be no simultaneous plurality of claims without a simultaneous plurality of men. Again, the dictates of morality remain. It is clear from this that justice can only be invoked when conflict arises, occasioned by the disagreement of two or more men regarding the correct mode of disposal for scarce means.

Presupposed by such a conflict is that there exist two claims justified by subjective morality or estimates of utility which do not conform to one another. Justice is the set of resolutions whereby a continued moral disagreement may be categorically overcome, as well as the determined repercussions for failing to abide by such resolutions. All parties must submit to a mutually recognised claim, above and beyond one's own individuality. The number of possible rules for allocation is endless, and so we must here distinguish between absolute justice and conditioned justice, dependent upon the transient agreements of men. Absolute justice determines initial appropriation and rights as such. Conditioned justice is the contractual sacrifice of one's own claims to a superior arbiter. Cases discussing the former are distinguished by the prosecuting claim always containing the idea that the disputed item was never the defendant's. Conditioned justice, be it an arbitration based on consequence or a contest of sport, does not deny absolute justice, but rather works within it in order to find agreeable terms to the resolution of some foreseen conflict. In essence, the former finds rights, while the latter agrees upon the particular conditions for their transfer. Conditioned justice may be found in a wide variety of social arrangements, from the honour codes of duelling to the agreed upon relations between landlord and tenant. In these cases, and in all others, conditioned justice sets the limits to acceptable behaviours, and outlines what repercussions may follow when such limits are breached.

The function of eternal justice may best be demonstrated by positing a society in which it is wholly denied. Fundamentally, any interaction in which absolute justice is not recognised suffers from a failure to understand that a belief in the correctness of one's position does not constitute a proof that one's position is superior to that of one's opposition. The action which does not recognise justice does not understand that should two men be bound to disagree, some solution must be followed which may not be understood by all involved parties to conform to their particular moral sentiments and opinions. This framework of settlements must, in its essence, contain supra-rational authority. Should such justice go unrecognised, all claims of others, or all claims against one's own, would have absolutely zero weight as such. One's belief that one's opinion is correct would be sufficient epistemological basis for enacting the belief in question to its fullest extent. When man behaves in such a manner, he can only utilise conditioned justice not as a form of justice proper, but rather as a rationalised means towards willed power. Since a belief in justice is a necessary consequence of the idea that the essence of another's being is equivalent to one's own, a complete denial of justice requires that one denies the participation of other men in all of those intrinsic ethical qualities detailed above. To completely deny justice, one must become solipsistic. It is this line of reasoning which best explains why those states which most seek to describe man in solely mechanical terms, to the destruction of his responsibility, are also those states which have most completely eliminated the property principle.

If man cannot see anything as property of another, then he must treat the world as if wholly unowned - including other men. To recognise something as the property of another is in essence to change its subjective functional character so as to subordinate one's own rationalistic evaluation of the thing to a conception quite similar to that given to the sacred. In doing so, we change the object from the product of an efficient end to the product of a final end. Now, to mistake a final end for an efficient end, and to put this object to one's own rationalised usage as a consequence of this mistake, is to cause a devaluation of the act which originally caused the object. For to change the product of the original act from its willed form is to cause the creator of the desired object to view his creative act as less successful relative to the standards he employed in that act. The only cases in which this is not so are precisely those cases wherein conflict is impossible, for both the creator and the would-be-usurper consider themselves beneficiaries of the latter's interaction with the former's creation. As an example, take a man having produced a plain wooden house. A traveller comes across it and views it as a possible source of firewood, but upon closer inspection comes to the correct belief that the object is a product of a creative will. He therefore makes it some part sacred, and passes it by. A second man comes and finds the object quite admirably structured - but finds its plainness too gloomy for his own liking. He positions a number of flowers and shrubs around the house's face, clears some gathered debris from its door, admires his work then moves on. At no point does he recognise the house to belong to another. A third man passes by totally oblivious to the character of the structure as being the product of a final end. He breaks in, takes what he wishes, and goes on his way.

We say that the owner of the house is quite happy when he comes to see the developments brought by the second man but becomes distraught when learning that the third man has plundered his belongings. Should all men involved have correctly recognised the property involved, and should all men here understand the effects of their actions on the creator of the property, that is, act successfully, then only the third man's action would be foregone. The only actions permitted by a lack of property recognition are therefore those which would cause the desired item never to have been created should the creator have had foresight enough to view the crime as a consequence of his creative act. Thus, insofar as the totality of men act under an understanding occasioned by injustice, the totality of men will cease to create the good, and the totality of power will be lowered. We may therefore say that actions which are only possible due to a lack of recognition of justice are categorically parasitical in principle, this being the only way through which one may command the some created object without having participated either in its creation or in the creation of something deemed roughly equivalent to that item through means of trade.

Now, in showing the essential beneficiality of a strict adherence to such a form of justice, we have nonetheless made no step towards demonstrating that adherence to property justice is *sufficient* in the procurement of a good society. This is a question of quite some import, for if our aim is to be the betterment of society, we must make ourselves aware of these traits which must be procured within a society most directly, most necessarily, and prior to all others. With this in mind, what may be said about the sufficiency of justice alone to the creation of the good society? On this matter there are two general theses worth mentioning: the first, that recognition of property is the founding principle of civilisation. This is the libertarian approach. Second, that civilisation is the inevitable product of a good stock or a good race, and that, while such a stock may tend to uphold the ideals of liberty, the necessity of good stock is of primary importance to any civilisation. This is the more traditionalist position. Should the former be truer, then the task of 'redeeming' a civilisation appears only as difficult as does an education of modern man on the goodness of property and a removal of the more dangerous members of society. Should the latter theory be true, then the task presented to us is nigh impossible, lying on the lines of a total and intentional reconstruction of a people's spirit at the very least, and, at most, a reconstruction of a race's physic-biological constitution spanning centuries.

Any considered view on this matter will arrive at the conclusion that both factors are quite important to any civilisation There is a point of degeneration and incompetence at which no amount of understanding of justice will generate a good society, while a society of competent individuals will not be able to very well progress when much of its resources are utilised to the prevention of theft and parasitism resulting from a lack of ability to abstain from the products of other men's labours. No survey of this matter can give any useful indication regard the exact proportions of usefulness of each of these factors. What may be said, however, is that a relation of the two factors is rather symbiotic. A society of good men who lose the ability to sense eternal justice will come to degenerate in matters of individual virtue, that is, action directed only to the temporal individuality, and that a degeneration of stock will cause an inability to sense justice. This relation will soon be addressed, but we turn first to a final point regarding justice and property, one of epistemology, universality, and hierarchy.

It has become a popular view that property is antithetical to tradition. This claim is largely based on an implicit integration of the dialectical rhythm into the historical dogmas of many conservative commentators. The claim supposes that some time approximate to the emergence of the Renaissance Italian city-states, private property and 'individual freedom' began to take hold of Europe. Since then, or at least from that point until the Great War, property rights and liberty grew, while tradition wilted. This is also the strain of thought which so carelessly conflates property with money-interests and 'consumer society'. Yet, its Marxist influences aside, this conception of freedom and property is largely the product of the employment of a crude positivist-materialist methodology in defining and understanding both property rights and freedom. It is seen that a larger number of people may use a larger number of things in a larger number of ways, and, as such, the theorist concludes that the law of property justice property is flourishing. This is nonsense. Secondly, this claim conflates a society moulded by justice with one defined by a rationalist will to overthrow some existing state of affairs in an attempt to secure some emancipation. It is this latter force which defines modernity, no matter how often this movement has attempted to wear the mask of strict justice. A society does not need to endlessly theorise over and explicitly invoke the property principle, in some bastardised form or other, in order to be founded upon an ingrained respect for just and inviolable allocations of power or object. As we must see, the rationalism which has defined modernity, and even the modern fervour for freedom, is in fact counter to the fundamental spirit of property itself.

This fundamental spirit is the demand of property that man suspend his judgement and individuality in the face of natural order. As we have seen, in order for an actor to display an understanding that an object is just property, he must suspend his judgement-action when estimating with the object's manifold possibilities. As such, the property-recognising society must be one of humility and order. This understanding is at root an epistemological claim which is both foundational to any traditionalist society and anti-rationalist. It is that there exists truth, outside of one's own subjectivity, which one's own reason is presently incapable of arriving at. It is only on this basis that an individual may refuse to act when he is of the immediate opinion that something has been wrongly done, given that there exist no external restraints stopping him from correcting the perceived error.

This suspension of judgement is not a good-in-itself. It is possible to incorrectly suspend judgement, at which point humility becomes a vice. The utility of a suspension of judgement is dependent upon the virtue of the actions or allocations which take place in lieu of the suspended one. The whole essence of the suspension of judgement is that the individual judges himself to be incapable of judging the utility of alternative courses of action. That is, the correct suspension of judgement requires a correct evaluation of the relative merits of one's own action and those of another. Yet it is precisely the individual's inability to properly estimate the goodness of the other when shrouded by his own errors which makes the suspension of judgement an imperative in the first place. In order to deny his belief that his idea is superior, it seems that he must, in some way, hold the belief that his idea is inferior. Either this, or the task of deciding which individuals or which actions are to be respected above one's own must be instilled upon the individual from without, to the repression of the agency of his individual rationality.

This is an aspect of political organisation the particulars of which have no immediately positable solution. Additionally, this is a point of weakness for those who espouse the traditionalist doctrines of society and politics. For while just attention is given by them to the importance of the renunciation of the hubris of individualist rationalism and to the necessity of tradition and natural hierarchy within society, the *processes* whereby a virtuous allocation of authority is to be procured, such that a subordination of the individual is both natural and generally beneficial, have been seldom explored by the theorists in question. This lack of insight has resulted in a doctrine which can do little but inspire a fatalistic societal pessimism. For some, this societal pessimism has risen to the reaches of the metaphysical, being reflected in those teachings which state that modern man finds himself placed in the midst of an inherently degenerative phase of a wider temporal cycle, the present stage being marked by an ever-increasing detachment of man from those spiritual heights which were reached anterior to recorded human history. Until this Kali Yuga comes to close in some many thousand years, the doctrine holds that mankind will be destined by fate to degenerate.

Additionally, the incompleteness of the traditionalist corpus can often lead to a position of self-induced intellectual paralysis - for in decrying intellectual hubris as the cause of the decline of the well-ordered society, one may begin to doubt whether or not one has any right to use one's own intellect as a means to weaken modern society, which is certainly the product of an amalgamation of forces far beyond the knowledge of any single individual. We hope that these limitations may be to some degree amended through an examination of the relationship between tradition and property.

The categorical essence of tradition bears much relation to that of property. In the face of both, the individual is bound to never intrude upon those realms outside of his rightful place. Tradition, however, is somewhat broader than property. Traditions have no determinate form, since any possible authoritative value acquired from without may be considered traditional, and so tradition may be either object-oriented, in which case we face the sacred, or subject-oriented, in which case we bow to a superior soul. Property, on the other hand, anchors itself wholly to the world in the realm of the fixed object.

An additional differentiating quality of tradition, under the employment of the term followed by those in favour of it, is its qualitatively positive element. Under this usage of the word, while all tradition bears authority, not all authority can be considered to be a manifestation of tradition. Generally speaking, the traditional is that which has come to acquire authority through a process of the synthesis of experience, a process immune to the claims of any individual rationality, so as to be honoured in due proportion to its natural virtue. In other words, an authority is only traditional when its position in the natural hierarchy of the Good has come to be properly reflected in the transient and temporal hierarchies of the social structure by means of a traditionalist process. Yet while these valid claims buttress themselves upon the authority of nature, little work has been done so as to systematically qualify, from a traditionalist perspective, where exactly this naturalness lies, and where it might be absent. Without this, there can exist no method for the determination of whether or not any given authority is truly traditional. A further examination of the point will serve well to demonstrate our thesis of the essential filial nature of property and tradition.

It is to be little contested that the strongmen of modern politic occupy an unnatural, thus untraditional, authority. No matter what their goals may be, their foundations are a manifestation of the undifferentiated will of the demos. Those not the direct product of such forces are rather its usurpers - they, through conflict, possess with their own souls the beasts bred by the swollen lower castes, and throw off the saddle. The claim of unnature here lies in two separate grounds - poverty of process and poverty of essence. Poverty of process occurs when the traditional method of selection is ignored. Only under proper process can an authoritative claim be made sacred and integrated into genuine tradition. In most traditional civilisations, the leader of a people drew his validity from the assent of some class of nobility, most often through the spiritual prospection of the high priesthood. These latter were themselves believed to have valid claims to power through a process of becoming the elect of some number of their direct inferiors or the heirs of their direct superiors. In the traditional society, authority must be sanctified by those with the authority to sanctify authority. Ideally, this regressive chain begins along with the birth of the society itself, in the emergence of its first peoples and structures from the unordered chaos which came before. Poverty of essence more simply the degree to which the society in question can be seen to differ in its workings from the ideal society. Poverty of essence, however, is not simply an estimable, quantifiable quality, a truth available to the minds of all. Just as the lowest of men must most often defer their judgements on their own actions so as to permit the actions of others, the low man must also be incapable of estimating the whole goodness of the society in which he lives. If he does not have the authority to understand and justly condemn the actions of many of his immediate associates, how are we to allow him the epistemological authority to censure judgements of the whole society, especially a society ordered according to the virtuous process?

Thus, poverty of essence, defined by a power existing in the hands of one too low in the natural hierarchy to be its just wielder, *is measured by* poverty of process. It is only poverty of process that can be the proper measure of a society's health, not any individual rationalisation, for such a rationalisation demands the authority to judge the entirety of a society. In other words, if the process is followed, then no poverty of essence can interrupt the natural order of things. The unnaturalness of every democratic rule of course lies in the fact that his authority is based upon the wills of usurpers, those who have gained their power to elect through their sheer quantity rather than any reference to quantity. It is to be savoured that a true democracy is not yet upon us.

According to the traditional view, the fabric of natural authority, metaphorically speaking its substance, is the involuntary esteeming of the Other. While involuntary, no coercion is here involved. The respect for the other comes from an internal force, awe at his virtue, quite like how one does not choose to regard a hammer as having high or low quality - rather, this awe necessarily flows from the truth of the characters involved. From this conception it should be clear quite how similar the concepts of property and tradition must be. Moreover, the action which contains the substance of tradition must be seen to obe almost identical with the action which, according to the precepts of justice recently detailed, ascribes to a man rightful rule over some functional property - over, roughly speaking, the means of societal organisation.

In a civilisation which strictly obeys property justice, those who occupy the highest position must be those who, according to historical precedent and proper process, have most been recognised by their compatriots as drawing the ethical totality towards its own perfection. Whenever one affirms that a man owns something justly, he affirms that the owner has either created its function or has been bestowed the right to its usage by someone with the just authority to perform this act. The degree of societal power which this estimation gives the owner is a product of both the intensity of the estimation and the societal power of authority of the person making the estimation. This being so, we may understand a sort of social 'gravity', a necessary consequence of authoritative mass, which, according to the position of the authoritative figure, exerts an effect on all other social bodies.

Now, the exact magnitude of one's authority in such a society, even when excluding acts of pure creation (or expansion of the good), is by no means fixed. Any authority of any magnitude may have its power stripped immediately on the occasion of a universal lack of belief in the premise of its just authority, that those things which flow from him are or have been good. Thus, the pope can retain only a shadow of his power in a secular world, and the vineyard owner none in a world turned abstinent. On the other hand, revaluations of lesser creations cause those previously insignificant to gain authority in proportion to the influence which these valuations asset on the actions of the existing social fabric.

Before going further in outlining these syntheses, a point must be made regarding the differences between traditional authority as a category and property justice as a means thereto and part thereof.

As previously mentioned, voluntary society may be organised through either strictly legal and objective delimitations of property, or through trust. The trust principle exerts its influence through means of the impulse towards duty. In a more trust-based society, actions are taken to the benefit of others in expectation that the benefit shall in some way be returned through the duty-sense of the initial action's beneficiary.

The immediate point of difference between the two forms of authority is their respective legal enforceability. It is characteristic for the property principle to have a high degree of enforceability through force due to its pseudo-objective nature - that is, its claims, on practical grounds, be generally treated as if they were object-oriented. It is clear what a man is owed if someone steals his axe, less so if a supposed beneficiary of a man's labouring help refuses to return the favour. Yet this is a difference of no universal necessity. Rather, the starker difference lies in the object upon which the claimant's right would be staked should his legal claim be true.

Moreover, it is not clear the even if the contested matter of trust were found in an object, a just reimbursement could be given, for the principle of reimbursement is the returning of a thing to its rightful owner, which requires that someone else has taken the object unrightfully. Yet nobody can come to have unrighteously taken a thing without having been an active agent in the transfer of a good. Now, in matters of duty, the duty-bound is always the passive agent - the one who has had something done unto him. Thus, the recipient of some benefit which appears to bind him in duty cannot thereby be bound in terms of property for that reason alone. Let us take the gift. Insofar as the gift is bestowed as true property, that is, insofar as its usages are given to the recipient alone and rights to these cannot be reclaimed by the original giver, the giver has no legal claim against the recipient should the latter not act as the giver desires in response to the gift. Insofar as the 'gift' does not bestow any usage rights unto the recipient and may be retracted at any point by the giver, the act becomes, strictly speaking, one of contract rather than gift giving. It is only with the true gift that duty can arise, yet it is only with the true gift that the giver cannot enforce his claims by a just employment of coercion.

Properly speaking, the type of authority which lies opposed to that of property is that obtained through bestowing one's graces upon a wholly passive agent. Insofar as the latter agent was indeed active, that is, was the origin of a participant creative force of the action of transfer, a legal claim towards the rectification of injustice may be made. Once more, then, we come against a point solvable by no system of organisation or framework of justice alone - the actions to be taken in disputes where the sole matter of relevant truth lies, if anywhere at all, within the defendant or claimant. It is possible for the former to overemphasise his lack of responsibility in the matter, to exaggerate his passivity, and thereby avoid retribution. A prime benefit of high-trust and ethical societies is that these occasions are minimised. For example, a man may bestow the assistance of labour upon another, when neither share the same verbal language, when the former sees the latter appearing exhausted in his works. The seemingly tired man is happy to finish the work himself, even if he must take some time to rest, but does not mind the assistance of the onlooker, who he presumes is simply bestowing a friendly deed without expectation of any eventual return for his actions. The assisting man, however, is habituated to a custom wherein such assistance, if not to be repaid, must be refused. It is clear that in this case, the assisted man was highly passive in his receipt of the service done, and we see little reason why he should be considered liable to retributive judgement as a consequence of this interaction. On the other hand, we can imagine a scenario in which the assisted man, in a remarkable display of ignorance regarding the customs of his environment, presumes the worker to be merely joking when the latter makes gestures conveying a notion of money in exchange for labour, and waiting for the assent of the tired man before going about his assistive labours. Only some time after this does the tired man come to understand that he was the only person in his locality who would ever have misunderstood the meaning of the gesture aimed at confirming that some reimbursement would be due for the actions of his assistant.

Thus, it is clear that matters of both duty and property are muddled by the problem of communication, this issue bearing more heavily upon the former than the latter. Though there is no sure remedy which may prevent these issues from ever occurring, a good stock of people bound by a general congruence of culture and communication would go some way towards reducing the risk that such things might come to pass.

Before venturing too far off track, we return to the concept of authority-through-duty and its claims upon the individual. We find that the purest form of authority-through-duty lies those cases in which the object of creation is not merely a thing, but rather another ensouled individual[19]. Through this action, the bestower changes the individual, rather than his world alone, so as to leave him better disposed to his transcendent purpose. In such a case, there is no object of possible retrieval should the beneficiary refuse to show due diligence to his supposed benefactor. Here bear in mind that we talk not of absolutely pure gifts, which entail the expectation that nothing ever be given in return, but rather that bond occasioned by a benefit bestowed the breaking of which constitutes betrayal. Our question here is to be this: what is the relation of our sense of property justice to this bond of duty? In answering this, we must address the claims of those who would have us believe that a position in favour of the proliferation of property recognition will inevitably lead to a decline of those duty-bonds which can be neither dissolved into object-property nor stipulated in a formal and contractual manner. The truth of the matter is entirely to the contrary.

The sense of the bond of duty is, like that of property, determined by the recognition of a relationship between a functional state of affairs and an active ethical entity. One can feel no such bond towards a mere object, nor towards an ethical being by which one has never been affected. The prime difference between the sense of property and that of duty is that the former demands a merely negative course of action - that is, makes it such that a certain object is not to be interacted with in such-and-such a way. The latter demands a positive action, such that the value of various means increases to the degree that they are seen as fit to the fulfilment of duty. The former sentiment, when violated, transposes itself into the latter, whereas duty, when fulfilled, transforms into a recognition of property; the recipient of the duty, the original benefactor, is believed to own his due reward given that it has been bestowed.

Now, here supposing that property is ethically and legally enforceable, and that duty is not, we can clearly see that the sentiment occasioned by duty is by no means at odds with that brought on by a belief in property justice. The psychological content of these notions being independent of the plausibility of their objective enforceability, *we are bound to admit that the set of beliefs which binds one to property also binds one to duty.* If one recognises a man to have created art upon a stone with no other considerable use, he must, understanding the situation in its entirety, feel an ethical obligation so as to not interfere with the created item. Similarly, if one recognises a man to have educated oneself at a young age now forgotten, ultimately to one's own great benefit, one must feel an ethical obligation to the end of repaying the deed done - unless freed from this obligation by the original bestower. Since the psychological contents of these sentiments is one and the same, procuring one in society must occasion the other. Thus, it is absurd to claim that a society which bases its ethics on a recognition of property rights will neglect natural duty, should the latter indeed not be a category of thing enforceable by means of the property courts themselves. To the contrary - insofar as one occasions in one's people a disregard for property ethics in favour of utilitarian rationalism, the only possible alternative, one simultaneously destroys any justification for duty, a causation quite obviously reflected in the tendencies of our own modern, rationalistic and utilitarian era. The rise of property rights *relative* to duty comes from the fact that the former, owing to its general recognition in courts of law (now much threatened), acts as a safe haven, albeit an inadequate one, for those beneficial relationships of duty which are now quite dead to us; which may no longer be procured through means of duty and trust alone. The river mouth does not steal water from the mountain stream, though this may well be posited by one who sees only the direction of flow and the relative magnitude of the river's downstream parts. This error is occasioned by an ignorance of a deeper underlying cause - namely, gravity. In our case, we deal with a force apparently little less ubiquitous - social decay.

If not in their psychological content, nor their causative element, the essential differences between the imperatives of property and of duty rest in their relative enforceability. This must make itself evident through a difference in the creative products the recognition of which causes each respective sentiment. To examine this properly, we will take a typical particular of the duty bond unmuddied by any distinguishing aspect of explicit, contractualist property: the paternal relationship. This we must differentiate from the gift, which is an interaction completed on the premise that no reciprocal obligation is expected or required on behalf of the action's beneficiary. To the contrary, we must examine that category of action undergone with an expectation on behalf of the active agent that the recipient or passive element will one day repay the good done, if this ever be called upon. It is obvious that the binding nature of such a bestowal is not entirely independent of the subjectivities of the recipient - otherwise, anyone could bestow anything upon any other and demand fidelity in proportion to the giver's opinion of the service bestowed, subject to any conceivable delusions of grandeur. If it were admitted that the duty-bond were independent of the sentiments of the man it binds, a man who believed lead to be gold could dispense his lower metal with a genuine belief that he was thereby coming to the great aid of his contemporaries. Doing this, he could arrive at the understanding that he was owed some vast deference or social recompense, and we could not object that he would thereby come to be the ruler of his country.

Thus, we must find out under which circumstances, if any, the recipient's qualities bind him to a reciprocation. We may first examine the case in which the recipient himself recognises the benefit bestowed and voluntarily returns the favour. While the justice of the employment of force is irrelevant, or better impossible, in cases where duty is voluntarily repaid, that the state of the recipient which would most be likely to justify the employment of force would be the one in which the subject himself recognises the benefit which he has received.

Let us posit a man quite harshly wounded in a secluded area, who has fallen into unconsciousness. He is noticed by a passer-by, and, by one means or another, taken into the care of the traveller's home. The wounded man wakes confused and, after having his situation brought to light by his temporary caretaker, comes to learn that the latter had foregone quite some expense in ensuring that the wounded man be brought to safety. As a result of the assistance given, the passer-by rendered himself unable to sell his wares as planned at the community's largest seasonal market. Additionally, he employed some of his scarce medicinal supplies so as to better ensure the safety of the wounded man.

Our beneficiary, valuing his health and his life, very much appreciates the actions of his caretaker, and, moreover, recognised the sacrifice which the latter had to this end endured. It is also clear to him that this action was not undertaken with aim to simply give resources away. His saviour is not particularly rich, and had acted in hope that this sacrifice would at least be reimbursed with something of equal measure.

This state of affairs being so, the formerly wounded man must feel a sense of duty towards his benefactor and adjust his actions so as to fulfil the requirements thereof. If he does not do so, then he does not recognise himself as being benefitted through the action of the other, either not valuing his own health, or not considering the other to be a genuine ethical reality. Now, for a claim to be enforceable through co-ercion, that is, for an object-based right to exist, property justice de-mands that an ethical reality be the cause of a functional change in the world and, further, that proportionally little function would be lost should the material substrate of this functional object be made exclu-sive property of the issuer of the change. We have further established that, should this latter clause not be met, any significant loss to the creator hereby engendered is to be reimbursed to him by the opposing claimant party in proportion to his relative additions to the contested object.

It is clear that matters of duty refer to changes in objects already owned through a just claim. In order for duty to have any legal claim, it must not undermine itself in demanding its own enforcement. Thus, all enforceable duty must operate under the criteria that the actor is permitted by the owner to change his property in such and such a way. We must, then, ask of our case three questions: did the passer-by vio-late a right of the wounded man by interfering with the latter's body; did the passer-by add function to the wounded man's body; does this addition remain the property of the passer-by once mixed with the wounded man? This being known, we may definitively say whether or not duty has any remote basis for coercive enforcement.

The first question strongly brings to mind the much-discussed sce-nario of a parent restraining a child who attempts to run into a busy street, or force used to prevent a highly intoxicated man from harming himself. It is clear that in such cases we admit the recipient of benefit to be his own self, and thus his own owner. With the help of the notions of justice and property laid out above this question is much more easily settled than has previously been made apparent. As far as we may be concerned, one's future self owns one's current property through a means essentially equal to - but far more predictable and secure than - the legal will which a man may leave upon his death, so as to properly designate who after him is to become possessor of his properties. The future self succeeding the current self, property titles are transferred as a matter of course. Legal claims, such as the right to receive from a man some amount of gold ten years hence, are property precisely in the way that an owned hammer or piece of fruit may be, and any property can be given away at any point. Thus, while a parent may be using the child's body in a way not explicitly sanctioned, any violation hereby occurring becomes entirely null when the child retracts its claim that it has, by the action of his parents, been violated. The same applies to the drunkard - if he sees the restraint imposed upon him as helpful after having sobered, then no violation can be said to continue to exist. Furthermore, any claim which may hereby be laid upon the offending party can be only proportionate to the damage caused - insignificant at most.

As has now twice been mentioned, any absurd complications which arise from these scenarios, such as the drunken man fabricating some story following his being restrained to the end of grandly extorting those who laid hands upon him, may only arise from an equally absurd viciousness in the actions of those who claim to be victims. Our answer to these apparent complications remains the same - dishonesty and treachery are beneficial to no society which houses them. These traits bend all rules, decay all precedent and lead to malfunction and tyranny. We have no reason to believe from the possibility of any such abuse that the system of property here advocated is any more susceptible to this form of manipulation than some alternative, be it fascist, socialist, liberal, or otherwise.

If the wounded man genuinely appreciates being tended to, then no violation of his rights stands as far as justice is concerned.

Onto the second matter: does the temporary caretaker add function to the body of the wounded man through its modification? Our answer here is precisely the same as for the first question - if the latter genuinely believes so, then the former has done as much.

The third question demands a more thorough investigation: does the creator of the function have any ownership of the effects of his actions if they improve the property of another? It is quite clear that he does so if they are negative, for it is on this foundation that any claims against him for the violations of some property justice must be built.

It has been affirmed, on grounds neither utilitarian nor objective, that the object of a creative act becomes the creator's insofar as the created function is the demonstrated function of the modified object, forming his exclusive ownership when the difference between the two is negligible. Further, the creator may only take his yield without impediment provided he does not thereby impede another's ownership of the created product. This latter clause denies the right of a man to ever own another against his will. Yet, unlike according to the positions of the objective-absolutists, who sever function from just claim, this does not mean that the creator has no claim to that which he created in the other man's property so long as the recipient recognises the righteousness of this claim, *a judgement necessary in affirming that the active man's product is both his own and also beneficial.* In other words, when A acts upon B, A has a claim over B, and B must act dutifully towards A, insofar as B understands A to have, by this act, improved B's property. This condition coincides precisely with the set of conditions under which B would in any way feel a sense of duty towards A, and be thereby swayed to act to the benefit of, or under the authority of, A. Thus, if and only if B demonstrates his duty to A by means of action does A have any right to the property of B. Under no other circumstance has A any claim over B's property when he acts thereupon, for in doing so otherwise than this he would be denying to an ethical other the category of claim which he affirms for himself - that is, A would, by seizing B's property, be denying B's claim to have the good accrue to B and be under B's control in proportion to B's good, while A would simultaneously affirm that B's property is in fact A's to control as a natural result of A's goodness.

It will now doubtless be alleged, by those who do not keep our central thesis in clear view, that this caveat of ours, which purports that duty *is* legally enforceable only provided that it is voluntarily undertaken, is at best a trifle, and at worst a mere tautology or manifest contradiction. We must claim otherwise on all counts. It is true that the legal enforcement of the above rule can never force a change in society, but to claim as much was never our aim. This relation rather serves to prove the incontestable identity of property justice and justice of duty, and the oneness of means which must therefore make itself present to both the propertarian libertarian and the traditionalist. For we may now see that the only means whereby a society may align itself towards truthful duty are those which allow this duty to be better sensed and understood, and that these means are precisely those which condition a society towards an adherence to property rights. Both property and duty spring from one's ability to correctly recognise the phenomena of one's life as being the result of the active presence of some ethical reality.

As a consequence of this, we must see to the core of the matter regarding the absolute inability of political reform to 'remodel' a society so as to conform the latter to our desired principles. For while the economist may correctly say that, for example, a lower rate of government spending will tend to increase the goodness of society, we may claim above this that, should there by a spiritual tendency towards a decline in the perception of supra-material reality, no measure of tax cut of bureaucratic reform may annul the collapse thereby necessitated.

We may, then, expand our first virtue of self-knowledge into the prime virtue of all-knowledge, knowledge of the ethical totality in all of its workings. With this, we complete our foray into the realm of rights.

# 14

## UTOPIA AND REVOLUTION

The effects of the preceding on the plausibility and structure of ideal society as envisioned by the libertarian cannot be understated. It is no longer possible to imagine a society made perfect by some indefinite number of formal and contractual relations, which bind man absolutely to his own objective property, independent of all values, and with no particular reference to social relation except insofar as such relations secure the end of securing material property. He who supports the justice of property, and all that which follows therefrom, must now lower objective property down from the principle of the highest, and make duty its equal - both deriving their justice and goodness only as children of the recognition of the ethical reality and its influence, and both inconceivable in this recognition's absence. Thus, the libertarian's desire to bring about the world of property rights must be also a desire for each person to strictly recognise his duty towards those actors which have made his position possible, to the sacrifice of the strictly 'self-centred' alternative courses of action, and, equally important, to the affirmation of the proportional subordination of the individual rationality.

In describing the type of society which is bound to become organised when the precepts of justice are followed, the first qualification which arises is whether or not mere justice is sufficient for the creation of a good society. The answer is palpably to the negative, clearly demonstrable from the fact that the alone man, to whom justice has no meaning, can live a life either terrible or blessed. Likewise, two, or any greater number of men, can fail to produce anything of worth despite a perfect ability of each to recognise the created things owned by the respective authors. The inverse of this question must always be answered: can a good society form which has absolutely no conception of justice? To this we answer that such a case is only possible with men made of stuff inconceivably sterner than any man yet born: a race indifferent to serfdom or kingship, to health or illness, to life long or short, to family and to all kin alike. For every type of man below this, the truly unjust society must be the truly unliveable society. Man would have to forego all joys based upon the recognition of the subject in the other, and live amongst men who, far from being his friends, care about him only insofar as they can enslave him to their own benefit, with all of their human cunning at their disposal for the attainment of this erroneous end.

What we may say with certainty is that any degree of degradation in a civilisation's spiritual intuition, measured by a drifting away from the wholly correct array of beliefs, will cause a proportionate decline, both material and spiritual (or economic and cultural), with both immediate and ever-worsening effect. We may posit three notable effects of this dampening of ethical intuition conducive to a poverty of world and spirit. One affects the material, one the spiritual, and a third condemns both.

To begin with the material, we reframe a position already alluded to. Any decrease in the recognition of property justice will cause created objects to more often be used in ways contrary to the principle of their creation, the will of their creator. Thus, the creative principle will categorically be viewed as a less worthwhile endeavour, and past creators will come to learn, *ceteris paribus*, that creative action is fruitless. Thus, in the future, fewer of these objects deemed desirable by plunderer and creator alike will come into existence, for their existence must be the product of a now-impeded will. Naturally, those products which are not entirely forsaken are instead reduced to lesser quantities or qualities, for in order to create, resources must be expended in ensuring the future production of the created product.

This demand for correctness of judgement need not apply only to man, but rather to all that may be considered teleologically caused, or all contained within the ethical totality. If one supposes the rain to have been created for a purpose which precludes exploitation by man, then any violation of this end would, if this be true, cause times of future drought. Thus, if false, and only if false, would dispelling such a seemingly superstitious belief be to the benefit of man. The implications of this will be revisited later.

The exclusively spiritual loss to which an unjust civilisation is condemned lies in the gradual approach of a wholly lonesome world. It is not suggested that property rights cause a belief in others, but rather that the disbelief in the former can only be occasioned by a waning faith in the reality of the latter. The presence of a spirit or subject within one's world can only be conceived through the belief that particular causative relations are occasioned teleologically rather than mechanically. The belief that nothing in the world flows from or is caused by a will is equivalent to a banishment of the subject-other from one's reality. Thus arises the psychological phenomenon whereby man, in an attempt to free himself from duty or interpersonal responsibility, frames the effect which inspired such sentiments of duty as rather the product of mere mechanical laws detached wholly from any notion of intent. This has made itself well manifest in the modern popularity of those egoist doctrines which deny even the possibility of action inspired by the potential benefit of the other, as well as numerous other reductionist attempts to destroy a sense of responsibility which one might find contentious with one's other values - framing an action as being done only out of habit, or only for profit, or, the strongest form of this tendency yet to rear its head, the reduction of action to mere combinations of ill-understood chemicals of the brain. It is thus absolutely no coincidence that these times in which the property principle is only 'understood' through its own shadow, if at all, have seen the rise also of assorted forms of dogma denying the place of the will in the world - to the effect of the denial of all responsibility, in both the positive sense which occasions duty or the negative sense which occasions punishment for given misdeeds. In the society which loses its conception of ownership, criminals and heroes alike become no more than passive elements in the environmental storm.

The absolute form of this reductionist tendency, which few theorists have dared to address, and in which no man has ever truly believed, is solipsism. We needn't mislead ourselves by supposing that this solipsistic effect has of yet taken no real hold of us. Its effect has been significant. Modern man, and this tautologically, has engendered in himself a semi-solipsism in his inability to fully integrate into himself a sense of duty to family, to community, to forebearer and to lord. The phenomenological presence of all of the above has been slowly consumed by the modern man's very essence. Being unable to habitually see the world as flowing from creative sources, anterior to matter, he cannot feel a duty or reverence towards those figures which surround or precede him, which engenders a very real denial of their existence within his life.

Lastly, that effect which causes a degeneration both material and spiritual: a debasement of authority and decision-making. Any action possible only due to a lack of the justice-sense must usurp authority from the superior elements within a civilisation, reducing their power proportionately. In creating a thing, and thus having a command of it, the agent becomes powerful in society in proportion to the judged goodness of that created thing. This is true whether the created thing be the occasion for reciprocated duty or the ownership of objective property. Thus, in a just society, those in highest command will be those who have best satisfied the best judgement of society, this latter being the 'decision-making regression' about which we have previously spoken. The act which denies property or duty must reorganise society such that the spiritually superior, judged so by the only epistemologically universalizable standards for societal organisation, becomes gradually replaced by the spiritually inferior, resulting in a society bereft of genuine hierarchy, now led by either a fake replica order in the case of a mild or implicit spiritual upheaval, or a revolution aiming at a complete levelling in the case of a more severe and explicit degeneration. As a consequence, the command received in an unjust society, one of fraudulent authority, must be inferior to those received in the principled society, for which we can see the necessity of an eventual 'tipping-point, upon the reaching of which authority, fraudulent and natural alike, becomes categorically dismissed due to its developed uselessness. For the presuppositions of authority are such that adherence thereto is not discernible on the basis of the particular merit of the command, but instead according to that categorical principle which sits above the command. Correct authority, flowing from a society which adheres to genuine spiritual hierarchy, must dispense orders from high to low, and thus inspire actions better than would have occurred in its absence. This can generally be understood through time by the subject of authority. By use of fraudulent authority, the lower commands the higher, necessarily to ill effect. This engenders a spirit of disbelief in the authority of a certain societal element, of, say, the capitalist, the state, or the elderly, as well as rousing a distrust of authority as such. If developed to a large enough extent, a revolution must occur. In such revolutions, much positive authority, should it still exist, is bound to be overthrown along with its fraudulent counterpart, for the difference between the two is necessarily little visible to the previously ruled classes.

By way of example, modern times have, through the democratic principle, gradually usurped proper hierarchy with a fraudulent counterpart from below. The organisation of society must therefore flow from inferior principles, which means that those institutions which man must respect if he is to follow the rules of society are unworthy of the degree of respect demanded. Under such authority, society will tend towards decadence. Once this decadence has become unbearable for the masses, they must seek to deny the claims of the decadent authority - which necessitates a judgement by the masses regarding the merits of authority as such. This must result in not only a localised uprooting of false authority, but also a destruction of what good remains within society's hierarchies. As authority becomes increasingly wiped of merit and subject to the revolutionary whims of the masses, further revolution becomes inevitable, since that authority established in an ad hoc fashion by the demos to replace the old state of dissatisfaction will be a blind throwing of darts, sufficient only by sheer luck and happenstance. Only when a blind revolution eventually strikes luck, or when a set of new rulers have forcibly extinguished all chance for revolution anew, does the period of revolution come to a close.

For these reasons, there exists no remote possibility for a swift and definite fix to the plights of modern society. Even presuming an immediate spiritual retracement or ascension, the dutiful fidelity thereby occasioned could at most be directed towards a bastard hierarchy, spawn of revolution. There exists no mechanism conducive to a mending of temporal authority other than a long and continuous upwards climb, of adherence to the rules of property, whereby spiritual supremacy may come to supplant this levelled inversion, as truth does to falsehood. As with the culling of any vicious habit, such a reversion to the state of justice is bound to inspire in society an immediate pain and loss. Reforming a fallen society must, in one sense, be a task more difficult than would be starting one anew, for a newly birthed civilisation does not find itself beset by the masonry of decadence.

# 15

## DYNAMICS OF THE JUST SOCIETY

Under a just society, one gains power through an expansion of the desirability of oneself and one's extensions - that is, property and the ties of duty. If one binds together a sharp stone and a small branch to make some tool, one benefits according to those higher means which may now be procured through use of the tool. One of these means is trade. Trade has two apparent functions worth examining. The first is simpler, the exchange of direct function, wherein both parties have a preference more for the other's item than for their own. The man who wishes for food and has much water exchanges with the man who wishes for water and has much food.

To this end, there is little room for error in the trade. Given 'perfect knowledge', this trade would still be made, for no abundance of knowledge would work to quench man's thirst or sate his hunger. This function of trade is generally accepted by the conservative restrictors of liberty, and so demands no elaborate defence.

Trade's other function, arising only in cases of scarce knowledge, thus always present, occurs whenever value is transferred, and power accrued, according to the participants' respective knowledge of the potentialities of the objects being traded. All trades partake in both of these functions to varying degrees, for all value supposes knowledge that a thing satisfies some desire.

We here venture to show that those more speculative actions, far from being the bane of traditional structure and stability, as might often be asserted, are rather a prime constructive force in its establishment and regeneration. Categorically, an individual gains as a result of a speculative action when his estimation of the general utility of a function is more correct than that of his trading partner. Let two examples furnish this point: a man believes a bag of seed useless and trades it to another for tuppence, who rather believes the bag bountiful. The latter is proven correct, his harvest yields him large sums and affords to many around him plentiful food for coming months. The source of the benefit of this trade is speculative in nature, rather than being based in the asymmetric desires of its participants. Had the seeds' salesman have known what their eventual repeat had known, he would have kept them for himself. Thus, the speculative principle served, along the lines of property justice, to give social power, authority conveyed upon him through his now-enhanced property stock, to the category of man best capable of orienting himself in the world so as to bring the ethical totality closer to the perfect state of being, the eternal aim of action as such. Those who gave him money for his harvested crops could only do so, given the just rules of property acquisition, in exchange for that accrued according to the merits of their past actions and interactions, be they direct or speculative. Insofar as this sale of food effected a result different from what was expected of it, on the side of either the farmer or the purchaser, the party closest to the eventual truth reaps again further reward at the expense of, and only of, the trade's other party[20].

A second example, an extension of the principles of the first: a merchant and a blacksmith come to meet. The latter would like to invest his gold reserves but sees no avenue to do so. His own business could utilise no further funding, and his knowledge of industry is far from expansive. Before meeting the merchant, the smith had decided it best to simply spend to a mild extravagance on direr foodstuffs, fairer clothes, and other such luxuries. He is offered an alternative: entrust the merchant with his funds and he will receive a three percent rate of profit per year, at absolutely no risk. The contract is signed, and the merchant seeks a proper investment. He finds a man who requires funding to build a mill. The latter promises the former a five percent yield on any funds invested, unless the project collapses completely, in which case the merchant's investment would be forever lost.

In such a scenario, in which direction does authority flow, to whom and on which principles? Further, how does this state of affairs compete with the alternative of one blacksmith's temporary luxury?

Pushing the problem no further than the purchase of flour from the miller, it is obvious that this state of affairs, given that the mill has come to turn a rate of profit of over five percent, has brought to the smith, merchant and miller alike an elevated position in society - a command over more, relatively speaking, when compared to the alternative, consumptive scenario. In this latter, the command which the blacksmith had over society is held in the form of his reserved gold, which is given to another in exchange for the 'usage' or enactment of his authority to the effect of exacting upon civilisation his will to have his immediate pleasure met. Now, whether or not the recipient of these funds grows in power as a consequence depends on the relative virtue of his own usage of the funds. If he merely follows the blacksmith in exchanging his money to command under his will the resources of society towards an immediate gratification of his desires, then his initial acquisition of funds comes to bring him no great gain. In this case, the relative power is placed in the hands of a yet more remote party, the individual from whom the second man purchases the objects used to procure his own immediate pleasure, and so on until a man receives the funds who does not immediately consume their power. The only party who receives for any length of time what the blacksmith had lost, in relative terms, is the one who makes of the authority he received in the form of gold some use to the benefit of a larger part of the ethical totality than that taken up by his immediate self.

This general view of consumptive expenditure being so - that in consuming for himself, man loses temporal influence and position until this is retrieved from others anew through just means of creation or interaction - we can better view the more complex dynamics of investment. In saving his funds rather than spending them, the blacksmith elevates his position in society insofar as he executes the judgement to value the whole more highly in proportion to the immediate part. Next, he makes further gain on these saved funds by temporarily yielding them into the service of another - the merchant. Here excluding any later benefit to the latter, this stage of the exchange is marked by the 'renting' of the power of the blacksmith by the merchant. The risk of this being presumed nil for the sake of simplicity, the blacksmith here receives social elevation due to two effects. Firstly, definitely and concretely barring himself from utilising his property to his own immediate ends, placing this function instead in the hands of the merchant. In doing so, he offers to a greater degree than was above stated that his judgement and understanding partake in the whole more highly in proportion to the immediate part, relative to the other wielders of power in society. If the merchant could find one more ready to employ such a view, he could and would secure his deal for less, to the *ceteris paribus* loss of the blacksmith. The blacksmith's ability to sacrifice his immediate consumption would be less remarkable, and so less necessary and less valuable.

Secondly, the fact that a given rate of interest has been secured by the blacksmith demonstrates, at the point of the transaction, that given the arrays of knowledge in the possession of each party, the merchant believes that he can, by use of the means in question, secure a larger multiplication than does the blacksmith. Thus, the transaction serves the purpose of putting a restrained power into the hands of one better suited to its employment. In temporarily yielding the power which he has justly come to acquire, the blacksmith allows the resources of society to serve the ends of man better than they would if this yielded proportion were governed wholly by the blacksmith himself. At this point the service of the blacksmith ends, and he receives his just reward.

The benefit accruing to the merchant is one highly contingent. He has no surety of repayment for he is tired to the fate of the mill. Taking this risk upon himself, unburdening both the blacksmith and the miller from the twists of unseen fate, is his first rendered service. In entering into such agreements, he effectively becomes a means in the world whereby the chaos in the lives of others is lessened such that their energies can be elsewhere expended with higher certainty. Himself more capable of bearing this unknown, he acts as a conduit of risk. Secondly, he provides a service similar to that of the blacksmith, for he must have restraint enough to hold reserves in the eventuality that his investment fails, else he would be unable to repay the blacksmith the promised funds and would be liable to criminal charges. His true function, however, is knowledge. We can see his growth of power from this chain of actions as being the differential in knowledge between himself and the blacksmith with respect to the possibilities of the latter's goods. In any instance where he turns a profit through this function, it must be so that the blacksmith himself was incapable of, without intermediary, utilising his own funds in a way deemed so positive by the sum of justly created powers. Yet the blacksmith has some conception of utility for his gold, and so yields it not free of charge. Should the merchant turn a revenue less than this charge - less than the rightful owner's own estimates of the utility of the alternative uses of the gold - then his position in the social hierarchy must decline, for he would incur a loss. Thus, the prime role of our merchant here is the active manifestation of putting a given set of resources through novel and ever-improving usages.

We say manifestation, for all of these sources of power are categories of valuable human behaviour as such, which occur in people in varying quantities at various times. In each of us the merchant role has an influence whenever our array of understanding undergoes a change however minor, and we are influenced by that positive spirit in the blacksmith whenever a conception of ethical other, be this our future self or another individuality, causes us to forestall consumption.

Given that traits are conducive to power, rather than people or classes as such, we can therefore view the dynamics of a free society in terms of the distinction and proliferation of good and bad traits, rather than through good and bad people. In the merchant becoming rich or poor, we elevate or subordinate in society not the merchant as such, but rather ingenuity or incompetence respectively. Any deviation from justice which hampers this selection takes the form not as a preference for different peoples, but a direct affront to ingenuity and expansive consciousness.

Back to our chain of economy: the miller, like the blacksmith, has foregone his risk in contract with the merchant. There are here two aspects to his gain: the second half of ingenuity, and labour. To the degree that the merchant could not simply have hired the miller and purchased by himself the necessary operational factors of production, the miller gains from his scarce and valuable knowledge - a gain categorically alike the main boon of the merchant. Thus his knowledge of the local market, the personalities of the townsfolk, nearby supply chains and so forth allow him to purchase the money from the merchant and, to the degree that his knowledge is useful, more efficiently organise his venture and reap the differential profit for himself. To understand the ratio of ingenuity-profit, or entrepreneurial gain, falling to each party, a short aside is required to address the value of knowledge.

Although rarely recognised as such in any explicit fashion, almost all knowledge becomes worthless in proportion to its commonness, for almost all knowledge serves merely to transform worldly objects into better means for the attainment of given worldly ends. Thus it obeys those laws applicable to the material objects which function to the attainment of those same ends. In a city of fifty thousand houses and only ten thousand people, an extra house is likely useless. With no houses and the same number of people, by procuring a house one might make oneself a king. If a city ten thousand large happens to have nine thousand carpenters, an extra carpenter is also quite useless - insofar as he is a carpenter; and such a man is a carpenter insofar as he possesses an understanding of carpentry. Thus knowledge, like houses, becomes worthless when superabundant.

It follows that we can make no definite judgement on the relative values of two sets of practical knowledge through an isolated examination of the knowledge itself. In a free society, the value placed on such knowledge is the product of those individuals of authority, insofar as they have authority, as ordained by the whole values of their being, rather than simply their formal intellectual tastes. Further, losses accrue to these holders of authority whenever their judgements of the value of knowledge are misplaced, as would happen in the case of the man who paid a great sum to be told the precise location of buried treasure, only to find the treasure itself worth little more than the labours required to excavate it, or the man who spends a surplus securing the labours of a renowned painter of portraits, only to later find the painter's skill to in no way exceed that of many lesser-known and lesser-priced names. We mention this fact as a response to the arrogance of that division of traditionalist which, under the pressure of their pseudo-socialist adoration of brute labour, take up great prejudice, in a categorical sense, against the 'idling money lender', and wish to remove his role from society as useless, no matter how instrumental many may find his services. For the reasons listed above, and those gone before, it would be better for such individuals if they came to properly understand their true position as socialist revolutionaries confusedly swept along by some fashionable traditionalist current. For their condemnation springs only from their deeply held individualist-rationalist convictions, necessarily anti-traditional, and their adoration of the labour classes.

If, in terms of entrepreneurial gain alone, the merchant reaps more than the miller, it can only be so due to the judgements of that activity selected through the procedural and incremental processes of liberty, without reference to the ad hoc intellectual theories of those with no rightful authority in the matter. In particular, the miller may be partaking in a very routine operation, the knowledge in him may be quite easily provided by another or be productive of little gain. Without the knowledge of the merchant, an amount of authority - societal direction - would have been expended upon cloths and trinkets for the blacksmith instead of the construction and staffing of a new flour mill - and thus the merchant is, perhaps more than anything else in the process, an absolutely instrumental and active cause in the creation of the mill.

The factor of gain belonging solely to the miller is that coming from labour. Essentially, this is a making useful of one's body to the command of the ethical totality, in exchange for some power bestowed by some individual of authority in proportion to the latter's authority and his estimation of the labour to be demanded. Once the miller's labour has been completed, he receives his reward according to the final usefulness of his constructed mill. A moment here on the dynamic effects of this flow of action with respect to the genuine goodness of its end product. Should the final effects of this economic chain, say, the consumption of bread made from the mill's flour, be a good, then it is so through an increase in the power of the ethical totality. In this case, all four parties, blacksmith, merchant miller and consumer of bread, gain in absolute and relative terms - relative gain being social ascent, absolute being proximity to perfection under given rules. All others see no absolute gain, and naturally fall in strictly relative terms. Should the consumption of bread prove mistaken and cause decadence, the total power of society declines, through a large decline in the consumer, who has given some but received nothing (or less than nothing), offset by small gains to those who successfully met his will sanctioned through his accrued authority. Yet there exists a further effect: insofar as the consumer loses by his consumption, he must, in the long run, fall into disrepute and decadence and come to possess less power.

This means that negative productive operations are, *ceteris paribus*, necessarily disadvantaged in a free society, since their source of their existence must be one with a permanent tendency to wane.

The characteristics above described bear no necessary relation to what is properly called the economy. Their relation lies instead to action and to value as such, and they are thus equally present in both cultural and economic realms. Any above examples have been drawn from the economic realm simply because this latter better demonstrates the qualities under discussion, due to the advanced formality, specialisation and quantitative nature of role which occur within the economy. It is nonetheless true that all bestowals and exchanges of value and authority, including those in the personal or cultural sphere, occur through the principles demonstrated above, and, as such, are subject to the same inherent laws and tendencies.

Thus, in order for a father to benefit his child intentionally, he must forestall pleasure for himself and show a sound understanding of the field of child raising. Additionally, he must labour to this end. In an absolutely just society, any deviation from a proper recompense for these actions, in proportion to their value, cannot be blamed upon justice itself, but rather decadence of stock - the child, come of age, recognises these contributions made to himself by his father and defers onto him an approximate degree of respect and authority so as to repay the benefit done. Only should his understanding be somehow dulled can he fail to recognise this good done unto him, and, inspired by this, act to the fulfilment of his duties. Naturally, the father is at liberty to free the son from any such reverential actions. Thus, when the rules of property justice are strictly upheld by a civilisation for their own sake, the father gains position in society through the willing reverence of the son, insofar as he has created the benefit in the latter through the means of the spirits of labour, ingenuity, and an expansive consciousness of the ethical totality. The absolute degree to which this link comes to elevate him is contingent upon the son's own power in society, conferred according to the latter's developed virtues, partially the product of the father.

There exists another time of authority which we have yet to discuss. This is the authority of identity or of genus, as opposed to that of personality or of particular. Under this form we qualify those rules which, without reference to individuals, describe a general framework for the hierarchical relations of particular social castes and demographic groups. Thus, the categorical subservience of child to parent, of layman to ecclesiastic, of citizen to lord, of demos to aristos. These relations cannot be described under what has above been said, and we may not pass them by without comment, owing to them as we do so much of the function of any virtuous and well-ordered civilisation. Nonetheless, we have but few steps to make from our outline of particularist duty in order to properly integrate its categorical counterpart.

In essence, this categorical reverence is evoked in those cases where the recipient of respect has interacted with the subject in no such way so as to directly benefit his individuality. A prime example, perhaps, would be the visit of a nobleman to a distant, foreign King. The King has in no way benefitted the nobleman, and so that duty resulting from the recognition of direct benefit cannot be here evoked. In these cases, the prime cause of reverence is inspired as an effect of the principled subordination of the self to the judgement of that beyond one's own individuality. Essentially, an acceptance of the judgements of a just and systemic process without having the arrogance to attempt to usurp that process through the employment of one's own individual rationality. In fact, this goes beyond a mere acceptance of the results of a justice process, but, above that, is inspired too by the belief that those things selected through such processes must tend to have a nobility and virtue which exists even if unseen. Thus the travelling noble, to some degree, places himself in awe of and at the service of the general authority of the foreign king. Note that this cannot occur should the noble identify the cause of the King's local authority as lacking justice in any significant way. The "respect" shown to a recognised tyrant can be little more than facade, exclusively self-serving and diplomatic in nature. Thus it should come of no surprise to us to see our modern democratic peoples, and their leaders, engaging in purely respectless, cynical and disdainful diplomacy. For, ultimately, the position of reverence towards the unknown authority is entirely related to the capability of a people to understand and to respect property. It is only when a people comes to understand its own highest authorities as reflections of tyrannical oppression, rather than of virtue, that this judgement will be cast indiscriminately onto those societies of which one is not a part. In a society's primordial stages, caste relations cannot be set by authority, for there exists no precedent for any such relation. Rather, any form of categorical respect demanded by certain classes within one's society is a manifestation of the above reverence of the noble to foreign the King, which may occur only once a systematic process of selection according to virtue has taken place in strict accord with justice. These societal relations thus become solidified in proportion to the development and longevity of the rule of justice and degrade in proportion to its abandonment.

Upon these foundations we now endeavour to show that the 'monetary man' is not favoured by the precepts of freedom, as our statist conservatives would venture to claim. For, from this, we seek to prove rather that it is instead the virtuous man who, as such, rises to the apex of the just structure. This is to be done under the presupposition of absolute adherence to the standards of justice, which includes an unwavering defence of the laws of property. From what we have already laid out, such a proof requires little by way of new excavation, but instead only a recapitulation.

We have said that the goodness of an action is the effect thereby caused on the ethical totality, wherein, as the word suggests, the action consists of the active rather than passive element of the effect in question. Under a state of absolute adherence to the standards of justice, defined not by abstract, formal and explicit 'ideology of ethics', but a recognition of objects within one's world as being caused by some teleological act, all such effects of action, occurring to a part of the ethical totality, must be understood to be the effect of the act, and the recipient as such must seek to instate proportional justice onto the entity, be this through objective property or reciprocal duty.

Whenever this equivalence does not occur, the relevant understandings of worldly justice have not been met. Only then can the virtuous act be improperly rewarded.

We have, from the perspective of this absolute standard, arrived at a position from which to judge real states of affairs, which rises beyond the trite battle between 'capitalism' and 'socialism' which fails to remotely grasp the central point regarding what constructs and constitutes the good society. Both alternatives are answers to a question framed upon false grounds.[21]

This leads us roughly back towards an analysis of historical and contemporary reality under our new sharpened lens. Yet before we venture forth and begin the chapter which signals the closing of this work, it would be prudent to outline, according to our notions, a number of concrete effects which we must expect to see arise insofar as the spiritual state of man rises so as to encompass a more profound understanding of ethical reality.

Of particular note, it would make sense to cover the creation and enforcement of cultural norms, and the means of the enforcement of justice in those societies which in some way deviate from a perfect conception of its dictates, and therefore require the pressure of a measure of force.

Towards the beginning of this work, it was briefly lamented that the genuine aesthetic merit or beauty of the public space has undergone a degradation. This phenomenon ranges from the minute, in litter and human noise, to the grand, through the multiplication of meshes of steel and glass reaching to the clouds and the growing absence of those aesthetic adornments of architecture which offer a range of awe and refuge to any passer-by, now replaced instead with 'functional' and quickly blackened, basic geometric shapes, clad at most by neon lights and graffiti. In a perfectly just society, such a state of affairs can come to be only given a terrible decline in the general mental faculties and physical capabilities of man. When the benefit received by every passer-by is in due proportion repaid to the creator, all that is avoidable in our situation becomes to that degree avoided. Yet we must look too towards the creator himself. His aim in producing the building being the best possible action, his endeavours will be uninspired and short-sighted insofar as he has no active conception of the true reality of all of those who are ever to be influenced by his product.

As good as these analytic truths may be, their practical effect might only be understood through an application to a genuine state of affairs, wherein men do not meet the supra-encyclopaedic standard of knowledge demanded by the perfect action. As has been said, a fall in these understandings must cause a flight from faith to contract. A further degradation makes contract, too, impracticable, and leaves us with little more than violence and brutal parasitism.

When the state of man's ethical faculty falls so as to preclude the well-functioning of prior channels of trust and duty, we must endeavour to retain as much as possible through means of pure objective property. The essential issue at hand then becomes that benefit can be received from the public work with no proportional benefit ever being returned to its original creator. Furthermore, since these public features by their very nature split their benefit over a large populace and over a long period of time, and since this benefit is caused not by a consumption of some part of the product but rather through an exposure to its beauty, it becomes both impracticable and entirely unjust to employ coercion to extract some amount of power from all those who witness the object. The most fitting solution to this problem, given a merely middling general understanding of justice, is one which is at present precluded by the popular form of government.

This is, namely, the democratised or nationalised ownership of those large swaths of land previously held, in a pseudo-private manner, by the by-gone landed classes. The supposed merits of democracy have already been above laid bare in a general sense, from which it should be clear how the democratic principle differs so wildly from our conceptions of justice. To state our aim: when the possibility of duty-based reciprocation of a good received leaves us, and consequently grandness in areas such as architecture loses much of its natural production, a second-best state of affairs would be that one in which those objects through which the benefit is ultimately received are all held, through just means, by a single beneficiary. Given that a beneficiary action exists, it can only be received by an individual by means of some physical intermediary object. For the music concert, this intermediary object to the appreciation of the music's grandeur is the concert hall itself, or, more specifically, some definite place within it. If the concert hall's ownership had absolutely no relation to the benefit dispensed by the musicians, then the musicians could receive no recompense in proportion to their acts. If each seat were owned wholly and permanently by a unique individual, rather than being held by a single owner of the whole concert hall, then any hiring of the orchestra, in a society which deviates from one of perfect duty, would dispense benefit to the seat-owners which would never be returned. With respect to a work of public architecture, the equivalent is, roughly speaking, the building's city or town itself, or some district thereof. The benefit of a beautiful public space is almost wholly accrued to those in the vicinity, or, as is equivalent, by means of the vicinity. This being so, the vicinity's true value, as a means to some good, must increase in due proportion.

When the area is owned either by innumerable private individuals, or some democratic caretaker, the increase in value which the public beauty causes to the wider area in no way benefits the creator of the benefit. If, however, all value changes in the area were to be accrued to a single entity or individual, which can only occur by this entity being the rightful authority over the area itself, then the negative effects of the loss of the duty-sense become almost wholly mitigated. For in such a case, this entity will ensure that beauty be created insofar as creating this beauty has a net positive effect on the ethical totality, which is the same condition for the creation of the work in the scenario of optimum ethical understanding. To put this into more concrete or standard terminology: in building, say, a cathedral, or in keeping streets free of the base individualistic ugliness of neon light advertisements, any benefit hereby received, by any individual, will cause an increase in the value of the roads from which this beauty can be taken in, the houses close to the area, the shops in the vicinity, and so forth. If the value of these is held by only one private entity, in other words, if, in accordance with our conception of justice, an entity creates, inherits or purchases this total, then the interaction between the creator of the good - say, the architect and builders, or the shopkeeper made to keep his shopface pleasant - and the beneficiary thereof becomes no different from that of any wholly private interaction, wherein the problem of sprawling, uncontrollable and unreciprocated benefit does not exist. This being so, the owner in this case will act so as to maximise the value of the city, whereas a large multitude of individual owners, or a democratic government, can only maximise their own allotments of space and time respectively. Naturally, the democratic government fares worse in the securing of our objective than do the multitude of private individuals, since not even increased value of the 'owned' area comes to benefit the democratic caretaker in any real way. This maximisation of the value of these means, then, requiring the owner to distribute as much power and wealth as possible to those creators with the power to procure it, coincides perfectly with that condition under which the beautiful item comes to be procured - the proportional benefit of the creator of the good.

We must now address the collection of more abstract cultural norms which makes up a behavioural culture. The problem presented by these requires only a different application of the principle already presented above with respect to public beauty, for all behaviour must take place by means of an intermediary object connecting man to world. The formal condition for maximising success in an imperfect civilisation, made up of imperfect men, is the ownership by a single entity of all means improved by a positive action. The mistake should not be made of therefore presuming that, under such a qualification, all those benefiting from an action are to have the entire magnitude of this good siphoned away and returned to the creator, so as to result in a net benefit of nil to the action's recipient. For example, it may be conceived that, under the above suggestions, an individual who enjoys looking at a cathedral ought, ideally, to sacrifice the exact amount gained thereby in order to benefit the cathedral's owner. If we wish to follow this line of reasoning, then we must admit that, in following his sense of duty, a man must exhaust all good received such that he is indifferent to having ever been benefited in the first place. Simultaneously, the initial giver of benefit would be immediately deprived of that which he would eventually in equal part regain, for it would be impossible for any right-thinking man to ever wish to be benefitted should he as a result have to suffer a loss to the precise degree that he could ever suffer a gain and force himself back to a state of indifference. It would be such that no just human interaction could ever result in net gain for either participant or for the ethical totality. One would do well to remember, in these cases too, that the formal condition of interaction, and thus trade, is the shared belief that the action undertaken improves the ethical totality. When speaking analytically, it becomes easy to forget that in order to benefit another, one does not need to incur an equal loss. This is so due to the disparity of desire between each individual. When one receives a smile from a loved one, smiling back does not neutralise the goodness of the interaction. On the contrary, it raises it. This is so as the recipient of the returned smile values this gesture more than its giver values the means required to bring it about. Similarly, if one man has only water while another has only flour, and both men desire to bake bread, the former giving the latter a cup of water does not require that the latter return to him the same cup of water. It would require instead that the latter return to the former some amount of flour. Both men hereby arrive at a position better than that which existed prior to the interaction, for the principle of the action is not to give back all that one has received, but instead to benefit one's neighbour in proportion to the benefit he has given you.

That aside, we bring as an example of a particular set of norms: behaviour in a public space. This includes any number of things from public spitting, irritating noises, a general disposition of respect, orderly vehicle traffic, sparse vehicle traffic, a prohibition of the shopside display of the obscene and degenerate, and so on. It must be here quite clear that when each building, each road and each square are all unconditionally owned by unrelated individuals, all of these things will begin to despoil the public environment given a flight of duty and natural ethical consciousness - and again, caretaker democracy must fare still worse. If the merchant of the obscene can extract a large sum of money from the tourist class through shocking, ugly, and disruptive displays, there is little to stop him from doing so. Indeed, it is a popular libertarian belief that under the rule of liberty, such things must come to be. It is similarly a popular belief that this is a good thing. Some have even become so muddle-headed as to believe any suggestion that such things might be bad to be an implicit affront to liberty, an affront which might suggest that we wish to invoke the state to force this mess away. The prevalence in the popular conscience of this latter reaction, even among the so-called libertarians, shows only how confined political thought has become to the dynamics of statism. Insofar as the spirit of the age becomes ruled by this statist rationalism, it becomes impossible for a society to draw any distinction between an opinion and a threat, because, for the people affected by this spirit of solipsism, it becomes axiomatic that the imperative of an opinion is to bend the world to its dictate.

However, and this is our central point, a just society prefers diverse and multitudinous ownership over central and hierarchical ownership no more than it prefers, as such, steel to iron, water to wine or pork to beef. All of the above are competing sets of functionality and are treated equally at this level. If one has benefits over the other, it becomes beneficial to produce it, and it becomes more prominent. This applies too to our proposed form of ownership. As has been shown, the central capturing of the totality of any given action ensures that the action be procured in proper proportion to its merits. As such, this central capturing becomes a more efficient thing to produce. Thus, given a lack of unjust, coercive, democratic remnants, there must be a tendency in a free society towards this particular form of ownership. As such, it can only be through the limitations inherent in modern, anti-property decadence that our current state of affairs has come to be.

Should the obscene-peddling shopkeeper attract and display the degenerate, he is lowering the power of that sum of things through which the obscene has an effect. We can take this to be a lowering of land and house prices, a flight of business, a flight of cultured tourists, whatever is caused by the degenerative or diseducative effect of such materials on the populace, and so on. Yet given the private and just ownership of these means by a single entity, a change in these affairs towards a more virtuous alternative poses no greater problem than, say, the restructuring of a factory so as to produce a more profitable product - something which few would claim to not be most efficiently executed through liberty. To ban obscenity, that is, to forbid obscenity as a condition for access to the shop, becomes profitable. Likewise, according to their genuine merits, we must admit the prohibition of various other behaviours and peoples according to this mode of organisation. Can it be imagined that the degeneration which has been allowed to occur throughout the last century within the inner parts of many once admirable cities might have occurred, to any significant degree, were every ounce of this degeneration to inflict some equivalent measure pain upon an entity with ultimate power to change the city's fate? Is it thinkable that those policies of political egalitarianism, which forcibly accelerated the demographic dilution and ultimate replacement of the city's best, would have occurred if every measure of ill hereby caused were to accrue to the policymaker himself? Certainly, if such a thing is to be expected under such conditions, then no politic of any cut can hope to salvage any good for man who is bent only on his own destruction. If man is not impossibly doomed, however, then we would be best served by that mode of organisation which can only reject those changes, both moral and demographic, which lower the instrumental value of the city. Imperfect though they may seem, these methods are certainly less so than all alternatives available to the real state of man: democratic ownership, incommensurable individualistic ownership, and state conservative plans alike.

Now, given that the organisation of assets tends towards their most profitable utilisation, we must expect that a free society, insofar as it is unimpeded by the anti-traditionalist coercion against which we rally, tends towards that mode and scope of organisation which maximises the goodness of the whole. Given the empirical facts of the matter, this seems to be general organisation on the level of town and city, with obvious opportunity for subsidiary subletting insofar as this benefits the whole. If such a mode of organisation is too limited in scope, causing large conflicts of values between cities, then this ownership must, and will tend to, ascend a level higher, to the level of the county. In such a case, the lower levels of the hierarchy, entities responsible for individual cities, would naturally be given enough power, through contractual ownership of means, to rule his own city under certain provisional limits set by the owner of the county, provisional limits which act only to funnel potential losses of value up towards a higher but limited entity. We say limited, for there is absolutely no reason to suppose that the highest entity possesses more practical power in the governance of any particular city than does the owner of the city himself. Should this former give to the latter any greater or lesser amount of power than is proper for the optimal function of his property, then his property will tend to decline. Similarly, while a King must sit above his army, and provide that which the general cannot, it does not follow from this that we must expect a King to possess the practical power to organise the army in its minutiae and particulars.

Should this thesis be a true representation of the tendencies of freedom, it no longer seems possible to quantify the 'capitalist' society of today as one fundamentally organised upon grounds of justice and liberty. Any simple investigation of the matter would confirm this perspective. The present society is not organised upon such principles, primarily because those within it do not possess the spirit of liberty, which demands a naturally acute intellectual awareness of the ethical totality. This is not to suppose that a sudden, strictly political movement towards liberty would be of no utility; rather that the possibility of such policy will continue to fade in proportion to the progress of any underlying spiritual decline. Thus, a matter of utmost importance is presented - the present survey demands that we come to understand how this sense may best be procured. If the free society is incapable of procuring its own support, or, still worse, inevitably leads to the decline thereof, then, regardless of the extent other merits, what reason can we have to lend it our unmitigated support?

Irrespective of any of the merits of justice detailed above, a free society cannot justify its own existence if such a mode of organisation does not harbour kindly that which gives it its vitality. It has not been sparingly claimed that the case is indeed that freedom works to its own destruction. This belief, reinforced by the strength of the currents of dialectical history, appears at first glance to hold some weight when considering the course which society and economy have jointly taken from the eighteenth century onwards. According to this belief, the organisation of society through the recognition of property came to prominence with the works of Locke and found its best manifestation in the American revolution. Having spread, the currents of property caused an industrial revolution throughout the late-eighteenth and nineteenth centuries, eventually causing the western capitalist powers to establish a temporary world hegemony of industry and finance. Yet, while the rule of property was growing, democratic and social discontent with the system grew too. This resulted in various socialist revolutions through one route, and an expanding regulatory welfare state through the other. Through the inequalities caused by the capitalist system, the masses were kept poor and wealth was hoarded at the top of the pyramid. The present day remains almost wholly capitalistic, and as such these inequalities remain or even continue to grow. Today, a near majority of the youth espouse a preference for what they consider to be socialism, and only few capitalists can confess their beliefs unashamedly. Thus it appears that, since unleashing itself around two hundred and fifty years ago, the capitalist system has been sewing its own demise.

A certain response to this interpretation of events, which presupposes their unalloyed truth, manifests itself in that conservatism which wishes to limit freedom only insofar as is necessary so as to prevent the degeneracies of the capitalist system from overshadowing and undermining its virtues. Thus, one may advocate for some measure of forced wealth reallocations, or a central government tasked to banning anti-hierarchical propaganda, or a large measure of spending on public defence units, for example.

The particulars of these answers have been addressed enough in this work's second part. Below, we argue instead in an entirely categorical opposition to the above claims: that the property sense, when allowed to follow its own self-fulfilment, proliferates itself more surely than any alternative mode of governance possibly could. To be quick with this, it is defined by us that the free society is the one under which violations of justice be prohibited and punished. Insofar as this constitutes the state of affairs, a sense of justice, which dissuades the instincts of theft and murder, can come only to a person's benefit. Further, there is much good reason to believe that the self-contained competent individual, who must act such as to have in view his whole life rather than his present appetites, has, in his expanded consciousness of self, a propensity towards higher consciousness of the other - for these two conceptions share a single root. And thus we can expect those most personally successful to be, relative to the population, dutifully conscious.

Now, with respect to those who actively propagate anti-property and anti-tradition sentiment - not from the animalistic position of petty theft of through some other instinct, but as crowned by some intellectual thesis or other - these elements, being an active menace to free society, are due to be expelled by any well-thinking landowner or organiser, in quite the same way that any worker who actively roused his fellows to strike would be swiftly dismissed by any well-organised employer, unless the former happened to be of some extraordinary merit. Those elements disruptive to the deeper framework of a society are especially likely to be expelled, since those spiritual elements which give rise to any such beliefs, an effeminate envy and hatred of all things which would qualify a genuine distinction between qualities, are of the most decadent possible. In a free society, these spiritual characteristics are bound to bring unto their hosts a rightful amount of contempt and scorn, for those who fail to properly relate success to quality in a society which properly rewards quality with success must themselves neglect becoming virtuous - for they cannot identify virtue.

Yet let us look to the opposite proposal: many might instead wish to engender justice and tradition through the employment of revolutionary force under the authority of the 'greater good'. They might wish to open up coercive and unjust channels through which the removal of undesirables might be achieved more surely and swiftly than could be done by means of a free society alone. In deviating from rule of freedom, this policy must be characterised by a violation of the judgement rights of those higher than the dispenser of the punishment, since this punishment must come to the effect of, through unfree and coercive means, removing certain elements from society which were otherwise ruled fine enough to partake therein. It ought to be obvious at this point that the introduction of such a rule must make it permissible, in principle, for any individual in society - independent of his position - to disregard the authority of his natural superiors for his own personal agenda. This is true irrespective of the form of coercive power opened up by these abuses.

Now, apart from necessarily instilling in a population a general characteristic of petty revolutionism, it must also be the case that such channels, which bypass the judgement of social hierarchies and the existing distribution of means and authority, are bound to be most exploited by those with a natural anti-hierarchical and revolutionary bent, for quite the same reasons as why the just man best succeeds through routes of justice. This has been discussed at length above. Thus, far from securing a society's freedom, such an opening will simply and swiftly become the central point unto which all of society's revolutionary undesirables will be attracted. Such a story is told perfectly well by the history of the American state government. So far as such an apparatus has all of the powers of freedom in addition to the powers of unpunished injustice, it will wage, and win, a long enduring war of attrition against those whose principles it was supposedly established to protect. Let it be reiterated: *in a society characterised by ordered judgement, those undesirable loathers of liberty can only succeed through means by which their actions are shrouded from this very judgement.* Far to the contrary of the claims of those who levee the following attack towards ourselves, the true utopian fancy of the tradition-facing theorist can be none other than that of 'limited democratic government'.

We return now to that historical narrative whereby 'freedom' arose in the eighteenth century only to be trampled through the twentieth. No genuine, universal view of property justice would be complete without a due scrutinization of this myth, which has called no small number of those allies of liberty to come to a stalwart defence of their own executioners. There is now little space in this work for a full-going analysis of the last millennium according to our own understandings, and so we hope that what little might be provided will help orientate the libertarian towards a better understanding of his own position in history.

# 16

## DECLINE OF THE
## ETHICAL
## CONSCIOUSNESS

In accordance with what has been said above, it would be fundamentally mistaken to attempt to understand the history of property justice in terms of the social predominance of formalistic legal contract, the movement of 'capital' and the structuring of the teleonomy around centres of mass physical production. The attention of any genuine adherent of liberty and justice must rather be drawn to the predominance in man of the justice sense which influences him to act with due respect for the understood presences of his fellow men within his phenomenological world.

With this as our point of reference, it becomes by no means obvious that those enlightenment 'explosions of liberty' - the revolutions of the French and the Americans, the secularisation of 'the state', the emergence of national self-determination, the rise of democracy and the emancipation of women, children and men - represent anything remotely comparable to the genuine progress of justice.

We wish to present a brief, chronological analysis of loosely distinct phases leading to the development of the modern world, beginning with the feudalistic middle ages and ending with democratic modernity, insofar as characteristics of these phases have any relevance to the sense of property justice itself. We must presumably here present the disclaimer that while we below present this course of events as being in many ways involutionary rather than evolutionary, we are by no means uncritical of the reality of the feudal phase or any mode of society which has followed it. The many transgressions of older times, exaggerated as they now may be, are lodged firmly in the minds of all modern men, and do not here require much by way of mention. There has never been, and never shall be, a time of perfect freedom, with transgression wholly banished.

From a more distant glance, we may see certain trends which, rather than being particular to certain phases, rather stand as a vein running through the whole of the previous millennium, causing various upheavals in various eras as the central principle of the vein continued towards its ultimate development. Firstly, we cannot fail to notice a continuous shrinkage of the spiritual horizons of man. Crudely speaking, Medieval ages were characterised by a view of spirit as that which gives matter its form, or rather saw the world as a living aspect of and supported by a spiritual substratum. The modern view is inverse. For modern man, the substratum of reality, if he may ever speak or think of such a thing, is matter, understood to be the atom or the electron or the photon, or whichever subdivision of space seems today to be the last. Upon this dead base rests the spirit, if modern man should utter such a word at all. All movement is aspiritual in principle, and so the spirit does nothing and has no nature, relegated to being a mere illusion whereby illusory beings experience matter. Despite being the product of a twofold illusion, this matter is somehow supposed to be real.

Secondly, and quite related, is the development of the sense that there is nothing above man. Perhaps better phrased, so as to include the levelling of man to the level of an arrogant animal, this is the notion that all living things, as such, are qualitatively equal with respect to their morality of ethicality. Any difference between living things is caused from without, and thus no living thing can be said to be culpable. From this necessarily follows a will to minimise the externalities and prejudices which work to create inequality between that which is inherently equal.

Thirdly, and once more intertwined, is the predominance of individual judgement. That one always ought to do what one judges right, independent of the rules of any external authority, unless one thereby harms another's ability to do the same. The goal of such a will comes to be the maximisation of 'self-expression', or the identification of oneself with that which differentiates oneself from all others. It is this tendency above all others which can be said to characterise the transformation undertaken by the European soul through the course of the previous millennium. It should be clear from the outset that insofar as an individual loses the ability to submit himself to the direction of a justly selected authority, and prefers, instead, to go about his life according to the momentary whims which overcome him, the soul of that man must be said to have undergone decline in his faculty for the sensing of ethical reality, which is the father of the property sense. Thus, when a society appears to be 'emancipating' itself from an adherence to those behavioural norms previously fixed to it from above and behind, we can be quite certain that it is well on the path to an anti-property revolution.

Given these general themes which become active to varying degrees in each successive era to be examined, let us move on to a closer examination of the medieval. On the level of state, the most striking aspect of the medieval period is its decentralisation of power. Instead of all men standing as equals under an all-powerful state, lands are governed by layered hierarchies of well-defined and incremental powers. Between the men of lowest and highest caste lay Lord, Knight, Baron, Earl, Duke and Prince, and, intermingling like warp and weave with these ranks of nobility, the Priest, Bishop, Archbishop and Cardinal. We say intermingling as these powers were yet to become cleft apart as would later occur through the secularisation of society. During the period in question, their domains were distinguishable but essentially tied.

Further, the power of any of these categories of rank was, when compared to the limitless modern state, absolutely bounded. Indeed, this is necessitated by the structure - any abuses of the power of Dukedom would deprive Earl, King and Bishop alike. Yet such abuses were not limited through power constraint alone. To a large degree, the limit of medieval power was contained within the individual's understanding of self and of other. For inseparable from man's place in a societal hierarchy was his perceived place in the spiritual hierarchy. Seldom would the knight think himself 'fit to be King', while many now believe themselves fit to rule the democratic leviathan. Such a proposal would, for such a man, amount to a denial of his ontological identity. Naturally, this secured a reverence and willing submission to one's superiors, to an extent established by the relationship between the roles of the individuals in question. These fixed relations applied, too, in the opposite direction. For if a superior overstepped his bounds vis-a-vis the inferior he would become imposter and usurper, and thereby lose some measure of his right to authority. As such, the period was marked by incremental and localised conflicts between vertically neighbouring powers in a way unimaginable in the modern world, which understands only the horizontal struggle between competing national governments.

The principle of hierarchy, in short, descended from a belief that in the King lay the temporal manifestation of the eternal ethical principle, which was attuned and certified by the exoteric religious form of Church approval. This principle was dispersed, as blood from the heart, to the subordinate divisions of the ruling system, the members of which, in participating in their role, understood themselves to be representatives of an eternal spiritual order.

Under this mode of organisation, the roles, and thus the rights, of the lower castes were not simply absent of form. There existed rights of these classes the violation of which would have been viewed as a profanation of this entire system of order. On a wholly material level, these rights were rather slight when compared to the material rights of the lower castes in more modern eras. This fact can be alloyed by the fact that the old society was acutely averse to the material as such. Yet with respect to the recognised sovereignty which these men did hold - over kith and kin, if their competence merited so much - their power was deemed inviolable. A totalitarian seizure of children for a centralised state upbringing, or the subjection of men to labour camps as if they were cattle, would have been unthinkable. As a class, the serfs were at worst condemned to subsistence.

Of high relevance to us is this period's marked exaltation of dutiful and honourable action. Let us take the roles of child and father. There existed a near universal deference of the former to the latter on two counts: subordination of individual rationality to the spiritual maturity of the father, and a duty towards the one who had been the active force in the creation and development of oneself. The manifestation of this deference most at odds with the modern way of life is the authority of the father to select the husband of his daughters. Such a state of affairs seems as repugnant to the modern egalitarian as extor-

tionate taxation and a leviathan state did to the enlightenment liberal - yet, should we be unable to wholly endorse such authority, we
must nonetheless admit that it flows necessarily from a recognition
both of the father's wisdom, and the fact that the father had, in body
or spirit, created much good in the daughter. To take another example, the spirit of readiness to lay down one's life in defence of King
or faith, manifest most perfectly in the Knightly orders. Such an orientation is now, especially after our Great War, one which is nearly
impossible. Yet such a belief becomes wholly comprehendible given
the understanding the King, as worldly representative of the Way or
the solar principle, had maintained a region's prosperity, or that the
Church alone had led one's soul to Christ. Further, we must understand this sacrifice as being made not for a King or a Church representative, but rather for Kingdom or the Church itself, both as functions
or roles. For, as was most typical of the age, the King was not virtuous
in his individuality, but in his kingliness - that is, insofar as he represented the position of King which stood before him and would continue after him. This understanding better explains how the medieval
man might conceive of the King as being the source of his prosperity
- rather than giving reverence to King as an individual man wearing
the crown, an idiosyncratically modernist conception, he gave reverence to just Kingship as a real entity which persisted throughout and
above any number of its particular manifestations within individual
human beings. It is thus the role of King which he understood to be
worth dying to protect. This ontological shift best captures the change
from medieval to modern; that the former considered supra-natural
forces as being ontologically anterior to the 'individuality', which was
understood to be primarily some sum of such forces, while the latter
has come to make the individuality sacred as its own ontological unit
above which nothing exists at all.

Medievalism is also distinct from all thereafter in its experience of a truly spiritual world. Partially due to the fact that the period in question marked the high tide of both paganistic alloying of Christianity both Greek and Germanic, worldly activity was seen as reflective of inner spiritual forces from supra-physical realms. Thus the predominance of ritual, omen and alchemic currents, many traces of which still highly adorn the more picturesque and metaphorical aspects of our supposedly secularised language and symbology. Now, the tendency to understand physical change as reflective of a spiritual teleological principle is precisely that which qualifies the judgement of justice and of property. These powerful spiritualist currents have little to do with those individualistic, idiosyncratic superstitions often portrayed in popular modern histories, such as potioncraft, chemical alchemy, and witch hunting. Rather, the principles of spiritual influence in the world were, like much else, passed down from above and passed on from the grave, subject to the spiritualistic qualifications of the giver.

The importance of this point must be more formally stressed. That world entirely devoid of spiritual intuition cannot succeed, for violating a will by acting on the teleological as if it were merely natural leads to a general destruction of the goodness of the ethical totality. Yet the existence of these teleological, spiritual existences, be they human or otherwise, cannot be discerned by means of scientific examination. Given that we admit the organisation of nature to allow for real human agency or teleological will, we cannot disprove, categorically, either sub- or supra-human teleological principles acting within nature; or, more accurately, that the flow of nature might be ordered by non-human forces. We must also admit the possibility that, even if man were to be able to come to 'find' teleological principles within the world through trial and error - an impossibility - any such ethical, teleological principle might be profaned into losing much of its utility for man by being made subject to the sceptical manipulations of men who wish not to work with it, but simply through it.

Given that an understanding of the nature of the teleological elements within the world is one condition for mastery of the world, we
must admit the possibility that those most successfully oriented - the
royal and ecclesiastical nobility - may possess an ability, conscious or
otherwise, to fulfil the ritualistic or initiatory requisites for a successful invocation of immaterial spiritual forces. Further, we might suppose such an intuition as being a partial cause of these individuals'
initial elevation and success. To stress the grounds of this once more,
it would be impossible to convince a member of a naturally solipsistic "society" of the ethical reality of those around him. This is a fundamentally different venture than proving to him that night follows
dusk, for all ongoings within the world occur along the lines of natural, mechanical laws, such that the assertion of ethical reality outside
of the immediate reality is *never* required in order to sufficiently explain how some one thing has come to occur. Despite this, the individual within the solipsistic society who best intuits the ethical reality
of his contemporaries must be advantaged in ascending that society's
structures, for he has come to possess knowledge of the workings of
the world through sources from which his solipsistic fellows have been
entirely cut off. The nobility of the solipsistic society, then, should it
be said to have any nobility at all and not simply be stuck in a permanent barbarism, would tend to consist of those individuals most capable of intuiting supra-natural truths. This principle is of course true
of our own society, and of that of the medieval period. Since we have
no reason to assert that the extent of supra-rational truth is the human, we must admit the possibility that the nobility of a period have
arrived at their position through an ability to interact with the world
in a way that conforms to the channels of non-human supra-natural
ethical realities.

If this is so, then the principle of subordination according to position, and duty according to benefit received, are the only possible

means by which a society might proliferate its mystical means of supra-natural orientation into the lower castes, or at least to more than none or a select few. Enough on this point; an elaboration of its possible implications would derail us from too much from this chapter's central matter. Though it should well be reiterated: if nature is organised around the wills of men, a requisite for teleology, why must we steadfastly affirm all but the actions of man to be purely natural?

Before moving on to an analysis of the post-medieval world, a general point or two on the goodness of the feudal society vis-a-vis our own. It is clear that we cannot endorse the physical property claims which underpin the era. To claim a whole 'nation' as the rightful land of the collective Lords through the King is a grand injustice. Such a proposition is acceptable only insofar as the ultimate owner, the King, created the soil itself, or changed its constitution profoundly in the eyes of the whole peasant and serf castes, such that it would be, without the action of his role, quite useless. One may make a point that these peoples indeed believed the King to have created the *goodness* of the land as such, due to his spiritual radiation without which the land would be incapable of furnishing the requirements of the highly spiritual medieval life. Nonetheless, it seems impossible to stretch this principle far enough so as to justify the land distributions of the feudal period. Whatever injustices this period contained would prove the downfall of the whole medieval political structure, both for better and for worse.

Additionally, a comment must be made on the well-being of those living in medieval times. In judging such a thing, two paths are open to us. Insofar as we must make a choice, we may judge from our modern grounds, or upon the grounds of the medieval spirit itself. The former are profane and disoriented, and measure well-being entirely in terms of unrestricted access to the satisfaction of any instinct, without distinction. Further, the modern spirit measures the quantity of this undifferentiated stoking of instinct in terms of the material goods consumed in the act which satiates the desire. Under such premises, the feudal age seems dire indeed. Yet such premises are false. Insofar as he is modern, modern man knows nothing of right living and has no centrality. Despite his abundance of immediate pleasures, he is deeply dissatisfied with life. Despite his dissatisfaction with life, he is more afraid of death than any group of men which came before him. And yet, far from learning from this state of permanently stimulated dissatisfaction, he would grasp at the chance to forego a timely death and instead become some ceaselessly degenerating, externally sustained pleasure-cripple.

The criteria of the good life to the medievalist, on the other hand, ascribes to most modern pleasures a negative value, as instigating corruption of the soul. Material plenitude is corned by the medievalist. His positive value comes from the appeasement of perceived spiritual powers through engaging in qualitatively correct action. He does this through ritual, minor and major. In comparison to the man of today, the medievalist was scarcely afraid of death as such, and thus cared far less than the modern that the length of his individual existence could not be prolonged by the advance of medicine. He was instead afraid of incorrect living, of the degradation of his soul by the temptations of Satan.

Thus we can be sure that while most modern men would shun a voluntary return to the medieval, a proportion at least as great of medievals would decline a transplant into modernity, and would see man as having, in trend, teleonomically shrunken in the seven hundred years following Dante. And so, without divulging here into a genuine ethical critique, we must at least admit that the preferability of our own society over the medieval rests upon a highly contentious claim, one based primarily on the adaptations of our own souls to the exter-

338 - JOSEPH KEANE

nal abundance of our society and our habituated materialist-atheistic worldview.

While exceedingly few of our contemporaries extoll the feudal, it is not rare to find some number who begin to furnish praises with the flourishing of the Renaissance. Owing to the general conceivability of the renaissance mind vis-a-vis the medieval, we may state that the change of spirit occurring between the fourteenth and sixteenth centuries signifies the largest since or prior in any equivalent span of time. This is primarily due to the rise of humanism, a worldview which, in relation to our own, is antecedent rather than strictly opposed. That being said, the immediate effects of this spiritual leap, especially in material terms, were relatively slim in comparison to that which has since occurred.

The humanistic tendency may be defined by its juxtaposition of soul-in-man and matter, the latter being perceived by the former, as well as by the elimination of any general plurality of spiritual forces. Through this latter, humanism strictly denies the reality of forces of ritual and any 'paganistic' conception of a moved world by forces between man and divine first mover. It is with the inception of humanism that the defining intellectual elements of medievalism would be put on a path of steady transformation. Spirituality and alchemy would slowly warp into modern psychology, while the temporal body of religion was bound to become both less important and less substantial. By the time it had become infused with the suppositions of the enlightenment, the humanist tendency had morphed these medieval forms into the Spinozist One. Come modernity, we see a further reduction, or absolute inversion, into Freudianism and materialist atheism respectively. In this humanism, we must see the glint of an approaching egalitarianism; for in denying anything between man and God, we approach a world no longer distinguishable in terms of spiritual quality or anterior metaphysical type.

The 'type' was indeed the prime casualty of the renaissance itself. The belief that the King embodied, truly manifest, an eternal and metaphysical solar principle became seen as antiquated. With the removal of this aspect of Kinghood, which has profound impact on the possibility of truly robust hierarchy, one must lose any notion of the ontological relevance of one's societal position or rank. Whereas the King was formerly a being of strictly higher quality, he became in the Renaissance a wholly human recipient of power, blessed by good education or good blood, and lucky enough to be born the heir of his father's power. What affected the crown affected the limbs similarly. Dying in the King, the role died also in society's lower echelons. Man was no longer anything but man - he was not, ontologically speaking, a craftsman, but rather a man who happens to craft for his living.

The significance of this for us is not to be understated. The decline of the role causes two necessary changes in man's spiritual understanding with respect to teleological causality and thus of property and duty. In participating in a role, voluntarily or authentically, man finds himself to be freed from the multidirectional pulls of his fragmented being and instead elevated to a position wherein his individual soul can best fulfil its limits and become itself on Earth. The role is passed down from above and through from the past. As such, the recipient of the role understands himself to be elevated through a spiritual gift, refined and cultivated through the actions of others. He could not 'make' this role himself - indeed, this defines the role. This recognition necessitates in him, assisted by the confines of the role itself, a strict sense of duty. The role is not in oneself, but from without, and thus bestows upon its man both the responsibilities to be carried out by nature of the role's particular nature, as well as a subordination of the self to the understood will of the active principles of the role's emergence. Any deviation from the role through actions of unformed personality are treated as sacrilege, a sentiment wholly related to the sensing of injustice. When a society is structured by the appreciated role, men better understand their indebtedness to the spiritual orientations of their forebearers and betters.

When a society loses the ability to properly structure initiative principle and to bestow an appropriate role upon many of its members, the latent forces of individualistic rationalism and a general Machiavellianism disperse themselves through its hierarchies. The function of any position in life becomes increasingly to be a mere stepping-stone towards the fulfilment of one's individualised ethical understanding, which is identical with a systemic denial or ignorance off the wisdom and active influence of past men. As a result, certain parts of society become opposed to one another rather than participating in a unified orientation towards a singular peak.

The denial of the role continues into the modern day, an understanding of which helps us to contextualise the import of roles in a traditional society. More recently, for example, mankind has ventured so far as to attempt a complete emancipation from the roles which govern the sexes, which work to bring into actuality the virtues which man and woman eternally contain in essential potentiality. In short, these roles aided their respective demographics in the full development of their distinguishing latent powers. This is accomplished through the grafting onto the individual of a role shaped so as to best subordinate and control the negative aspects of their distinguishing nature, in this case those of the feminine and masculine natures, and to give a definite aspirational form to a boundless and volatile individuality. Modern humanity has thrown off these restraints, which unified a universally understood path for the development of the person with the general good of the race, so that it may instead 'explore' those once-subordinated depths to its own demise.

The decline of types led directly to the weakening of the structural hierarchies of traditional society, from within and from without. From

within, because each individual took it upon himself to find new solutions for those problems better solved through the workings of his
former role. For example, this striving individualism and the dominance of the individual powers over the restraining role acted to hasten the monetary corruption of the church, a corruption which would
have been less mighty in force should the general church representative be more dominated by his ecclesiastical role than his individualistic rationality. Naturally, this decline of the role affected equally
the integrity of the virile noble castes. The noble castes of each locality increasingly striving for their own individualised notions of gain,
the collapse of any remaining alliance of Kingdom and Rome became
inevitable when the representatives of the former began to become
aware of the corruption of the latter. The local powers no longer limited by the parallel workings of the Church, we begin to see the rise of
the modern nation-state.

The forces from without act through the lower strata of society.
They could no longer see themselves as elevated by participation in the
structures above, both due to their own detachment from the role and
due to the genuine corruption of the structure's highest reaches above
addressed. The lower castes must accordingly focus ever more on the
demerits of the structures around them, for the merits have come to
escape them.

From this spiritual evolution, which signifies a decrease in man's
spiritual intuition, we see a number of political consequences. On the
one hand, monarchical absolutism arises - Kings came to see Kingship
as existing through their own individualities, rather than through a
definite role which they have come to represent temporally. Having
no reference to any spiritual link to the papacy, and now able to centralise power from those subordinated land owners, whose legitimate
claim to their respective measures of power have become fragile with

the expiration of their roles, the inevitable consequence is an increase in the power of the King's whims over those of all below him.

From this arise the individualistic forces of the demos, which become active in matters both secular and religious (a division of type which up to this point could not have been properly cut). With respect to political individualism, we see enclaves of man entirely unlinked to the feudal superstructure, partially due to their own volition and partially due to the bleeding of the powers bridging low and high. This evisceration of the middle-powers, that between serf and King, lowers the pressure on the former to conform in minutiae to the lessons of the previous era. Thus we see arise the merchant port towns of Italy, Holland and England. On the religious front, dissatisfaction must ferment with respect to the Church's claim to be the authoritative interpreter of all spiritual matters. The institution increasingly corrupt, and layman more often seeing the difference between himself and Pope as one of mere temporal power, the actions of a Luther become inevitable.

Underneath the high spiritual lies the racial. Differences in soul no longer being naturally attributed to the metaphysical, interpretation must fall one level below so as to attribute them instead to the merely physical. Additionally, with the eyes of man becoming unattuned to that ethical absolute which permeates all virtuous temporal structures, he must increasingly come to take these structures themselves as being intrinsically good. Thus, when the high-spiritual fades out under the eclipse of individualist humanism, the forces of racial and national spirit naturally take their place. These forces are easily harnessed by the aspiring absolutists to the effect of a grand hardening of cultures and borders, best seen in the alliances of the German princes with revolutionary Luther, and so the groundwork for the modern state is fully laid.

The humanism of the renaissance provokes in man a re-evaluation of the fundamental principles of the relation of his soul to the world.

Spiritual tradition wanes, and material modernity approaches. The intellectual function of man must become to study a world which contains only himself and matter.

It is widely supposed that the renaissance, dividing modern from medieval thought, was lit by a rediscovery of the ancient Greek texts - yet such a theory seems to quite suppose itself. This theory does nothing to explain why confrontation with Greek culture, a thing certainly permeated by tradition and even a habitual spiritual mysticism, happened to inspire in recently medieval, European man his modern, materialist, humanist course. The forces of Aristotle had already been well enough integrated into Scholasticism some four centuries prior to the dawn of the renaissance, and where, precisely, are the ideas of Plato to be found in the world of Newton, Luther and Bacon? Or are we to suppose that Plotinus was somehow less Greek than Montaigne, given that the medieval period, unconcerned with the Greek spirit, took so closely after the former, while the renaissance, spawn of the rekindling of Greek ingenuity, might be encapsulated in the latter? It seems rather that the European spirit, its prior phase waning, was inspired simply by a desire for the new and novel, which met its catalyst in an appreciation of the explosive intellectual virility and Otherness to be found in later Greek culture. Absolutely none of its more profound, high-spiritual aspects became integrated into European culture by means of the renaissance. To the contrary, this new energy gutted from its own civilization those vestigial traces of Greek spirituality which combined in the first millennium with the Hebrew Christian spirit.

Following the renaissance, we are said to arrive at the enlightenment. That division between renaissance and enlightenment is one less firm than that which initiated the former. Rather than understanding it to be a diversion of spirit, it would be better understood as being the natural and direct heir of the distinguishing renaissance suppositions. On a political and social level, the enlightenment signifies the point at which dead traditional forms could no longer hold the non-traditional spirit. Whereas we previously addressed something akin to the 'emancipation of Kings', we arrive now at the emancipation of the individual as such. For quite some time, the power of the King had been growing in inverse proportion to any recognised justification for the ownership of that power. As such, the culling of Kingship was quite inevitable. The King's power now viewed with suspicion, there comes to the forefront of thought a fairly justifiable demand for the redistribution among the masses of the King's false power. This is the point at which the twentieth-century libertarian believes the spirit of property justice to have come into full bloom, yet this cannot be said to be the case. It might be better said to be liberty's entrancing autumn. Instead of an increase in spiritual intuition, the essential cause of the spirit of property and justice, we see instead revolutions arising from a disbelief in the participation of temporal power in justice - a shift in position only half justifiable. To the degree that this change of spirit was unjustified, due to the growing ignorance of the active goodness of traditional hierarchy, we must instead talk of a decline in the spirit responsible for property. It is only in this sense that the events following the enlightenment can be properly understood. It was from those bloody revolutions of individualist rationalism that there emerged a particularly distinct, and hitherto unseen, form of society - the hollow nation.

The libertarian too quickly dismisses the possibility that just value can be grown on grounds which have had their virginal purity violated by the precedents of injustice. He can often only see in medievalism the injustice of its land relations. Yet on these driftwood foundations were mounted, not by the fault of the latter, many productive relations the recognition of which would very justly inspire duty. In seeking to perfect society's foundations, the liberal razed the last vestiges of those structures which he now wishes his barren landscape could be capable of growing. Yet worse, he planted upon these barren foundations a single seed which would never come against limits, a principle of coercion far more grand and var more virile - the seed of coercion-for-itself.

As we ventured to show in the chapter preceding this history, the natural course of the unimpeded, formless free society is one quite resembling a purified medievalism. It is precisely this which the liberal's naive levelling has made impossible. This is no victory for property, for the grounds for these liberal revolutions were primarily laid through a decay of the property sense - man simply degenerated in his ability to correctly understand the effects of past teleological activity.

Within the hollow nation, occupied by little other than quantitative masses down below and rationalised, abstract state up above, man found his energies liberated from all forces which hitherto stood between - his relationships to the Church, to his superiors, to his subordinates, to his guild, to his town and, owing to his lack of role, even to himself. These energies no longer being formative on him during his youth, we come now across a man finally and truly opposed to the spiritual, traditional man of fixed role which came before.

The revolutionary spirit never strikes at only the heart of its nemesis. For the sake of surety, it wishes to swiftly do away with the life-force of its other organs. These secondary organs, in contrast with the formal, overarching domineering structures of the heart, are instead latent energies pervading in the revolutionised society whereby the old order's nature might continue to be sensed. In the context of the liberalist revolutions, this aversion is directed towards those duties above listed. To subordinate oneself in any such way becomes antithetical to the new culture. Through this perspective we more clearly understand the cultural development of the American states.

In the hollow nation, the masses, which no longer have any umbilical relation to the way of tradition, must expend their energies through alternative channels. Having lost the art of approaching perfection through perceptual virtue, or a production of virtue within oneself, one must instead attempt to create something equivalent to a "virtue within the world", or an improving of the world's material shape so that any quality of man can satisfy his will therein. Again it must be restated: this state of affairs came to be through the reduction of the spiritual intuition ultimately responsible for an understanding of private property.

This degradation could not stop with the liberalist revolutions. The history of the world from the eighteenth century onwards can be summarised as one of "progress", supposedly an emancipation of the lower forces in society from the unjustified tyranny of the higher - an unceasing destruction of all pre-enlightenment social relics, which, it can be truthfully said, had no place existing within the modern world. This is most visible in the grand equalising of the governed classes of the liberal society.

Towards the beginning of this period, the democratic right was upheld only for a short minority of peoples, those classes most representative of temporal virtue, who, more so than other classes, might be said to have held historical precedent for their elevated positions insofar as these were freely and justly acquired. Such a system of organization, however, is an affirmation of certain medieval notions of intrinsic virtue or quality, independent of temporal matter or 'environmental effect'. These were bound to become uprooted with the continued advance of the modern spirit. The growing identification of salvation with the material has evidently hastened this collapse.

The shift from absolutist to democratic forms of government was brought into being by the expansion of individualist rationalism in the non-ruling classes. The lower cannot contain within itself the higher, and so these classes were bound to prove incompetent judges of their own rulers. The king-piece of their judgement was that the ruling powers were using their privileged position to consolidate their own power at the expense of the masses - an activity which must be unjust, since all men are equal under God. The shift from limited to absolute democracy requires only these suppositions, from which the former was born, and a temporal delay long enough for the spirit of the times to more completely dominate its antecedent. The non-voting classes come to consider limited voting to be a tool for keeping power amongst the few, for the gain of the few. Individualist rationalism thus awakened even more in the lower classes, who are naturally incapable of containing within themselves a full understanding of the virtues of higher men, the eventual universalisation of the democratic voting base must be seen as becoming entirely inevitable.

We see here the framework of the socialist awakening and of modern egalitarianism. Before addressing these, some focus must be given to the changing nature of differences in men in the hollow, materialistic nation. When a society values primarily spirit, a levelling of hierarchies is a danger quite remote, for the nature of the spiritual genius is to produce that which cannot be alienated from him - his own golden soul. The produce of the great men of material, however, is wholly alienable. That the King's spiritual virtue was stolen from the peasant classes, and that, therefore, the peasants must somehow digest the King's soul and reawaken themselves, could not easily become a particularly attractive idea, or, at the very least, such a proposition requires a more advance degradation of spirit than does the equivalent aim directed at expropriating the rulers of the materialist society.

As such, the revolutionary forces of the nineteenth-century focused increasingly on the expropriation of the property of the rich. Only few men possess the knowledge within themselves to justify the material disparities of the capitalist economy, and when intellectualism is open to all, when the spirit of the times is fundamentally revolutionary, and when the will of the masses is the new sovereign, the reign of the socialist view - through revolution or a melding with the democratic state - becomes a nation's fate. This fate came to pass towards the beginning of the twentieth century, and a hatred for the rich has never since ceased. At this point in the age, the development of its central idea began to reach its terminal velocity. Each gain of the revolutionary spirit demanded yet further encroachments. The two world wars smashed to pulp the brain matter of one hundred million of the most virile Europeans, and dealt to the continent itself a death blow, serving as the final culmination of the revolutionary will towards 'national self-determination', which it has ever since come to surpass.

Around this time, the most profound formulation of spiritual blindness came into circulation through the writings of those such as Dewey. There exists an absolute equality of souls, in essence, and all difference in men is therefore unessential, from without. Thus, difference between souled things is an injustice as such, to be rectified by the state, which has now become the active embodiment of judgement. The active nature of the human soul became mere illusion, for now only matter could be understood. The soul became a mere nothing within an all-consuming tempest. This shows quite clearly the synthesis of the materialist metaphysic and the egalitarian ethic. Both reach their completeness in denying the responsibility of man as such.

With this formulated, the socialist energies rose into an attack on hierarchy in all of its forms. Frantically searching for some purpose or pleasure to seek, the supra-rational spiritual forces of the medievals reawakened in the sub-rational unconscious of base animal man as understood by the psychoanalysts. In short, the point was approached wherein any form of organisation or order served as a mechanism of power whereby one might oppress another. The dissolution of the role reached near completion once its bourgeois shadows such as the gentleman, the modern family and the housewife became subject to these destructive, centrifugal forces, an enhanced version of those very forces which sculpted such forms some generations prior. Even the personality as such, understood as that force of solarity in the individual which subjugates the various chaotic forces within to a single highest point, began to be dissolved amidst the cult of the worship of many-formed subterranean 'self-expression'. Instead of becoming a marble pillar, the modern human increasingly wished to become a formless sludge, indiscriminately reaching out in any direction in an act he calls self-discovery. One can only expect this movement to continue. To where exactly it leads, none can claim to know.

# 17

## PROVIDENCE

The foregoing historical narrative ought to make it clear that the libertarian requires recalibration with respect to his choice of idols. The founders of the liberal states, no matter how grand their particular souls may have been, are not to be emulated. Furthermore, they simply cannot be emulated. Their time has passed.

If what we have said in this work is even half-true, then the prospects for liberty seem quite dim indeed. Yet it is better to be in sober hopelessness than to be drawn to false light.

The major bane of our ideals springs not from some nineteenth-century socialist agitation, but lies, to some degree or another, within each one of us. It lives as we act. For whatever reason, that which gives life to property and justice is forsaken in us, and has been tending to do so since a point beyond many people's the furthest historical horizons.

To which end, then, could this work have been written? If none other, let it serve to transmute the political energies of the anti-moderns and true libertarians into something more profound. The politicisation of all aspects of life is a great poison in itself, irrespective of its eventual direction. To prove such a method hopeless, as we hope to have done through this work's second part, can serve only to better the state of things, if only in some small fashion. Additionally, our first part may remove some degree of power from those profane economic schools which, while wearing the robes of freedom, must be thought of as little more than zealots for the modern age. Finally, our third part may well give direction to the libertarian who knows no vessel for his energies other than the political.

If our best spirits are to be miraculously reawakened, such an event may spring only from a reorientation of ourselves and those who we can, in our smallness, truly inspire or influence. Such a reorientation is almost incomprehensible in scope. Once the equilibriums and ratios of reason and tradition have been broken, and once the temporal structures of society have completely ceased to reflect a spiritual virtue, it seems that no man can restore them. Further, it seems that the waters of our society have reached a point of such pollution that any virtue now found within would more likely sink like lead than rise like oil.

One must not conclude from this political hopelessness any sort of nihilism. That such a reaction is even a possibility shows how far we now are from being a society capable of maintaining justice. The imperative of each man and of each action will eternally be the perfection of the ethical totality. He must engage on this path indifferent to the ebbs and flows of circumstance. If men act with grand enough souls, freedom is as natural as the fruit of a well-grown tree. If he degenerates, then freedom will desert him. This is another form of justice.

# Notes

1.  Strictly speaking, the present value of the alternate market uses of an economic resource is, in some cases, marginally below that value for which the resource is eventually traded and employed. This is due to the fact that this purchase itself constitutes some demand for the product, and may require that the price of the good be bid up given that an increased number of prospective purchasers are now competing for a fixed number of goods.

2.  We here use standard terminology of 'time preference', a term favoured by the Austrian school of economics, so as to not unnecessarily muddle the present discussion. In the current work's third part, time preference will be critiqued and subsequently transfigured into 'understanding of the ethical totality'.

3.  In economic jargon, an externality, which may be positive or negative, is the total effect of the production or consumption of a good on parties other than the producer or consumer, an example being the cost of obesity on the taxpayer. Externalities are naturally only measured quantitatively, in terms of a net effect on future aggregate economic production or economic growth. This concept contains, by the standards of economic orthodoxy, no special reference to anything outside of the monetary nexus, and thus has no relation to the spiritual or cultural as such.

4.  Throughout this work, 'objective' and 'subjective' should not be taken to signify what these words have come to mean through their bastardisation by popular discourse. By 'subjective' we mean neither 'untrue' nor 'relative'. Instead, we mean that which is *absolutely true of the subject*. By 'objective', on the other hand, we mean that which is *absolutely true of the object*. The objective and the subjective assertion are not differentiated by their claim to truth per se, but rather by the ontological category of that thing about which some truth is claimed.

5.  As is obvious, we here speak about no individual economist. We instead describe the qualities of the economist as a role, in which anyone may par-

take to the degree that they adhere consistently to the orthodox precepts of the field.

6.    This is a partial truth. A market for the future labours of others, without their own consent, exists in the form of the trade of government bonds, which derive their value wholly from a promise on behalf of the government to plunder its populace.

7.    The moral character we mention here refers, in brief, to the character which violates without scruple the prescriptions of the Kantian categorical imperative, or asserts that the particular of his own individuality does not adhere to the same ethical universals which others, in a multiplicity of peoples, must adhere to for society to be functional. These universals refer to certain sacred absolutes, absolute in their weight not with respect to some infinity of consequence, but with reference to the categories inherent in human interaction. Within this category the Kantian would place the lie, violence, selfishness and, perhaps, suicide. The character of ill morality who violates these absolutes may nonetheless be extremely competent, acting with no great participation in the immanent consequentialist vices of imprudence and cowardice. We do not assert that the person who advances in the political hierarchy will be he who can least well tie his own shoes.

8.    It is misleading to use the term 'output' when describing the good that a bureaucratic system may do for the public, for, strictly speaking, this is not their product. We do not say that checkers players are less productive than chess players since they checkmate fewer kings. The output of an entity is its ability to produce, internally or by means of itself, that product which, as such, ensures the entity's own proliferation.

9.    There are limited possible combinations of man's resources, and endless hypothetical combinations of the satisfaction of his desires. As such, there are an uncountable number of desirable combinations which cannot be met by man's productive potential; and of that relatively small number of desirable combinations which are mechanically possible, only a slither are capable of avoiding a grand wastefulness. We are tasked with continually calculating the specifications of this iota.

10.    As of the writing of this book, this veil now appears to be slipping. It is now no longer shocking for a state's central bank to explicitly declare that it will embezzle unlimited funds for state employment without demanding any payments of interest. Further, collusion between the two entities has reached a point of explicitness that the state may openly boast that it is utilising the function of the central bank to directly purchase equity shares

in "private" corporations, as in Japan, or through directly purchasing bonds of "private" corporate debt, as in the United States of America. None of this is surprising except, perhaps, the fact that nobody seems to have noticed, and that those who have noticed do not seem to care.

11.    A natural aristocracy is that small minority of individuals who tend towards highest elevation within a system of freedom. As such, the category has relation to the particular characteristics which a given society has come to consider virtuous. Despite this condition for its manifestation, the natural aristocracy continues to exist in a latent fashion within any society rooted in coercive practices. Insofar as coercion exists as a rule, there comes to exist a chasm separating the virtues of the natural aristocracy and their actual societal position, as the goodness of their actions becomes disproportionate to the elevation they receive therefrom - part of this elevation being plundered by the coercive actors. In a hypothetical, wholly coercive society, the natural aristocracy avoids all detection; first due to the fact that its actions receive no reward, and secondly as a result of the absolute destruction of the historical regression. This regression is that which gives concrete form to virtue in the abstract. Without any such historical mechanism, a 'society' can say nothing about virtue above the level of mere tautology, that virtue is an action's proximity to the good action.

12.    The categories here employed are those necessary of the rational, active being as such. In saying that each rule is independent of the quality of the prohibited action, we say so in the same sense that the Austrian School of Economics refers to goods - that is, unified through any method of external, *ex post* categorisation, such as two houses may be bound, but rather united through psychological inseparability or indifference. If the actor has a preference between the houses, revealed through his actions, they are not the same good. As such, should the rule permit of certain caveats, our claim is not invalidated. Rather, a new universal is posited in place of the old, or two universals in place of one.

13.    The laws of a nation must rest a close distance away from the temperament of its populace. If there is no distance between the two, then the laws are useless. If the difference is too large, then the laws shall not be obeyed. As the nexus of a nation's laws grows larger and more complex, and its dictates more particular, the plausibility of seating authority within this ideal range becomes increasingly distant.

14.    By some*thing* we speak here only of objects of the senses or of phenomena. The Good itself falls under neither of these categories, and, as such,

whatever we say about "what it means for *something* to be valued" is meant as no judgement regarding the category of Goodness as such, which lies outside of all *particular* experience and is instead a requisite of Being as such.

15. This is so as the conception in question still allows us to hold the prime universal moral ground of the rational being to be the construction of power as such - as harm done unto a *recognised* other must make one to that degree powerless.

16. For the sake of brevity, 'other ethical realities' will here be shortened to 'others', such that 'others' should be taken to include both other individualities and the future self.

17. The terms 'good' and 'bad' are here used in relation to the highest imperative of man, or with respect to the man's proximity to perfection, than with relation to any particular code of moral purity or selflessness. When we speak of the bad man, we approximate more the bad seat, which collapses under the smallest weight, rather than referring to a man of particular selfishness or cruelty.

18. This mode of appropriation is also entirely sufficient in those cases where a single man acts to improve some object to which he has justly purchased exclusive rights of ownership. Exclusive rights are justly purchased when all means used in the transaction, by both parties, are themselves the results of just allocations.

19. We do not mean to include in this category parenthood as such, the act of conception. A distinction must be drawn between the creation of betterment in an existing subject and the apparent creation of the ethical substance of some individual. To treat the latter with any appropriate degree of depth would bring us towards a metaphysical discussion far beyond the reaches of this work. Avoiding this matter, we will consider the act of conception itself, or the point at which the soul becomes one with the body of the foetus, as imputing to the child no inherent rightful duty towards its parents. Naturally, all other aspects of parenthood, including the incubation of pregnancy itself, may correctly and justly instil in the child a sense of due duty.

20. Fraud, defined as being that trade which is instigated with the intent of either participant to deceive the other as to the characteristics of the goods to be exchanged, does not conform to justice. In brief, in giving up his property for trade, each participant acts according to a set of conditions and suppositions. If the other party promises to fulfil these but does

not do so after having received the former's property, the exchange is to be annulled. This same rule is employed when a property owner gives another contingent access to his property, as with the invitation into one's home. If one invites another into his home on the condition that the latter takes off his shoes upon entry, and the latter does not do so, it should be obvious that continued entry into the former's house must constitute some form of trespassing, and not conform to the standards of justice.

21.    As previously mentioned, capitalism, like socialism, may refer to one of a manifold of contradictory positions or matters of societal organisation. Here we use the term in its most common usage. While some theorists of liberty have attempted to make the term 'capitalism' come to be synonymous with whatever notions of liberty they wish to unfold, such an endeavour will always be fruitless. It is not clear why such theorists would go to any lengths to rectify a word which has its roots in, and thus its etymological implications chosen by, nineteenth-century revolutionary socialism. Indeed, if 'capitalism' is to mean any system of liberty, then we must label all of the above 'capitalistic'. In the context of both this word's origin and common use, such an employment seems little more than dishonest fancy. Continued employment of the term as referring to some ideal state of affairs serves only to confuse and dissuade.

Lightning Source UK Ltd.
Milton Keynes UK
UKHW020810030920
369259UK00007B/156

9 789090 335674